MEN
WHO LEAD LABOR

ACKNOWLEDGMENT
(TO ORIGINAL EDITION)

THE AUTHORS are grateful for the generous assistance of Louis Budenz, Theodore Draper, Lawrence Emery, Granville Hicks, E. W. McDowell, and Ruth McKenney.

They are especially indebted to Harold Seidman, Cowles Scholar in Government at Yale University, for permission to use material from the first draft of his forthcoming book on labor racketeers; to Herbert Resner for material on the West Coast maritime unions; to Robert W. Dunn, Grace Hutchins, and Hy Kravif of Labor Research Association; and to a member of the carpenters' union who for obvious reasons must remain anonymous.

BRUCE MINTON
JOHN STUART

July, 1937

MEN
WHO LEAD LABOR

Richard Bransten, 1906-1955.

by **BRUCE MINTON** *and* **JOHN STUART**

WITH DRAWINGS BY SCOTT JOHNSTON

Essay Index Reprint Series

BOOKS FOR LIBRARIES PRESS
FREEPORT, NEW YORK

First Published 1937
Reprinted 1969

STANDARD BOOK NUMBER:
8369-1309-4

LIBRARY OF CONGRESS CATALOG CARD NUMBER:
73-93362

PRINTED IN THE UNITED STATES OF AMERICA

CONTENTS

I. WILLIAM GREEN

Ghost of Gompers

THIRTY-SEVEN YEARS as president of the American Federation of Labor had convinced Samuel Gompers that the Federation was pretty much his property. And so, being both canny and methodical, the old man prepared for his long-threatened death by grooming a successor. He died in December 1924, leaving specific instructions that "crown prince" Matthew Woll of the small Photo-Engravers Union should inherit his position at the head of the council table.

Gompers, however, was not able to dictate from his grave. The executive council appropriately mourned his passing, and each vice president quietly set about assuring himself a major rôle in the direction of Federation affairs. On one point, the strong men on the executive council saw eye to eye: they had grown heartily sick of Gompers' autocracy. To show their defiance, they would straightway disregard Gompers' choice for president.

Particularly did John L. Lewis, dynamic president of the United Mine Workers, largest union in the Federation, resent Woll's pretensions. For Lewis never forgot an enemy; he recalled very clearly Woll's opposition back in 1921 when Lewis, with what amounted to sacrilege, had run against Gompers for president. Now, if the contradictory politics of the executive council precluded his own election, Lewis at least wanted to have a controlling voice in the final choice. William Hutcheson of the carpenters' union and T. A. Rickert of the United Garment Workers, both dominant figures in the Federation, felt much the same way. Among them, they eliminated Woll and even scrapped Gompers' further decree that the first vice president, senile James Duncan of the Granite Cutters, be honored as the stop-gap until the next annual convention could endorse a more permanent choice. The honor, Gompers had decided, was due Duncan because of his countless years as vice president and his seniority. But the men who manoeuvered the executive council feared that during Duncan's short term, Matthew Woll might plot some course whereby he could edge himself into the presidency at the convention. Accordingly, six days after Gompers' death, the council "unanimously" named a dark horse — William Green of Coshocton, Ohio.

The compromise candidate had nothing markedly to recommend him, except membership in Lewis' union — and Lewis controlled the largest bloc of votes. Yet each official on the executive council hoped to advance his own interests through the prosaic, malleable Green. To the accompaniment of Duncan's tearful protests, they draped the portly secretary-treasurer of the United Mine Workers in Gompers' mantle and presented him to the American labor movement. The membership was fully as astounded as Green. With the exception of the miners, the rank and file had hardly heard of William Green before.

Even as they placed Green in Gompers' shoes, the A.F. of L. high command felt doubts as to his fitness. They were afraid he was too progressive, and his Red-baiting (all council officials were accomplished performers) lacked the required vociferousness. No doubt Green's opposition to American recognition of the Soviet Union was wholehearted. Yet how explain his support at the 1920 Montreal convention of the progressive Plumb Plan which sought to grant semi-governmental ownership of the railroads? Did not Green's advocacy of old age pensions smack of socialism? The leadership hesitated, not quite convinced that they had found the appropriate pawn in the quiet but untested Green.

The convention that would confirm Green's appointment or name another president met at Atlantic City late in 1925 with Green nervously presiding. As the session got under way with the customary routine speeches, Green recognized the fraternal delegate, A. A. Purcell, president of the British Trade Union Congress. Instead of the formal emptiness expected of him, Purcell, a member of the Anglo-Russian Committee and a recent visitor to the Soviet Union, challenged the principles on which the A.F. of L. rested. The astonished officials squirmed as they heard him urge militant industrial union-ism, a labor party, recognition by the United States of the Soviet Union, and friendly relations between the Russian unions and the A.F. of L.

A tense moment. Amid mild applause, Purcell resumed his seat.

William Green, the unproved temporary president, stepped to the rostrum. The old-timers leaned forward, wondering how the sleek, round-faced chairman would meet the challenge. At fifty-two Green had the well fed, comfortable appearance of a small town banker. His pince-nez gave him dignity; the heavy gold watch chain gleaming across his paunch added the proper air of solidity. And as he spoke, with easy, ambling affability, the members of the executive council nodded to each other and smiled.

"There may be a time," Green admitted, shaking his finger at the delegates, "when we in America can organize an independent political party, when our nation becomes an industrial nation, as Great Britain now is. We will have to change in America from an agricultural nation to a semi-industrial country before we can make a success along that line." Nowhere did William Green give ground to the fraternal delegate from England. Surely he wore Gompers' mantle well. In the recess that followed, John P. Frey, pedant of the A.F. of L., was overheard telling his colleagues as they slowly paced the boardwalk, "Now we know that we have a strong man who can wear Samuel Gompers' shoes!"

The "strong man," with the convention's endorsement, could almost certainly bank on being reelected in the future. He had come out of the Middle West; the steady rise from a coal miner's son to the presidency of the A.F. of L. had left few scars. If he no longer looked much like a worker, who then on the executive council did? Mild, genial, well mannered, he lacked the color of his garrulous, exhibitionistic predecessor, just as he lacked his shrewdness. But superficial differences did not prevent Green from sharing the presidential chair with the ghost of Gompers.

HUGH GREEN had left an English mine to settle with his Welsh wife in Coshocton, Ohio. There William was born on March 3, 1873. The boy grew up in this little mining community, attended elementary school, and during vacations helped his father in the pit. The burden of a large family did not allow Hugh Green seriously to encourage young William's vague ambition to enter the ministry. Instead, at sixteen, William took his place in the mines.

In this expanding industrial town, the United Mine Workers of America, including many militant and class-conscious workers, not only fought to protect the miners from exploitation, but also formed the nucleus of the workers' social life. American miners had a proud heritage of struggle — more strikes, more aggressive tactics against the employers than workers in any other occupation. Billy Green met socialists, anarchists, revolutionaries of all hues. But he had a cautious streak that led him to shy away from strange ideas. He preferred teaching Sunday school in the local Baptist Church to wrangling about the class struggle and ways to change the world. The serious-minded young man who didn't smoke or chew or even swear, shrugged away the "subversive" opinions he heard all about him in the union, and concentrated on getting a firm grasp on the workings of inner union politics.

At twenty-one he married. He worked in the mines but quite naturally he dreamed of success, the American kind of success that brought comfort and prestige. In 1900, he landed his first job as a union official when he was elected sub-district president of the U.M.W. His days in the mines were over. From then on it was a matter of waiting for the breaks in order to push higher in the union. And in 1906 he stepped into the presidency of the Ohio state district of the union where he remained for four years. To bolster his position, he dabbled in Ohio politics. A loyal Democrat, he acted as delegate at large to the 1912 convention, and the next year won a seat in the State Senate. In his two terms — four years — he soon established himself as "regular," a dependable administration man willing enough to take orders. It was Senator Green who made the sob speech for the administration at the end of important debates, a technique which he perfected and which proved invaluable throughout his career.

With hair combed neatly to one side, in plain well-fitting clothes, apple-cheeked Senator Green cut a nice, and unobtrusive, figure as Democratic floor leader. He drafted occasional bills, carefully progressive in tone, not too extreme but calculated to add prestige to their sponsor. His measure eliminating certain abuses in the mining industry, his bill instituting a short work week for women, his compensation act passed the legislature without great opposition. More important, he introduced legislation abolishing the payment of miners on the basis of their output after coal had been screened (a trick that allowed operators to disregard a large part of the miner's tonnage). Green's proposal substituted payment on "mine run"; in other words, on coal as it came out of the pit. When the miners struck in 1914, their militant support aided considerably in forcing the bill's adoption.

During his second term, Green proved that he had not altered too greatly since his younger Coshocton days. Then he had meticulously shunned socialistic ideas. And now, with the Akron rubber workers striking for higher wages and against miserable working conditions, Green looked askance at the organizers of the Industrial Workers of the World who had come to Akron and turned confusion into effective action. As chairman of the legislative investigating committee, Green smelled "outside agitators." He denounced the I.W.W. leadership, condemning the autocracy of the rubber owners as an afterthought. His attack largely accounted for the strike's failure. The rubber workers made no gains and returned to work under even more oppressive conditions. Nevertheless, labor's representative in the State Senate had saved workers from revolution — and higher wages.

State politics aided Green to obtain, in 1913, the office of secretary-treasurer of the U.M.W. He moved to Indianapolis and settled down to his new job, though he kept a soft place in his heart for Coshocton which he revisited regularly. He was not one to drop old friends; as the town's most distinguished citizen, he took care to show that success had not turned his head. But his career had just begun. Events soon again broke favorably for him. A vacancy in the A.F. of L. executive council in 1914 left the powerful U.M.W. unrepresented. Gompers offered the seventh vice presidency, which carried with it membership in the council, to John P. White, head of the U.M.W. White, however, indignantly refused the position of *seventh* vice president as beneath his level of importance. Gompers appointed another candidate, but the miners still remained without a council position. Finally, to solve this vexing problem, Gompers cast about for a compromise, and ended by selecting William Green for the eighth vice presidency. Green had no false pride. Unknown outside his own union, he refused to let dignity stand in his way: he would eagerly have accepted the eightieth chair at the council table. Time, he realized, would eliminate the older members and with each death move the line up one seat. By 1924, Green had risen to third place.

A sober, plodding man, not endowed with great imagination or overwhelming ambition, Green never seriously imagined himself president of the A.F. of L. But he found that with patience and by avoiding open conflict which too often brought enemies, he could get ahead. And just because he took no leading rôle in Federation affairs, the unassuming Green, Elk, Odd Fellow, ardent dry, family man with a pleasant wife, four daughters and a son, found himself without any effort on his part elected to the presidency of the Federation at a salary of $12,000 a year with expenses, and looked upon as a force in the American scene.

"Labor is safe under his leadership," a Richmond paper pointed out, "capital has nothing to fear during his regime, and the public is fortunate in having him as the responsible spokesman of a highly important group of citizens." Throughout the country, anti-labor newspapers congratulated the A.F. of L. on its "sane choice." William Green studied the editorials. With his election, he became America's most obliging — and probably most prolific — public speaker. He appeared everywhere, before Rotarians, Elks, Masons, Odd Fellows, American Legionnaires, church groups, Y's, and now and then, before the workers. In a high pitch of pulpit ecstasy he told a conference, about to initiate a Southern organization campaign:

> "I know as I speak to you this morning, that our thoughts instinctively turn to the greatness of our Country and to our homes and while all of us come from different communities and sections which we call our homes in a large sense this great America is our home and we love America because it is our home and we are thinking about its greatness, its resources, the common heritage of liberty and democracy that has been conferred upon us, the breadth and the length of our land, the greatest nation in all the world and we are happy to live here in America and to call America our home. We want to make America what it ought to be, a land of happy homes where liberty, in its fullest sense, is enjoyed by all classes and all groups of people; where he who lives in an exalted and influential position may enjoy all the rights to which he is entitled and where the humblest in all the land may walk in the orderly paths of freedom and liberty and enjoy all the blessings that come to the rich and to the mighty."

The refrain always had the same lilt, as though Green were still answering the hotheads who had talked so freely in those early Coshocton days: he promised to be a "good" labor leader, he pledged that he would inconvenience no one. The theory which held that class distinctions existed, Green declared to be a "foreign" doctrine without relevance to America. His leadership, he stressed immediately after his election, would reject the philosophy of class conflict and steadfastly "adhere to those fundamental principles so ably championed by Mr. Gompers, and upon which the superstructure of organized labor rests."

Nor did he intend these words merely as a tribute to the deceased Gompers. William Green had been trained in the Gompers tradition; it had become as deeply ingrained in him as the indelible blue spots under his skin which he carried as a result of his early days in the mines. He clung to his heritage because he believed in it, and because he understood nothing else. With the nation in a period of unprecedented financial gambling, Green foresaw only higher and higher and still higher profits, limitless growth of industry, and as a result, more and more jobs. Wages would rise too. Of that he felt certain; for he was convinced that the just owners could easily be made to understand the "wisdom of labor's position" when it asked for a reasonable share of the profits.

In the subsequent years, from 1925 to 1929, as the membership of the unions dropped precipitously, as unemployment spread, as strikes and labor organizations were brutally crushed, as the workers' standard of living remained stationary while profits mounted and the stock market shot up out of sight, disillusioned Green pulled Gompers' tattered mantle more closely about him and continued to grind out padded, patterned speeches proclaiming industrial peace and good will. Gompers, the great opportunist, had handed down the rule book; Green, content to be a figurehead, accepted it without question.

Any other man, even a strong man in the same position, would have responded to Green's conditioning in much the same manner. For though the dead Gompers had been unable to push his own candidate, Matthew Woll, into the presidency, he had saddled his philosophy securely on the executive council and on the rest of the A.F. of L. Green had no desire to fight the council; he wanted only to carry out its wishes. His willingness to follow, his faculty for strict neutrality allowed the stronger heads of international and national unions to function without restraint. Under Green, the A.F. of L. drifted aimlessly, like a rudderless boat, and the official labor movement tapered off into a dues-paying club without drive or purpose or even a semblance of accomplishment. There was good reason for this, a reason that necessitates an understanding of the Gompers philosophy which Green, reverent toward tradition, adhered to implicitly.

BASIC in the Gompers tradition was the rejection of independent political struggle in favor of economic action. From the premise that the American labor movement was "different," that it was "exceptional," stemmed the abortive deductions that class antagonisms did not exist, that trade unionism in America must solicit only simple and immediate concessions, that a long range objective was impossible, and that complete collaboration with the employer was the desired goal.

Before 1886, when the American Federation of Labor officially came into existence, Samuel Gompers, aggressive leader of the then powerful craft union of cigar makers, had already developed hostility to the independent politicalization of the labor movement. Strike defeats, in which the national and state governments helped to smash workers' organizations through the courts and by calling out troops to break picket lines and demoralize the men, threatened the lives of the unions. Gompers grew suspicious of the government, expanding this suspicion into a theory that labor should concentrate solely on the building of trade unions. Avoidance of labor struggle, Gompers concluded, meant the avoidance of governmental interference in union activities. By directing the energy of workers to the maintenance and strengthening of their organizations, by shunning strike action, Gompers reasoned that labor could prevent the government from meddling in union affairs. It followed that labor should keep rigidly out of the political field. If necessary, workers could "punish their enemies, reward their friends" — but always within the existing two party system. Instead of fighting the government's anti-labor offensive, Gompers capitulated before it; instead of invading the political arena and through an effective labor party electing candidates to office who would protect the interests of labor, Gompers ruled out independent politics. By retreating, by refusing to take measures that would reinforce the organized labor movement, Gompers renounced even the attempt to remove the causes of labor's weakness.

In addition, disagreements with the progressives helped to woo Gompers from his former lukewarm pseudo-liberalism which some have called socialism. Personal animosity developed into an unreasoning hate of all principles smacking of progress. Gompers conveniently labeled them socialistic. His own overbearing egotism, which could tolerate no rivalry, sensed in the progressives a danger to his growing power. Once he had ascended to a commanding position, Gompers shied away from the rivalry of forward looking workers whom he contemptuously dubbed "intellectuals." He functioned on a narrow opportunistic basis: that which worked at the moment was correct; let the future provide for itself. Political action posited a long term program. Obsessed by anxiety lest the labor movement would fall apart, Gompers stressed the necessity for immediate gains, for "pure and simple" business unionism struggling for better wages and shorter hours and very little else. True, there were periods, particularly in the early '90s, when the A.F. of L. branched out independently into the political field, but these were brief excursions and Gompers went along with a movement he could not halt only in order to retain his position in the saddle. What he really desired boiled down to "A fair day's work for a fair day's pay." As Gompers' mentor, Adolph Strasser, president of the Cigar Makers Union, explained in 1883 to a U. S. Senate Commission:

"We have no ultimate aim. We are going on from day to day. We are fighting for immediate objects, objects that can be realized in a few years."

By rejecting independent political action, the A.F. of L. denied class antagonisms and turned its back on the possibility of fruitful development. Early in his career, Gompers would have accepted the formulation of Karl Marx's collaborator, Friederich Engels, a keen student of the early American labor movement. Engels phrased the problem, "The very existence of Trades Unions is proof sufficient of the fact: if they are not made to fight against the encroachments of capital, what are they made for? There is no use mincing matters. No milksop words can hide the ugly fact that present society is mainly divided into two great antagonistic classes."

In fact, the preamble of the A.F. of L. constitution emphasized that "a struggle is going on in all nations of the civilized world, a struggle between the capitalist and the laborer, which grows in intensity from year to year, and will work disastrous results to the toiling millions if they are not combined for mutual protection." But Gompers repudiated this theory of class antagonism, and ostrich-like, hid his face from the conclusion that Engels logically drew: "A struggle between two great classes of society necessarily becomes a political struggle." Particularly did Gompers balk at the application of this logic to the labor movement. Engels continued, "In every struggle of class against class, the next end fought for is political power." Gompers rejected "the next end." He contended that the American labor movement was "exceptional." It was not imperative to raise the labor movement from the low level that aimed only at immediate economic demands to the higher stage of political action. As a result, Gompers, and with him the official labor movement, repudiated independent political struggle, class contradictions, and the need to organize all the workers in favor of the defeatist (and as it proved, completely ineffectual) theory of collaboration with the employers, and capitulation to the demands of the ruling class. Yet all labor struggles in which the American workers were involved proved the fallacy of his stand, proved the existence of classes whose interests were fundamentally conflicting. Homestead, Ludlow, Pullman, Pittsburgh — scores of other dramatic instances could not alter Gompers' insistence that reality was false and that his own fantasy alone conformed to objective conditions.

Furthermore, the constant influx of foreign born workers aided Gompers in splitting the labor movement. The presence of the foreign born was utilized to create antagonisms: differences in background and cultural heritage between the immigrants and those workers already "Americanized" proved a gulf which took time to bridge. What was on analysis a superficial rift prevented the American working class from presenting a common front to the industrialists; mutual economic and political needs were overshadowed by false jealousies and by hostilities of group against group within the working class itself. Far from discouraging this evil, Gompers stimulated it. Foreign workers, unfamiliar with the language and customs of the strange new land, found themselves cut off from their brother workers, looked down upon, discriminated against.

Many immigrants swallowed the American myth with its false hope that the worker in a factory could some day own the factory or one just like it. The myth impeded the development of class consciousness, while the success of the very few reinforced the illusion and confused the majority. Those immigrants who brought with them political theories or socialist convictions that differentiated them in the new environment, dropped or rationalized their former beliefs in order to be more quickly assimilated. For Gompers and his disciples insisted that socialist theories, if they influenced the conduct of organized labor, endangered the workers' cause already under vicious attack from the employing class. He never tired of stressing that the working class as a whole must turn its back on theory and struggle for immediate relief. It must preserve the weak and tottering labor organizations by battling only for "pure and simple" economic ends.

There was some basis for Gompers' reluctance to supplement economic struggle with independent political action. American workers possessed as yet no matured class experience to guide them. When exploitation became too severe in the industrial centers, workers moved to the less developed hinterlands. Particularly were the unskilled, mostly immigrants, drawn to the West by the prospect of free land and by fabulous tales of easy money and independence. And so soon as the unskilled left workshops for the agricultural fields, their places were taken by newly arrived immigrants who supplied the owners with a fresh source of cheap labor. To Gompers, with his opportunistic approach to the labor movement, the migration of the unskilled indicated their instability. His reasoning led him to neglect unskilled workers for the skilled.

Naturally, Gompers did not singlehandedly determine the course of labor's development in this country. But he reflected it and at the same time helped to mold it. He steadfastly refused to respond to vital changes occurring in American industry and finance. Gompers, and with him the official labor movement, clung to tenets which during the eighties contained some truth but which became antiquated as industry expanded and its structure altered.

At the time of the A.F. of L.'s inception in 1886, the labor movement was in part, at least, progressive and more or less adapted to objective conditions in industry. American economy was composed for the most part of numerous small enterprises employing a relatively small group of skilled workers. The unions protected these skilled groups. The A.F. of L. ideal of "job-monopoly" tended to limit unions to memberships composed of highly-trained men, thereby achieving a partial restriction of the labor supply and so maintaining high wages and the preferred position of those in the unions.

The 1890's saw a shift in the organization of industry which gained momentum in the succeeding decades. As the frontiers narrowed and workers, even the unskilled, became rooted in the industrial areas, fundamental changes simultaneously occurred in the mass-production industries. Coördinated operations tended to squeeze out the small enterprises and replace them with the large trusts. Mechanization eliminated the demand for skilled labor. Modern technique in production (the conveyor system, intra-factory transport, the crane, automatic and semi-automatic machinery) led to the unification of the labor process in large plants. Operations were simplified; the inevitable result was that semi-skilled workers replaced the skilled, and in many instances replaced the unskilled. In the decisive section of American industry, semi-skilled workers far outnumbered all other categories.

Soon even the monopoly of the unskilled laborer — excavation work — was invaded. A ditch-digging machine, for example, operated by one man and a helper, could accomplish in the same amount of time the work of forty-four shovel men. Similarly, highly skilled workers, whose training, accuracy, and nimbleness made them expensive to the employer, were displaced by the semi-skilled who in a very short time could learn to operate machines in factories fully as efficiently as men with years of experience. Thus in the glass industry machines eliminated the demand for skilled glass blowers. Semi-skilled labor predominated in many textile operations, in the chemical, steel, food, automobile, shoe, rubber, garment, and scores of other industries. To illustrate how far the demand for workers with little or no experience subsequently went in the Ford plant, of the 7,782 operations performed, 43 percent in 1926 demanded but one day's training; 36 percent one day to one week's training; 6 percent from one to two weeks; 14 percent from one month to a year; and only one percent from one to six years.

The A.F. of L., however, failed to reflect these significant changes in industry. It continued to defend job-monopoly. At the time of Gompers' death and after, the composition of the A.F. of L. unions reflected a philosophy of organization based on conditions that had long since disappeared. By maintaining rigid craft lines, the Federation excluded the vast majority of workers and no attempt was made to organize them. The A.F. of L. did not keep pace with the changing industrial scene; it clung to forms suitable enough to an era of free enterprise and free competition but completely obsolete in an era of monopoly and financial centralization. Gompersism, which almost from its inception came into violent conflict with reality, continued to rule the A.F. of L. It existed at the expense of the masses in favor of small, isolated labor groups which found themselves increasingly displaced by the semi-skilled.

Moreover, the conflict between the skilled, and the semi-skilled and unskilled workers weakened the working class. Jealous of their positions in their crafts, sensing the leveling process of growing industrialization, the skilled groups fought incursions, raised craft barriers, accented the division between themselves and the supposedly menial workers. Organized labor created its own aristocracy, its own factions that blocked unity in the ranks and discouraged a solid front against the owning class. In the international and national unions, the officers accepted the ideals of American business methods; they often left labor to go into business for themselves, or in their capacity of workers' delegates acted not as representatives of the membership but as owners of a corporation. The goal of business unionism was financial solvency, and large treasuries originally intended as strike funds for self-protection soon became an incubus preventing progressive action. The treasuries, so the officials felt, had to be preserved at all costs; in order not to diminish union funds (which incidentally provided the large salaries of union officials), the rich unions repeatedly pronounced strikes illegal or found technical reasons for withholding aid to the membership. Those unions with strong treasuries discouraged the militancy of the rank and file, refused strike benefits on the grounds that the union must be prepared for some bigger strike in the nebulous future which always failed to materialize. And this attitude militated against sympathy strikes or concern for the welfare of workers in other trades.

The tradition of skilled workers nurtured the rigid craft divisions that had long typified the A.F. of L. Each union guarded its jurisdiction enviously. Gompers at one time refused to allow workers who made stogies into his cigar makers union on the ground that they did not make cigars but a smoke of inferior quality! Craft unionism, and its concomitant, the hatred of "dual unionism" (invariably the result of the executive council's failure to bring organization to the great mass of workers), became the fetish of American labor. Craft snobbery impeded the unionization of the vast working class; high initiation fees and strict rules of entry in most instances kept the unskilled workers outside the labor movement. Continual jurisdictional disputes hampered organization. The custom whereby each craft entered into separate agreements with the employer in an industry precluded unity of action. If one craft struck, the other crafts in the same industry, even in the same shop, continued work — as they had pledged to do in their contracts. Similarly, workers in one plant signed contracts with the management while workers in the same craft in a neighboring plant either were unable to obtain such a contract or signed different agreements. Craft scabbed on craft, workers performing identical operations in plants often located in the same vicinity broke strikes of brother workers. This lack of unity made the unions cautious, timid, afraid of struggle, afraid of strikes. While the employers were more closely unified than ever by the growth of monopolies with their interlocking directorates, and of huge trusts with centralized management and control, the official labor movement faced stalemate. The static role of the A.F. of L. only reinforced the powerful position of the employers. Failure to recognize fundamental changes in industry placed Gompers and his executive council in the position of defending themselves against the tanks, airplanes, and machine guns of the employers with a rusty blunderbuss which they had sworn not to fire.

"Sanctity of contracts" replaced struggle. "Amicable" agreements between the owners and labor officials became the all important consideration. The unions found themselves bound hand and foot by these contracts, which often stretched over long periods, with sympathetic strikes outlawed, and unity non-existent. Likewise, negotiations for contracts brought labor leaders closer to employers. The official-dom, depending almost solely on across-the-table diplomacy, found coöperation with employers much easier than resistance. That this collaboration could not and did not bring with it an equality at the bargaining table was of no importance to the Gompers command. Even more significant, the contractual obligations entered into by the executive council and based on capitulation to the employers bene-fited only a handful of highly skilled workers and left the millions unorganized open to complete exploitation.

Yet despite Gompers, class relationships remained unchanged. The employers controlled the economic and financial institutions; the courts; the local, state, and federal governments. The owning class could demand and get injunctions, could sue the unions and cripple them financially, could railroad militant and progressive leaders to jail, could obtain state police, armed deputies, even troops if the need arose. By relinquishing the strike, by relinquishing political activity whereby labor could gain at least some control of the forms of government, Gompers and the other labor leaders found them-selves sitting across from the employers at the conference tables without the power to back threats or to force concessions or to pre-serve those gains already won by labor. Class lines were blurred; union leaders became apologists for their organizations, and soon identified themselves and those they represented with the employers.

WILLIAM GREEN no more thought of questioning the Gompers heritage than Moses dreamed of challenging the Ten Command-ments. In 1935, Green was still insisting that "the majority of employ-ers sincerely and honestly wish to maintain decent wage standards and humane conditions of employment. They neither seek the ex-ploitation of labor nor the exploitation of the consuming public. They are inspired by a keen sense of justice and are influenced in all their business dealings by a spirit of fair-dealing and fair-play."

At times, Green's reiteration of this theme sounded suspiciously like whistling to keep up courage. No doubt he desired above all things peace and pleasant relations with the employing class. But the price he paid for them was steep. "The right to strike," he informed the labor movement, "involves so many considerations that it ought to be utilized only as a last resort."

This would be true were it not that throughout his twelve years as president of the A.F. of L., Green never conceded that conditions warranted the use of this "last resort." Though the wage of 33,000,-000 American workers in the "prosperous" days of 1929 averaged $25 a week which placed their incomes below what the U.S. Bureau of Census found to be a minimum comfort level, Green and the executive council gave no thought to raising this level. That half the workers received even less than the meager $25 a week wage, existing at a bare subsistence standard of living or worse, failed to alter Green's steadfast resolution to discourage organized struggle by the working class. When pressure from the membership grew so powerful that Green was forced to make a show of supporting a strike, he immediately attempted to smooth things over by settling it before the strikers had gained their objectives. Jurisdictional disputes between the unions continued feverishly enough; but Gompers had ordered peace with the employers and Green guarded the tablets of the law. "If reason and judgment are enthroned," he asserted doggedly, "directing the lives and actions of men, we can establish a relationship in industry which will speed the cause of peace, satisfaction, and prosperity."

His conviction stemmed from the belief, borrowed from Gompers, that it was vital to abide by

"our consistent refusal to commit our movement to a class conscious philosophy which would have entailed tactics based upon a belief that irreconcilable conflict exists between owners of capital and labor. The American trade unionist has always believed that conference and joint negotiation were the way to decide conditions written into the work contract."

The hollowness of Green's homily that completely negated the preamble of the A.F. of L. constitution, was illustrated by the failure of the American labor movement to grow. When Green became president in 1924, the average membership of the A.F. of L. totaled 2,865,799, already a drop of approximately two and a quarter millions from the high mark of four years before. Green disregarded the warning. In consequence, the Federation limped along until 1929 with a stationary membership, shockingly inadequate in the light of the 30,000,000 American workers still eligible for organization. The subsequent economic crisis, instead of increasing membership, lowered it, until by the middle of 1933 it had sunk to the 1916 level of 2,126,796.

Such was the result of Green's stewardship during the first nine years after Gompers' death. His energy had been directed against the "Red menace," and in conjunction with the employers, against such militant independent unions as those created by the Trade Union Unity League in 1929. The independents of the T.U.U.L. emphasized the need for bringing the unorganized into effective industrial unions. Their program, supplemented by a policy of attempting to spur the A.F. of L. into motion, not surprisingly terrified Green and his associates on the executive council who saw in it a threat to their jobs. For the T.U.U.L. exposed to the majority of American workers just how illusory was the "prosperity" hailed by Green and just what steps should be taken to protect the working class from the terrific exploitation.

Once menaced, Green hit out blindly against this effort to vitalize the labor unions, and simultaneously drew closer to the employers for protection. His sense of decorum, shared by the executive council, prevented the A.F. of L. from undertaking a serious campaign to organize workers outside the labor movement. When the officialdom did contemplate such a drive, Green first notified the employers and meekly asked permission to proceed. If permission were refused — as inevitably it was in the mass-production industries — Green repeated his polite plea to employer "reasonableness" and promptly relinquished the drive. His experience in 1926 with Henry Ford proved typical. After the Ford Motor Company rebuffed Green's overtures toward organizing its plants, Green clucked like an angry hen, but he scrapped the elaborate plans just as he had previously canceled his intention to organize General Motors. Sweet reasonableness led only to capitulation.

In lieu of an aggressive policy, Green busied himself explaining labor's objectives in countless speeches and magazine articles. He sounded strikingly like a cautious social worker with his requests for free public schools, insurance, holidays, extension of contracts, and arbitration. Characteristically, he neglected to back his program with any suggestion as to how it could be achieved, overlooking the fact that to realize these aims, labor had first to face more basic problems. In reality, Green had no serious intention of forcing his program on reluctant industrialists. Instead, he waited for generous employers to drop concessions in his lap. He begged from door to door, hat in hand, with a tenderness that elicited no response from the owners: they only laughed at Green, and through him, mocked the whole official labor movement.

The Gompers tradition led Green even farther afield. From it stemmed not only the ineffectualness of the official labor movement but the abuses: lack of democracy in the unions, grafting, racketeering, shady political deals. Even the cautious Green was infected by the demoralization that poisoned the A.F. of L. Well aware of the corruption, though he managed to avoid personally implicating himself too deeply, Green closed his eyes to the dishonesty that surrounded him. Yet class coöperation involved him in acts which brought discredit and defeat to the labor movement.

In New York City the A.F. of L. as late as 1936 granted craft charters to notorious labor gangsters (such as Charles and Arthur Herbert, poultry racketeers). When Green was asked to help stamp out this abuse, he sidestepped the issue. The liberal press charged him with encouraging racketeering. Green realized that interference meant treading on the toes of Matthew Woll.

At the 1936 Tampa convention, he sided with the officials of the International Seamen's Union against the striking membership who protested that their leaders had illegally refused to hold union elections. Green approved the motion to declare the rank and file strike outlaw, and by so doing allied himself with David Grange, president of the Marine Cooks and Stewards, though Grange was unable to explain what he had done with $143,000 in union funds; with Oscar Carlson who had been defeated for office in a supervised union election; with Ivan Hunter who hired gangsters to bolster his rule on the waterfront. Nor did Green attempt to revoke the charter of New Jersey's Hudson County Central Labor Union when it endorsed for the mayoralty Boss Hague, notorious open shopper and chief of a steam-rolling political machine.

Honesty was at a premium among the high officials in the A.F. of L. and Green reflected this. As editor of the *Federationist*, official magazine of the A.F. of L., Green accepted an advertisement from the open shop General Electric Company though this corporation had forced a company union on its employees and was having labor troubles at the time the magazine carried its advertisement. In response to an inquiry by an indignant union member, Green explained that the printing of an advertisement did not necessarily imply endorsement of the company's labor relations. He was astounded when in 1929 the Typographical Union rebuked him for speaking over the radio on a program sponsored by *Collier's*. Union printers had been locked out several years before by the Crowell Publishing Company in Springfield, Ohio, where *Collier's* was printed. The union had spent large sums to inform labor that *Collier's* remained on the unfair list. But Green felt it no contradiction to talk under the auspices of the open shop magazine and, by lending his name, to help sell an unfair product.

More flagrant were Green's dealings with William Randolph Hearst, whom even Gompers had excoriated as a vicious enemy of labor. When the Federation Bank & Trust Co. of New York, controlled by William Green, John Sullivan of the New York State Federation of Labor, and other leading A.F. of L. officials, failed in 1931, the statement of assets and liabilities showed loans of over $250,000 made to Hearst newspapers. Ferdinand Lundberg in *Imperial Hearst* revealed that the bank loaned

> "$50,000 to Moe Annenberg, general circulation manager of the Hearst chain of newspapers . . . also endorsed a note of $12,687 for Joseph A. Moore of the New York *Morning Telegraph*, the leading sporting and theatrical sheet of the city; two *unsecured* loans of $50,000 each to Hearst's *American Weekly, Inc.;* two *unsecured* loans of $50,000 each to Hearst's New York *American*. Moe was also a borrower of $20,000 on collateral." [Lundberg's italics]

Not only did Green approve lending large sums of money to Hearst. The executive council, at the 1936 Tampa convention, forbade the Seattle Central Labor Council from taking further sympathetic action in support of the American Newspaper Guild, and condemned its past aid to the Guild's strike against Hearst's *Post-Intelligencer*. At the same time, Green and the executive council killed six resolutions advocating a boycott of the Hearst press, nobly asking, "Can we come before this convention praising freedom of the press with our lips and denying it with our votes?"

Surrounded as he was by corruption, Green neither condemned it nor attempted to curb it or stamp it out. Rather, he pretended ignorance. By overlooking abuses, he could maintain friendly relations with the other members of the executive council. In every way, Green desired to be just the kind of president the council wanted. Things functioned smoothly in official circles, the dues came in, and the A.F. of L. was slowly dying of dry rot from the top.

The economic crisis raised contradictions even within the sheltered executive council. The officials found that they could restrain their membership no longer: throughout the country strikes broke out, the workers defeated outworn leaders and elected militants in their stead. Everywhere union men demanded the organization of the unskilled and talked industrial unionism. Green was at his wit's end. Unrest meant friction; friction led to clashes with employers, and Green had spent his life building peace and understanding. His speeches no longer had effect: the rank and file failed to heed his warning that the Red hordes of Moscow would destroy them if they didn't toe the line drawn long ago by Samuel Gompers and carefully preserved by his successor, William Green.

THE DIFFICULTY arose primarily because the economic crisis raised economic problems. Green retained the misconceptions of Gompersism: he failed to realize the change in industry caused by the closing of the frontiers, the inability of the unskilled to migrate when exploitation became too severe, the growth of monopoly in an age of imperialism. Working class struggle was no longer merely economic, but took on a political character which Green was totally unequipped to comprehend. He still sought to unionize the skilled workers though the vast body of unskilled and semi-skilled were now the key to all successful organization. Green's years as statistician for the United Mine Workers, during which he collected neat pages of figures and facts, hardly prepared him to cope with a period of intense economic breakdown brought about by just those causes whose existence he failed to recognize.

Green cast about desperately for a solution. After two years' worry, he announced the cure that would pull America out of the morass. Mr. Green, formerly an advocate of prohibition, called for beer. Once America regained beer, the country would receive the spark that would "exhilarate industry and lift us out of the depression just as the automobile took us out of the bad times of 1921."

In the meantime, he agreed at President Hoover's conference of industrialists and A.F. of L. potentates that "coöperation" between capital and labor should be strengthened. The owners pledged no reduction of employment and wages; the union leaders agreed to outlaw strikes and to frown on attempts by workers to improve their conditions. The employers thereupon instituted wholesale discharges and wage cuts, the speed-up and stretch-out systems. But to William Green, a bargain was a bargain; he lived up to his end by maintaining the frown on his round, humorless face.

Beer came and still unemployment increased and American economy declined. Helplessly, Green threw up his hands, insisting that after all he was not to blame. "The responsibility for the application of remedies to the existing situation," he protested, "must rest with the owners and managers of industry and with those who control the economic and financial institutions of the nation." It was up to the owning class, he pointed out, since "policies, both economic and financial are originated by those who own and control industry." If the capitalists did not do something, Green or the rest of the executive council had no plan to offer. The labor movement must remain inert, waiting for the industrial and financial powers "to overcome our existing difficulties and bring about a return of prosperity." Now that Green had convinced himself that the solution was not in labor's hands, there remained nothing for the A.F. of L. to do but wait. Certainly Green would never allow labor to bring pressure on those in power.

Unemployment embarrassed Green even more. For two years, he pretended that it did not exist; he would have liked to continue the pretense but that was impossible. Finally, at the 1931 Vancouver convention, he breathed deeply and burst out with a warning that hunger could cause revolution. It took him another year before he could summon the courage to threaten that if labor were not relieved by a six hour day and a five day week, the A.F. of L. would resort to "force." The word stuck in his throat. By "force," he apologetically explained, he meant economic force, perhaps even picketing and boycott.

The defiant pose did not become William Green. He never risked it again, but resumed his polite, friendly reasonableness. Even when the N.R.A. was enacted and stimulated organization, Green failed to take advantage of Section 7-A which assured employees "the right to organize and bargain collectively through representatives of their own choosing."

Not that Green disapproved of the N.R.A. — far from it. But his participation virtually ended with his endorsement. He failed to launch an aggressive organizing campaign, though individual unions did and he was forced to grant many federal charters. At one moment, Green secretly ordered organizers to slow down the enrollment in the Federation. The wave of strikes that followed the enactment of the N.R.A. worried Green. He knew only one response — to discourage, if necessary to break, the workers' offensive. Accordingly, he resisted the 1934 West Coast maritime strike and proclaimed the general strike that followed "illegal," "unauthorized." He brought pressure on Francis Gorman to end the 1934 general textile strike in the East on the assurance that the government would investigate. Green's desire for peace at any cost in this case brought the workers nothing except blacklists and violence. The Federation president refused to protest the killings of workers by police, the brutality of vigilantes, the terror that raged throughout the South. Nor did he lend aid to the teamsters in Minneapolis (in fact, Green sent a special representative, Meyer Lewis, to the strike area to raise the Red scare and disorganize the workers); he disregarded the Toledo Electric Auto-Lite strikers, the agricultural workers, and the hundreds of labor battles.

He remained the bewildered tool of the most reactionary group within the executive council. The more serious conditions grew, and the more insistent workers became for immediate, decisive steps against economic oppression, the more stubbornly Green refused to commit himself.

By 1934 at the San Francisco convention, dissatisfaction had become manifest within the executive council. John L. Lewis, of the United Mine Workers, an industrial union, realized that unrest among the workers not only gave the A.F. of L. the opportunity to unionize the unorganized, but also that such a move had become imperative if the A.F. of L. was to serve any useful purpose. Moreover, the new drive must build industrial unions (which would include all crafts and occupations within a given industry, whether skilled or unskilled) in the basic industries of steel, rubber, automobile, glass, and textile. The health of Lewis' own union was at stake:

the United Mine Workers could not survive unless the mass-production industries were organized.

William Hutcheson, head of the largest craft organization, Matthew Woll, sovereign of the reactionaries, the many other craft officials objected to the campaign for industrial unionism because they feared it would destroy or absorb their own unions. In that case, what would become of them, their salaries, their jobs? Daniel Tobin, president of the teamsters, inveighed against "the rubbish that have lately come into other organizations." The convention compromised. Acknowledging the need for industrial organization in principle, while further declaring that craft and industrial unions could exist harmoniously side by side within the A.F. of L., the executive council put through a suitably vague resolution agreeing that organization should begin and intimating that it would start in the coming year.

Nothing happened. The delegates recognized even before the 1935 convention met in Atlantic City that so long as the executive council ran things, they would be fed speeches, not results. Certainly they couldn't expect timid William Green to take the initiative against the majority of the council. He was far too occupied scurrying about trying to find some non-existent middle ground in the controversy.

The factions lined up at Atlantic City for the showdown that could no longer be postponed. Those backing the industrial drive declared their intention of aiding the campaign in steel and spurring similar campaigns in other industries. It was time, they announced, for action. They would see that American labor got it.

Immediately after the convention, eight of the largest unions in the A.F. of L. formed the Committee for Industrial Organization to carry through their decision. Clearly Hutcheson, Woll, Morrison, Wharton, and the other die-hards on the executive council would never tolerate the C.I.O. Green, with only the past to guide him, tagged pathetically after the craft bloc. Afraid of Lewis, Green blustered and retreated. Though he was a member of Lewis' union, Green had long since renounced struggle as a union weapon. For years he had been out of contact with the realities of working class life. True, he still visited Coshocton, Ohio, and gossiped with the home town boys. But the mine where he had spent his early youth had been shut down for many years, and mining remained a hazy memory glimpsed by William Green through the charts and figures that littered his desk. In a panic over the bitterness of the struggle within the Federation, Green feebly attempted to play the historic rôle of great conciliator.

He was miscast. Trade unionists failed to respond to his flowery orations as industrialists seemingly had once responded. In an attempt to show authority that he had never possessed, Green drew himself to his full stature as president of the A.F. of L. and ordered Lewis to abandon the C.I.O. Lewis answered by resigning from the executive council. One after the other, central trades and labor councils, federal unions, even the membership of the craft unions, defied Green and in the face of his threats openly sympathized with and supported the C.I.O.

As a last resort, Green capitulated to the die-hards on the executive council who decided to show the insubordinate unions within the C.I.O. that they could not disregard tradition without paying dearly. To the solemn reminder issued by the council that those unions affiliated with the C.I.O. were guilty of violating the dread taboo of dual unionism, Lewis and his supporters replied that they were only too eager to remain within the Federation. But, they pointed out, the attempt to organize workers for whom no unions existed, or to bring them into unions already set up but not functioning, hardly constituted dual unionism. The executive council could make no impression on the rebels. There remained but one last warning to be exercised before expulsion: Green and the executive council "tried" the offenders (though those on trial, realizing they were already judged and found guilty, refused to appear when summoned) and proceeded to suspend all unions affiliated with the C.I.O. — one third of the A.F. of L. membership. The council understood quite well that under the A.F. of L. constitution these suspensions were illegal. That knowledge did not restrain Green or his associates; they abandoned all pretense of preserving unity within the Federation or of considering the wishes of the majority of the membership.

"The issue," Green repeated as if his repetition would have magical effect, "raised by the action of the eight international unions referred to is not craft unionism versus industrial unionism, but rather the question whether organization policies determined by a majority vote of the delegates in attendance at a convention shall be carried out." And again, "The question is: Cannot workingmen and women of this nation, through their chosen representatives, meet as a family, and then, as a family, after threshing out their problems thoroughly, settle their differences; and finally, can we not go out as *one* in the economic field and fight for policies we adopt?"

Democracy, majority rule, one big family. Democracy in conventions where delegates were handpicked by the heads of the international and national unions. Majority rule in the face of the executive council's refusal to carry out the mandate of the convention which called for organization of all workers not already in unions. One big family despite Green's refusal to listen to the C.I.O.'s suggestion that at the 1936 Tampa Convention the suspended unions be allowed full vote in return for a promise to abide by the majority decision of the delegates.

Furthermore, Green's lofty words, judged by his own "democratic" methods in Detroit and Akron late in 1935, had an ironic ring to them. When Green arrived in Detroit to present an international charter to the auto workers, he replied to objections and questions concerning the wording of the charter: "Take this or nothing." Waving aside an election, he appointed Francis J. Dillon president of the union over the protests of the majority of delegates. He handpicked the entire executive board, eliminating all leaders who had participated in strike action during the two previous years.

Immediately thereafter, Green hurried to Akron on the similar mission of delivering an international charter to the rubber workers. The delegates, forewarned by his arbitrary dictation in Detroit, demanded "democratic procedure." Green responded, "You can neither accept, nor reject, nor change any of this charter. I confer it on you. That's why you're here!" But the rubber workers defied Green's "democracy" and elected their own progressive officers.

BY THE BEGINNING OF 1937, the executive council, with Green as its spokesman, no longer troubled to conceal its strike-breaking tactics. When the United Automobile Workers, backed by the C.I.O., struck the General Motors Corporation's plants in Detroit, Flint, and elsewhere, and demanded collective bargaining and better conditions, Green openly fought the strike. Reinforcing General Motors' refusal to recognize the auto workers' union, Green chose the critical moment of the strike, when vigilantes were on the verge of attacking the workers, to insist that no agreement made between the corporation and the strikers could "abrogate the collective bargaining rights of A.F. of L. unions employed by the corporation." The management of General Motors seized on Green's request for recognition of the craft unions — which had hitherto refused to organize auto workers and which had managed to enroll only a handful of the highly skilled — as an excuse for withholding exclusive bargaining rights from the C.I.O. union. When, despite Green's feverish efforts to break the strike, the auto workers' union won exclusive recognition in twenty of the company's plants, higher wages, and other far-reaching concessions, Green dismissed the victory — the biggest ever won in the auto industry — with an expression of "regret" that the "settlement represents a surrender."

Things were going from bad to worse with William Green and the executive council. The membership of the United Mine Workers, which Green had joined in 1890 while still living in Coshocton, condemned him along with John P. Frey "for their gratuitous, insulting, anti-union, strike-breaking statements," and empowered the union's international officers to take steps to expel Green. Without union affiliation, Green would be unable to continue as president of the Federation. Happily for Green, the expulsion had to be ratified by a committee from his old inactive local at Coshocton, where William's brother Hugh ruled as secretary. Moreover, the badgered president was not without friends; just as a precaution, James C. Petrillo, president of the Chicago Federation of Musicians and an ardent craft-union supporter, inveigled his union into electing the ex-miner to membership. Even his close associates on the executive council had not guessed that sometime during his long and not too arduous career William Green had become a one finger virtuoso of the piano.

As the C.I.O. campaign accelerated, William Green's former serenity changed to bitter petulance. Terrified by the progress of industrial unionism, Green struck out at the progressives with blind viciousness. He removed the charter of the Columbus Central Labor Council in Ohio. He allowed John P. Frey to "advise" the Carnegie-Illinois Steel Corporation's company union — which rejected Frey's aid because he advocated craft forms and the company unions objected that craft organization was impractical and outdated! He attacked the sit-down strikes, so successfully employed by workers in mass-production industries, calling them "illegal," fuming that "Both personally and officially I disavow the sit-down strike as part of the economic and organization policy of the American Federation of Labor."

Green's final betrayal of American labor took place at the Cincinnati conference of the A.F. of L.'s officialdom in May 1937. He, along with the executive council, declared open warfare on the C.I.O. by ordering the expulsions of all C.I.O. locals from state and city federations. Who really was splitting the labor movement was abundantly evident when Green further asked for a "war chest" to promote A.F. of L. unions in opposition to those already organized by the C.I.O. This conference of hysteria and desperation unmasked Green and exposed him in all his helpless confusion.

The rule by tradition had led to collapse. Green neither added to his inheritance, nor changed it, nor detracted from it. He merely went along wherever it led. He had followed Gompers' rule book: he had insisted that labor should remain non-partisan, that it should "reward its friends, punish its enemies," that organized labor should be kept in narrow craft channels. He had decreed, in effect, that the interests of the many defer to the demands of the few. Proudly, in 1930, he had accepted the Theodore Roosevelt Medal for his "new policy of coöperation in industry, representing the American concept of industrialism and self reliance and fighting with success the disruptive influence of the radical element preaching communism and classwar."

Once he had been a miner. Once some had thought of him as a variety of liberal. After twelve years, William Green of Coshocton, Ohio, still addressed Rotary luncheons and wore a dress suit with ease, but the structure that Samuel Gompers had built and that he had inherited crumbled about him. After twelve years, John L. Lewis expressed the opinion of the majority of American workers when he called his former associate "cowardly and contemptible." For, in Lewis's words, William Green "sells his own breed down the river and receives the thanks of the National Association of Manufacturers."

II. WILLIAM HUTCHESON

Success Story of a Bruiser

WILLIAM HUTCHESON, general president of the United Brotherhood of Carpenters and Joiners of America, resented any slight to the gospel of Gompersism. In particular, the heresy of industrial unionism enraged him. And once crossed, Hutcheson struck out blindly and violently.

Not surprisingly the debate on industrial unionism at the 1935 A.F. of L. convention irritated the president of the carpenters. But when John L. Lewis refused to let the question rest, Hutcheson could no longer restrain his temper. "Point of order!" he insisted while Lewis spoke. The mine chief turned on the president of the carpenters sneeringly. The objection, Lewis remarked, was "small potatoes." That proved too much for Hutcheson. Pushing forward — six feet three and close to three hundred pounds — he retorted that he had been raised on just that kind of potato and "that is why I am so small." Aflame with craft-union loyalty, Hutcheson enlarged on this devastating reply, concluding his remarks by swearing at Lewis. Then Hutcheson acted. He lunged out at Lewis. When the other delegates finally separated them, Lewis scrambled to his feet with a torn shirt; Hutcheson rubbed a bruised face, wiping blood from a swollen lip. Vengefully he kicked a smaller delegate hovering nearby. Force had won: William Green sustained Hutcheson's point of order and Lewis had only the congratulatory telegrams from rank and file carpenters to console him.

The incident did not lessen Hutcheson's abhorrence of industrial unionism. At all costs he was determined to preserve craft forms. It was this quality of determination that had moved William Green some years before to describe him as, "A strong personality, an outstanding character, a dynamic forceful man." A similar determination reinforced Hutcheson's insistence that he retain unqualified control of the Brotherhood. As Hutcheson had made clear on more than one occasion, the function of the rank and file was not to ques-

tion his conduct of union affairs; their duty was to pay dues. And being a man of action, Hutcheson supplemented barrack discipline with wholesale expulsions of all who grumbled against his iron rule. He tolerated no opposition, since experience had taught him that the recalcitrant could usually be brought into agreement simply by cracking them over the head with a lead pipe.

Nevertheless, Hutcheson's forthright conduct did not conceal, at least from the delegate who nominated him for his twenty-second year as president of the Brotherhood, that "the thing closest to his heart is the grasping of a man's hand in profound friendship, which he admires more than anything else I know. . . . His nature is . . . sometimes very abrupt, and when it is abrupt it might hurt somebody's feelings. . . . Sometimes the big stick is used." In over two decades, "earnest, capable, qualified, and up-to-date" Bill Hutcheson, had not once deviated from the path of strict craft unionism. He was willing even to neglect the task of organizing carpenters in order to spend his full energy on jurisdictional disputes, a disease peculiar to the craft structure of the A.F. of L.

The indulgence of jurisdictional squabbles had plenty of precedent in Brotherhood history. From the moment the carpenters became involved in their first serious feud with the machine wood workers seven years after the Brotherhood's inception in 1886, hardly a day passed that did not find them embroiled in some inter-union quarrel. William Hutcheson saw no reason to change the pattern: he believed, like his predecessors, that any worker in wood from a lumberjack to a cabinetmaker was a potential dues-paying member of the Brotherhood. "Once wood, it is always the right of the carpenter to install it. . . ."

Accordingly, the Brotherhood fought structural iron workers, elevator constructors, tile layers, wire and metal lathers, painters, asbestos workers, car workers, hod carriers, brewery workers, plasterers, cement finishers. As industry expanded, friction increased: borderline processes, mechanization, the introduction of new materials frequently telescoped the functions of rival unions so that their members performed substantially the same functions. Jealous craft officials fought to control workers engaged on the same or similar jobs. Especially did the building-trades unions discover that their jurisdictions overlapped; lines of demarcation between crafts tended to blur and disappear as machinery displaced hand labor. The employers in their desire for cheap labor took advantage of the bickerings between unions, often deliberately raising jurisdictional problems to keep the workers divided and weakened.

On his part, William Hutcheson evinced little interest in allaying discord. As head of the largest craft union in the A.F. of L., he had sufficient influence to enable him successfully to claim marginal and related workers. Each victory swelled the union treasury, each victory increased his power. Under Hutcheson, the once aggressive Brotherhood substituted raids on other unions for campaigns to organize the trade. Recruiting cost money, endangered friendly relations with employers, and too often resulted in strikes that heightened the militancy of the rank and file and made control by the top union officials more difficult. Hutcheson preferred to let other crafts do the spade work; whereupon he took over their membership.

No doubt industrial unionism would have eliminated jurisdictional disputes. But Hutcheson pointed out that if "all workers were organized on an Industrial basis it would mean the elimination of our organization." The general president had no intention of relinquishing a good job on the doubtful chance of finding a place in a more inclusive union. He reminded the carpenters in his report to the 1936 convention that the Brotherhood "being a Craft Organization . . . cannot agree to the organizing of the workers on an Industrial basis . . . My opinion is that if the American Federation of Labor should accept the plan of the Committee for Industrial Organization, namely to organize all workers on an Industrial basis, the only solution for our organization would be to sever our affiliation with the American Federation of Labor."

In holding fast to Gompersism, Hutcheson adopted those methods that had long blocked successful organization. By 1930, these principles had almost completely perverted the A.F. of L. into a snobbish skilled worker society that presented an erroneous picture of working class distribution in American industry. Though unskilled and semiskilled workers far outnumbered the skilled, the A.F. of L. drew only five percent of its support from the mass-production industries of lumber, textile, food, leather, liquor, tobacco, and glass. For all practical purposes the Federation ignored automobile, rubber, and steel workers. On the other hand, 70 percent of the A.F. of L.'s

strength was recruited from sheltered industries of secondary importance in the industrial scene — building, printing, public service,
transportation, theater — and half of this was concentrated in the
building trades and transportation. Yet the executive council, with
such men as William Hutcheson directing its approach, stubbornly
resisted any change that would help to bring the mass of workers into
the unions.

WILLIAM HUTCHESON was born in Saginaw County, Michigan,
in 1874, where he grew tall and heavy on "small potatoes." His father, a ship carpenter, caulker and joiner, taught the boy his trade;
other than that, William received little schooling. In 1902 he joined
the Brotherhood of Carpenters. Once a member, he pushed ahead
fast enough: in four years he had been appointed business agent for
the vicinity of Saginaw. Florid, brutal William Hutcheson was
equipped by physique and temperament to practice the plug-ugly
tactics of business unionism.

By 1912, Hutcheson had been elected second vice president of the
Brotherhood; a year later he had advanced to the first vice presidency.
Then in 1915 James Kirby, head of the Brotherhood, died after an
appendicitis operation and Hutcheson automatically succeeded.
At the convention held the following year, his name appeared for
ratification. For the sake of form, another candidate ran against him,
but Hutcheson swaggered through the general election without difficulty, and once in office he found it a simple matter to hold on to the
position.

The Brotherhood presidency endowed Hutcheson with undivided
power. Ostensibly, Hutcheson was responsible to the general executive board of which he was also a member. This board, while for-
mally elected by the rank and file, in practice managed to remain
self-perpetuating. No one whom the general president did not approve of ever succeeded in being elected to it. By controlling the
business agents and the election machinery, the board was able to
declare elections illegal or void when undesirable candidates out-
manoeuvred the bureaucracy and won a majority of votes.

If the Brotherhood's constitution got in Hutcheson's way he swept
it aside contemptuously. The constitution empowered him to "decide
all points of law, appeals and grievances"; to "suspend any local

Union, District Council, State Council or Provincial Council for violation of the Constitution or International Laws"; he was to "supervise the entire interests of the United Brotherhood." He presided over and conducted all conventions and appointed all committees. He granted all charters, and filled all general offices with the consent of the executive board; he could appoint organizers at salaries of $100 a week; he could seize for examination "all books, papers, and financial accounts" of any subordinate local or council in the union.

In other words, the Brotherhood was Hutcheson's to do with as he pleased, for which he received $200 a week with expenses. Yet he was not content with the title of president, with the respectability that membership in the Masons, the Elks, and the Odd Fellows gave him, with the handsome salary and flexible expense account. William Hutcheson yearned for increased power, always greater power in corporation-controlled America. To get it, he made the necessary concessions: he became labor adviser to Hoover in the election campaign of 1932; four years later, as compensation for his services in supporting the Liberty League, he was allegedly promised the secretaryship of labor in the event of a Republican victory. Nor was Hutcheson reluctant to accept the high praise showered on him by grateful employers.

Moreover, the presidency of a powerful union opened many avenues beneficial to Hutcheson. He was too shrewd to let sentiment stand in his way. If association and coöperation with gangsters could advance him, he yielded to necessity. If preserving "industrial peace" brought remuneration, Hutcheson saw no reason to refuse. If union funds were available, he reasoned that their use to promote his own interests also served the rank and file — for he was convinced that the membership existed for his benefit. Logically, then, since progressives in the Brotherhood endangered his rule, and since the most violent opponents of progressivism were supporters of the Republican Party, Hutcheson found it desirable to act as labor prop for the most reactionary group in politics. By 1936, he was acknowledged as the white-headed boy of the anti-union, fascist-minded Liberty League.

THOUGH HUTCHESON pressed farther on the road to complete degradation than the majority of his craft union associates, union racketeering and bribe taking were as old as the Federation. Gompersism encouraged coöperation with employers, and coöperation led to concentration of power in the hands of the top officials. Union constitutions soon began to reflect this trend of limiting the rank and file's voice in the conduct of union affairs.

This tendency to abrogate union democracy received great impetus after the Haymarket bomb exploded in 1886 and public hysteria aided anti-labor groups to frame and hang militants. Because several of the railroaded victims were anarchists, the cry went up that organized labor was dominated by the philosophy of terrorism. Those employers who had granted the eight hour day seized the excuse to restore the ten and twelve hour day. Instead of resisting, union leaders grew panicky. The A.F. of L., still young and in the process of organization, was unable to repulse the attack even if the executive council had so desired; officials of the older, better entrenched Knights of Labor capitulated to the anti-labor frenzy, and aided it by joining the witch-hunt against the anarchists with a vehemence that put the employers to shame.

In the crusade that followed — to save the nation from "foreign radicalism" — employers sent hired spies into the factories, mills, and mines to report the most active labor leaders. Blacklists and intimidation resulted; company police forcibly ejected union men wherever they were discovered. Organized labor, reaping the harvest of its own mistaken tactics, found itself confronted with the burden of supporting blacklisted members. The unions decided that it would be cheaper and more efficient to appoint delegates whose sole job it would be to deal with the owners, and who would not be dependent on the employers for their bread and butter. Accordingly (as Harold Seidman concludes in his history of labor racketeering, *Labor Czars*), the unions began to select representatives not easily intimidated, to pay these appointees a salary, and to empower them to organize other workers and negotiate with the employers in the name of the membership.

In most instances, the unions granted these walking delegates (now called business agents) absolute power. Above all, the unions felt it important that the delegates lose no bargaining advantage through delay entailed by consulting the rank and file. Often walking delegates called strikes without referring their decisions to the workers involved. Not infrequently, militant business agents resorted to violence, even to dynamiting, in attempts to force employer concessions. Brawn and fearlessness became the required attributes of the walking delegates. Inevitably, unscrupulous illiterates who had no concern for the objectives and needs of the labor movement crept into key positions. The idealism which had dictated the violence of the more politicalized early trade unionists was transformed into criminal violence for personal advantage. Power bred arrogance. Walking delegates who were given the authority to fine employers for infraction of union rules, who were, moreover, free from control by the membership and who kept union accounts in their heads instead of in books, were not above temptation to take advantage of their position. They began to withhold funds that rightfully belonged in the union treasury. Easy money whetted the delegates' appetites, since more money meant more power. The authority to call strikes enabled the more unscrupulous to blackmail employers with threats of walkouts unless the employers paid tribute to the agents in the form of "strike insurance." The moment the less honest minority of delegates understood that they could personally benefit at the owners' expense — and at the still greater expense of the workers they supposedly represented — they had no desire to relinquish their soft jobs. To hang on to their sinecures, delegates bribed top union officials and struggled to rise in union politics. With democracy suppressed, once they did succeed in obtaining office they built machines to perpetuate their reigns and thereafter proved almost impossible to dislodge. Corrupt business agents, numerically but a tiny section of organized labor, ruled the unions and held on to their supremacy by bribery, terrorization of the membership, and most important of all, by connivance with the employers.

The implications of business unionism were not lost on the more astute capitalists. If a delegate could be bought, if he likewise had the power arbitrarily to call strikes, owners saw a chance for profitable alliances. Corporation heads conspired with and paid delegates to squeeze out their competitors by calling strikes against business rivals, at the same time buying protection against labor troubles. Such deals helped to build monopolies, and also aided in raising prices. Particularly did the combinations of dishonest union officials and employers flourish in the building trades. Building involved speculation and investment; returns only commenced with the completion of the project, so that delay usually meant financial disaster. If a contract went unfulfilled after a certain date, the builder often had to pay a large forfeit, or the renting season passed without the owner's obtaining tenants. The employers, therefore, willingly bought insurance against strikes — and the proceeds went into the tills of the walking delegates. By the middle of the 1890's, the construction industry in most large American cities was infiltrated with racketeering alliances. Unions were deluged with crooked, greedy men who saw an opportunity for quick money and power through the organized labor movement. The rank and file and the public paid the bill.

Racketeers also gained a foothold in the unions through the open shop drive which utilized police and gangsters to beat pickets and break strikes. Forced in self protection to retaliate, the unions hired professional strong-arm men to guard their striking members. Gangsters thus brought into the unions refused to relinquish their jobs when they were no longer needed. Instead, they saw to it that they were appointed walking delegates, and proceeded to dominate union after union. Reactionary employers had no objection to this, preferring to deal with gangsters than with leaders who loyally and militantly represented the workers.

Once corruption was entrenched in organized labor, the unions took on new interest for ward politicians, who saw that votes could be bought and sold through union dictators. And soon, business agents developed into political heelers on their own account, with influence in local and state politics. Graft rode high; the rank and file got nothing and often paid tribute to remain in the union. If they refused to knuckle under, workers faced expulsion and exclusion. Small shopkeepers, too, paid levies to union gangsters to protect their establishments from bombs and vandalism, or themselves from physical injury.

Most prominent in the list of labor racketeers were "Skinny" Madden and Sam Parks, who made fortunes as czars of the building trades in Chicago and New York. "Pinhead" McCarthy, once mayor of San Francisco, on one deal alone received $10,000 from the Pacific Gas and Electric Company to lobby against a bill for state owned electric light and power, though the bill had been endorsed by McCarthy's own Building Trades Council. Robert Brindell coined millions as dictator of the building trades in New York City, receiving as high as $50,000 for one "favor." In later years "Lepke" Buckhouse and "Charlie the Gurrah" Shapiro dominated the painters' locals through 250 gunmen, and had their hands at various times in the fur, garment, and other industries. Colonel Martin Mulhall, member of the Philadelphia Labor Union, bribed hundreds of union officers to support the open shop political program of the National Association of Manufacturers, and succeeded in defeating many real labor candidates. John Mitchell, president of the United Mine Workers, amassed a fortune of $250,000. Al Capone ran the cleaning and dyeing and other Chicago unions for years. In 1932, the A.F. of L. admitted that twenty-eight of its Chicago affiliates were ruled by racketeers and gangsters. Joseph P. Ryan, president of the New York City Trades and Labor Council and president of the International Longshoremen's Association, boasted not long ago that "the Central Trades and Labor Council is Tammany first and labor afterwards." It was in March 1937 that Paul Coulcher, for years one of Ryan's right hand men, was sentenced to Sing Sing prison for victimizing members of the hotel and restaurant union.

Under such conditions, no little danger threatened an individual who attempted to fight those in power. Aside from blacklists, loss of jobs, economic intimidation which workers could hardly resist, aside from expulsions, suspensions, fines levied by union courts where the union boss and his toadies acted both as judge and jury, those who opposed the machine risked physical injury and even death. Many highly skilled unionists passively submitted to the tyranny of the racketeers, and rationalized abuses by pointing to their own high wages. "So long as we get ours," many of them said, "we don't care if the racketeers get theirs." Racketeering fostered the feeling among some of the skilled workers, especially in the building trades, that they could preserve their wages only by tolerating the crooked business agents and union heads, and by excluding the unskilled and semi-skilled from their organizations.

Also, small merchants who refused to pay tribute to the ring found themselves out of business, or their establishments wrecked by gunmen. State and local governments, dominated by officials linked to racketeers (in turn supported by large financial and industrial interests), rarely offered help. As a result, workers came to distrust unions, and fell easy prey to the open shop drive.

The executive council of the A.F. of L. remained the final hope. But here again desperate workers learned that they could expect no assistance. The fight against politicians, gangsters, and powerful employers took greater courage than Samuel Gompers, or his successor, William Green, could muster. Besides, the A.F. of L. officials needed the votes of the crooked business agents. Nor was corruption confined so exclusively to the local union officers that it did not taint the members of the executive council. A few of the A.F. of L. vice presidents were not too far removed from racketeering. Of the fifteen members who composed the executive board in January 1937, six headed unions abounding in corruption. So severely had the Gompers heritage weakened the backbone of the official labor movement that several of the executive council had more to gain by protecting the racketeers than by fighting them.

Of course, a president of an international or national union, or a member of the executive council, had less temptation than the business agents to indulge in openly dishonest practices. In most cases, the leading officers of the Federation, softened by employer flattery, collaboration, and the social prestige that high rank brought, deteriorated into job-holding figureheads, fearful above all things of losing face or position. Typically, Matthew Woll, president of the Photo-Engravers, responded to an appeal by the New York Commissioner of Markets that he end the poultry racket, this way: "We can't do anything about it, Commissioner. You see, we got to look to the votes of the boys down the line to hold our jobs."

Undoubtedly, when the probe of the poultry racket could no longer be avoided, "the votes of the boys down the line" influenced Woll to appoint Michael J. Cashal, vice president of the teamsters, to the investigating commission. Cashal's clique benefited from the graft; in consequence, Cashal's contribution to stamping it out was to label the investigation "communistic." Previously, Matthew Woll had done his bit to stop graft by insisting with all the vigor at his command that no racketeering existed in the union of Joseph "Socks" Lanza, despite the statement of Samuel Seabury, state investigator, that "careful investigation will disclose, I think, that extortion was practiced by Lanza." Yet Lanza was fined $10,000 and sentenced to two years in Sing Sing for racketeering — but not because of any diligence on the part of Woll. Moreover, Woll, sanctimonious in a high collar and cloaked in the prim dignity of a country preacher, saw no contradiction in a labor official continuing as acting president of the anti-union, labor-baiting National Civic Federation until the 1935 A.F. of L. convention forced him to resign. Woll found little time for crusades against dishonest union officials (though he did manage to shout "Red!" at all progressives), since he was fully occupied with his Union Labor Life Insurance Company. Because of Woll's high station, the Company did a brisk business. His agents made a specialty of labor lawyers; those who didn't buy ran the risk of incurring Woll's displeasure. Executives also considered it wiser not to antagonize Woll and were loathe to refuse a policy from the Union Labor Company.

Other members of the executive council also refused to concern themselves with racketeering. This became less surprising when their own records were scrutinized:

1. John Coefield, Republican president of the plumbers, assisted "Pinhead" McCarthy in San Francisco in the old days when McCarthy grew rich on extortion, bribery, and systematic raids on the union treasury.

2. G. M. Bugniazet, secretary of the electrical workers, excused the dishonesty of Henry H. Broach, czar of the New York electrical workers, by blaming resultant labor trouble on "union spies." He produced "documents" to prove his charges, documents purported to have been written by one Edgar Applegate of the American Financiers Protective and Investigating Bureau. Neither Applegate nor the organization was ever located. Bugniazet gave blanket approval of the coercion, misappropriation of funds, intimidation and so forth practiced by his lieutenant.

3. Old Dan Tobin, president of the teamsters, the most corrupt union in America today and the backbone of the trucking, cleaning and dyeing, poultry, and laundry rackets, steadfastly refused to fight against the dishonest officials in his union. But he did resist strenuously when the rank and file revolted against such abuses.

4. Frank Duffy, silver haired secretary of the carpenters and William Hutcheson's righthand man, tolerated the corruption in the building trades and especially in the carpenters' union.

5. Harry C. Bates, officer of the bricklayers', masons' and plasterers union, shut his eyes consistently to large scale graft in the locals.

6. Edward Flore, president of the restaurant workers, refused to help the rank and file fight "Dutch" Schultz when Schultz's gang captured the New York locals.

The racketeering that infected the top leadership of the A.F. of L. also corroded other sections of the labor movement. As in the Federation, officials of the once powerful railroad brotherhoods accepted a craft union policy differing not the slightest from Gompersism, and like it, deteriorating into flagrant collaboration. Highly paid brotherhood officers under the spell of business unionism preached "labor capitalism." The brotherhoods launched large scale capitalist ventures, set up banks, investment companies, real estate developments, mail order houses. Warren S. Stone, formerly president of the Brotherhood of Locomotive Engineers, foretold a new rôle for labor: instead of fighting capital, the unions would take it over, thereby peacefully capturing economic and political power. "Running a bank is like running a peanut stand," Stone announced. "Only more peanut stands go out of business." With this generalization as a premise, the locomotive engineers proceeded to enter the banking business, founding over twelve banks with resources of more than $53,000,000.

Once started, the Brotherhood expanded with the same logic and eagerness that inspired any large financial organization to reach out for ever greater profits. Eleven brotherhood investment houses, with capital of $34,000,000 grew out of the banks. Real estate ventures intrigued the labor officials turned financiers: they built a two million dollar apartment house in an exclusive residential section of Cleveland; they purchased the Equitable Building in New York City for $38,000,000; they constructed the Standard Bank Building in Cleveland at a cost of over $6,000,000; they invested $16,000,000 in promoting and developing Venice, Florida. For $3,000,000 the Brotherhood bought the Coal River Collieries, and began to operate the mines — with non-union labor. Brotherhood officials forgot their function as labor leaders for the more pressing problems of running huge capitalist enterprises.

The honeymoon in the financial world lasted a little over five years. Railway workers poured money into the banks, real estate schemes, investment companies. The public — mostly workers — likewise put savings into Brotherhood projects, which, because they were operated by powerful unions, seemed to offer greater safety. Not until the

Brotherhood's Philadelphia bank lost out to the Mitten interests, not until the Coal River Collieries went into receivership, not until the Florida land boom fizzled in June 1927, did the railroad workers discover that "labor capitalism" destroyed their earnings.

By 1932, the banks, the companies, the projects had all failed. The Brotherhood owed $9,428,000 in excess of assets. The worker-investors had lost their savings, had seen over $30,000,000 of their money, carefully put aside during a lifetime of labor, completely dissipated. Moreover, reserves for insurance and pensions, paid for over long years had gone with the deposits. Brotherhood members lost whatever protection they had built up against old age and sickness.

With the crash, the true nature of "labor capitalism" was revealed. The top officials, who had visualized themselves not as labor leaders but as respected figures in the world of big business, had borrowed another leaf from capitalism's rules of instructions by profiting personally through the many transactions. They had taken huge cuts on real estate and other deals. Both Stone and William B. Prenter (who became president of the Brotherhood after Stone's death in 1925) made $50,000 apiece from the Coal River Collieries, though the Brotherhood members lost $3,000,000. When the Brotherhood sold the Equitable Building in New York City at a tremendous loss (a week after the sale the stock went up from $53 to $91 a share), the new owners presented each of the fourteen Brotherhood officials who had made the sale with a gift of from $2,000 to $2,500. The 1927 convention objected. Prenter replied, "I took mine and it's nobody's damned business."

The convention expelled Prenter and replaced him with Alvanley Johnston who immediately handed over all of the Brotherhood's capitalist enterprises to Claudius Huston, with the agreement that Huston would receive half of any profits accruing from their sale. Huston's financial activities were a little too subtle even for the Republican National Committee, of which Huston was a member. Several years later the Republicans forced Huston out of the organization.

The false attempt to turn the union into a capitalist enterprise led to corruption and the weakening of the Brotherhood. Similar experiences were repeated by several of the other large railway unions. And the records of A.F. of L. and Brotherhood demoralization sketched above only hinted the extent to which racketeering penetrated the union top leadership. To whatever extent William Hutcheson was implicated, he missed no tricks.

IN 1915, the year Hutcheson became president of the United Brotherhood of Carpenters and Joiners, 17,000 New York carpenters voted four to one to demand a fifty cent raise in their daily wages. After obtaining the approval of the Brotherhood's national office, local leaders negotiated and received contracts assuring the higher rate for 14,000 members. By May of the following year, the rank and file had decided on a strike of all New York locals in order to extend the new wage scale to the remaining 3,000 workers not included in the contract. On the eve of the walkout, when it was no longer possible to call it off, Hutcheson demanded that the strike be canceled. He gave no reason. The carpenters disregarded the president's order. Hutcheson thereupon rushed to New York, met secretly with the employers, and informed the men that he had signed a contract, in which the racketeers Brindell and Halkett participated. The agreement, presented by Hutcheson to a meeting of 800 men before he precipitously left for the West, invalidated the fifty cent wage increase already won by 14,000 carpenters.

In the rank and file revolt that followed, a referendum vote overthrew Hutcheson's agreement 11,745 to only 119. The New York State Council of Carpenters condemned the general president's interference as "a betrayal of the interests of the carpenters of New York and a violation of the principles of the labor movement." Only Brindell's dock builders endorsed the agreement.

Hutcheson, however, tolerated no criticism. Raging fiercely, he expelled sixty-five carpenters' locals with a membership of 17,000, and, joining the employers and Brindell, started to recruit scabs to break the strike. For this job, the employers claimed to have paid $85,000 — the coöperation of union officials cost money. Yet in the end the courts forced Hutcheson to reinstate the outlawed locals, which had won the strike despite Hutcheson's zealous scabbing.

That was what Hutcheson understood by direct action. In 1918, he suddenly showed his patriotism by heeding Woodrow Wilson's request to call off a strike of carpenters in East Coast shipyards. Naturally, he refused to allow the membership to vote on the question.

With the war ended and the great steel strike on, Hutcheson again grew public spirited and refused to condemn the government's strike-breaking aid to the steel corporations. That, he stated, would be un-American. The President of the Brotherhood protested that he had no use for the I.W.W. — which was not involved in the steel strike — and therefore refused to admit that governmental agencies were either autocratic or oppressive. Again, in 1921, he threatened to suspend any local of the carpenters' union that aided the general strike in the San Francisco building trades. That same year, during the Chicago strike of inside carpenters, Local 341, like the other locals, collected strike assessments of $60 a member, totaling about $12,000. Instead of turning this amount over to the district council, the officials split it among themselves and falsified the books. An investigating committee recommended that the local president, recording and financial secretaries, the treasurer, and one trustee be expelled. Harry Jensen, head of the carpenters, close friend and lieutenant of Hutcheson's, refused to do so and merely fined the offenders $200 each and transferred them to other locals. A group, calling itself the Progressive Building Trades Workers, commented on the sleight of hand, "It seemed like both Hutcheson and Jensen had a stake in maintaining their memberships."

With discontent growing among the Chicago carpenters in 1924, Hutcheson and his subordinate Jensen met with five leading contractors and signed an agreement which the newspapers hailed as granting the closed shop. The news succeeded in reëlecting Jensen the following day to the presidency of the district council. Weeks afterwards, the rank and file discovered that for all practical purposes the agreement duplicated the notorious Landis Award, against which, just two years before, the carpenters had waged one of the most bitter strikes in the history of Chicago labor. Hutcheson's new contract provided, among other things, that

1. There shall be no limitations as to the amount of work a man shall perform during his working day;

2. Employers are at liberty to employ and discharge whomsoever they see fit;

3. No restriction of the use of any raw or manufactured materials, except prison made (in other words, non-union goods were fully endorsed).

This agreement actually penalizing the rank and file was signed in the midst of a building boom. And any carpenter who dared to protest was expelled.

Support of Jensen was bad enough. But Hutcheson's closest associate for many years was the New York czar, Robert P. Brindell, the semi-illiterate dock builder who dominated the building trades. Hutcheson aided Brindell — though he did not accompany him to Sing Sing.

Brindell got his real start through Hutcheson. After he had made some headway with his little racketeering Dock and Pier Carpenters Union, Brindell associated his organization to Hutcheson's Brotherhood in order to benefit from the support of the largest craft union. By 1919, ambitious Brindell had converted the old Board of Business Agents into a Building Trades Council, chartered by the Building Trades Department of the A.F. of L. The charter did not hamper him; he violated it consistently and laid down his own rules. He had himself elected president of the council for life; he forbade rank and file members to become delegates; he ruled that all delegates must be business agents (whom Brindell appointed) with terms of three years and salaries of $75 a week. He saw to it that only one copy of the minutes of council meetings was kept, and that this copy remained in the secretary's hands where the rank and file could not see it.

Then Brindell went into the business of graft, systematically. With the employers, he formed monopolies, dictating who should receive city contracts. He sold strike insurance and instituted a system of levies on contractors. The employers formed an association which entered into an agreement with Brindell whereby their members promised to hire only Brindell workers and Brindell pledged in return to supply workers only to members of the association — thus eliminating competition. Brindell broke a wrecking union, which refused to pay ransom to him, by calling strikes of his own men on jobs where the wreckers worked. Then by organizing an outlaw union, Brindell took over a new racket.

His income was immense. Louis J. Cohn paid Brindell $4,250 for four large contracts. The Atwell Wrecking Co. contributed $17,120 for permission to pull down several buildings. Brindell decided who should have contracts and which of his favorites should become partners of contractors in order to share half the profits. He sold

Hugh Robertson of Todd, Iron and Robertson strike insurance for $50,000 when the firm started a forty million dollar project on the Cunard docks. Workers, too, paid tribute. In his own union, local 1458, Brindell collected from 5,000 members fifty cents a month. The 115,000 members of the Building Trades Council were taxed $1 a month each, for the privilege of working. Brindell exacted over $90,000 from the 1,800 members of the outlaw House Wreckers' Union, who also contributed $10,400 in dues. Privilege-of-work cards issued to 300 non-union men brought in $10 a week apiece. It cost the 136 business agents $14,000 a year to keep their jobs.

This was only a portion of Brindell's "take." Tammany protected him, and he protected Tammany. In the end, the czar overstepped himself and landed in Sing Sing. What part Hutcheson had played during the fat years of Brindell's rule was not revealed at the trial. Samuel Untermeyer, who helped convict Brindell, wired the A.F. of L. convention in Denver that the "Federation will also be exceptionally fortunate if the Carpenters' Union can rid itself of Brindell's crony, Hutcheson, who has been an evil influence."

Hutcheson managed to hang on to the general presidency despite reformers and the rising resentment in the Brotherhood. No other union head surpassed the absolutism with which he ran the carpenters' affairs. Backed as his reign was with gangsterism, Red baiting, and a policy which brought him and his hand-picked stalwarts power and profit (and the membership the privilege of paying for a good share of his personal success), it was small wonder that the more courageous attempted to organize militant opposition groups within the union to fight the general president and pry loose his stranglehold on the Brotherhood. Hutcheson retaliated ferociously, with beatings and expulsions. The man of action, with his insane temper, dealt with dissenters in short order.

For example, the 1924 election for general president found Morris Rosen running against Hutcheson on the platform of the Progressive Carpenters' Committee. The progressives advocated among other reforms a forty hour week, industrial unionism, job control, and the building of an independent Farmer-Labor Party. Hutcheson, always adept at patrioteering when it could be turned to his own advantage, called the platform ultra-revolutionary. To defeat it, his agents campaigned diligently, receiving for their loyalty as high as

$20 a day — not from Hutcheson but from the treasuries of the district councils. Moreover, to assure himself a clear majority, Hutcheson pilfered votes. That was nothing new. His friend Harry Jensen of the Chicago District Council threw out the entire vote of a hostile local when his reëlection was in doubt. Being a firm believer in the Gompers adage, "Punish your enemies, reward your friends," Hutcheson buttressed his fancy vote counting by expelling his rival Rosen and the entire New York local 376 for its support of the opposition candidate.

Hutcheson's housecleaning did not end there. He charged William Reynolds, vice president of the Detroit District Council and president of a local union, with membership in the progressive Trade Union Educational League, and expelled him without trial. But Reynolds' main crime was his active campaign for Rosen. Likewise, Fred W. Burgess, secretary of the campaign committee endorsing Willis K. Brown for secretary of the Brotherhood, was expelled from the Philadelphia local by Hutcheson — also without trial. Burgess had made the mistake of protesting against the autocracy of the general president and comparing Hutcheson to A. Mitchell Palmer and Harry M. Daugherty who covered up their own misdeeds in office by raising the Red scare as a smoke screen.

Even then, the systematic removal of critics did not stop. The general president expelled sixteen members of the Los Angeles district council for endorsing a Farmer-Labor Party and for joining the Trade Union Educational League. Their appeal to the 21st Indianapolis convention was never allowed to come before the delegates. Actually, their offense had been to call for amalgamation (a step toward industrial unionism), which was anathema to Hutcheson, though the 1913 convention of the Federation's Building Trades Department had gone on record favoring it. When in 1933 a Philadelphia local circularized the Brotherhood advocating an amendment to the general constitution which would cut the salaries of the top officials, prune expenditures, and provide for a system caring for unemployed carpenters, Hutcheson disregarded the endorsements of 365 locals in 42 states and Canada, and expelled the Philadelphia union.

Local 2717 of New York likewise caused the general presiden: trouble. In 1932 he was forced to threaten expulsion when progressives started a move in favor of unemployment insurance and relief. Several years before, the same local had failed to reëlect Sam and Louis Goldberg, Hutcheson's fast friends, to local officialdom. The Goldbergs, along with the defeated Morris Biren, formed a rump organization which Hutcheson recognized as the legal administration of the local. The progressives took the case to court. The referee ruled against Hutcheson and his protégés:

"When a constitutional limitation stood in the way of the defendants, [the opinion read] it was brushed aside without hesitation. This was true of the general president of the Brotherhood down to the least significant of the district council officers. This is not the first offense of this nature of which the officials of this union have been guilty . . .

"In all his actions, Halkett [a union official] was supported by General President Hutcheson . . . The whole history of the relations of the district council and the local reek of collusion and conspiracy on the part of the defendants to control the important offices of the local and hence dominate its business and affairs . . .

"The plaintiff did appeal to the general president for relief and that appeal was answered by a whitewashing investigation which was in character a mere formality. The forms of legality are thus made use of to override the will of the majority which finds itself helpless against tyrannical and self-serving leaders who combine to control and dominate the funds and policies of the union."

Obviously, rank and file workers could not take Hutcheson's every violation to court. They lacked money and organization, and they feared the consequences of such boldness, both to their jobs and to their persons. Moreover, they could put no final trust in the courts; more often than not, the rank and file found the courts hostile to them and sympathetic to their ruthless officials. The solution lay in cleaning out the union for themselves. But Hutcheson guarded against that eventuality.

So it went. The rank and file didn't have a chance. Hutcheson decided all policies, enforced his own will, and the membership could abide by it or get out. (By 1930, the Brotherhood admitted that it had left sixty percent of the eligible carpenters unorganized.) In New

York under the Hansen regime, the membership dropped from 30,000 in 1929 to 10,000 in 1936 although almost every other union had increased its enrollment since the passage of the N.R.A. The few union contracts that the Brotherhood retained went unenforced. The wage scale was unobserved. Carpenters found themselves at the mercy of the employers. But Hansen, who was accountable to Hutcheson only, believed the solution lay in a small, more select union, with higher dues and higher initiation fees. At the same time, he remained open handed in approving his own and other officials' expense accounts. Membership dues defrayed such charges as $3,115 to the Queens Motor Car Co. for the District President's automobile; $425 for a scarf pin presented to John Halkett, one of the boys; $500 to Samuel E. Wilson for the upkeep of his car for six months. But then most of the other district councils had similar expenses and Hutcheson's own expense account was commensurate with his high station.

Nevertheless, the Brotherhood maintained its position as the largest craft union. As the years passed, the tall, meaty-faced dictator, with his mop of brown hair greying at the temples and the muscle turning to fat from twenty-odd years of chair-warming service, grew more vicious. Yet beneath the rough exterior of the general president was a desire to be known as a humanitarian. He proposed that the carpenters erect a Home for the Aged in Lakeland, Florida. No doubt Major Berry's Pressmen's Home in Tennessee inspired Hutcheson. Berry's institution cost $11,000 to build and about $2,000,000 to keep going.

Of course, Hutcheson brooked no opposition to his venture in philanthropy. Delegate Mulcahy from Rhode Island made the mistake of questioning the advisability of the Home at the carpenters' convention, for, as he pointed out, the rank and file would support it and not the employers. He was twice assaulted for his presumption by Hutcheson's special friends, who were horrified that anyone could object to a home for aged carpenters. Though as a result he was laid up for two days, Mulcahy still persisted in being heard. His grievance was tabled. "I appeal from your decision," cried the obstinate delegate. President Hutcheson, flushed and resolute, pounded the gavel. "Delegate Mulcahy will be recorded in the proceedings as no longer a delegate in this convention."

Hutcheson bought the land for the Home during the Florida land boom without consulting the membership. Not accustomed to doing things by halves, he purchased hundreds of acres at a cost — so rumor had it — of $1,000 an acre. Some charged that the results of the referendum on the question of building the Home were falsified. Still others said that Hutcheson himself profited from the deal. Now those carpenters who have grown old serving the Hutcheson regime can die peacefully in Florida (at their brothers' expense).

DURING THE WAR, Hutcheson had decreed that conventions should be held every four years instead of every two. From 1928 until 1936, the Brotherhood did not convene at all. When it did in Lakeland, Florida, only 202 of the 1,647 locals sent delegates. Those that did attend found Hutcheson, if possible, more intolerant than ever of opposition. After "Mrs. J. D. ('Happy') Griffin, organist at the Home, entertained with a program of popular and semi-classical selections," President Hutcheson took charge and saw to it that things went his way. "All in favor of the motion will please rise," he commanded the delegates when voting on a crucial issue. "I would like the delegates who are opposed to the motion to give their names, so that it can be recorded." He appointed all committees. He raised dues from seventy-five cents to one dollar a month. He bitterly denounced the Committee for Industrial Organization headed by John L. Lewis. He warned any member who was a Communist or who signed a "communist" resolution that he would be expelled. When one delegate protested that the constitution guaranteed freedom of political belief, Hutcheson announced, "Communism is not a political belief." As one of Hutcheson's more philosophic disciples put it, "Every dog that comes out of the same litter is a dog, but they are not all colored alike," and a Communist was any man who "goes out to meetings . . . and sings the *International*." Weeks later thousands of opposition votes were reversed by Hutcheson's tabulating committee to assure the passage of constitutional amendments excluding Communists and dissident elements from the Brotherhood.

At the convention, Hutcheson had some trouble with the 74,000 dues-paying members from the Northwest. The loggers, sawmill, cooperage, shook and veneer workers, and the furniture workers wanted to vote. Hutcheson, lacking confidence in their allegiance, ruled that they could have no voice in the convention, but should continue to pay twenty-five cents a month each and be thankful for even quasi-admittance to the Brotherhood. These men, until 1935 members of federal unions, had been seized by Hutcheson in order to obtain their dues, not their opinions. Inasmuch as they endorsed the C.I.O. and demanded democratic rights in the Brotherhood, the general president ordered them to shut up or get out, in which case they would experience, as Frank Duffy put it, "the sweetest fight you ever had in your lives," because the Brotherhood would "notify all the big firms with which we have contracts covering hours, wages, and working conditions for the timberworkers that if they want to continue employing you outside of the Brotherhood we will put them on the unfair list and your manufactured stuff won't be handled elsewhere." In June 1937, the Northwest Federation of Woodworkers, which had grown to 100,000 members, began to poll its membership on the question of affiliation with the C.I.O.

Dictation that brought with it the splitting and weakening of organized labor failed to dismay Hutcheson. Gone was even the memory of the old socialistic tradition of the carpenters. And though the constitution contained a clause favoring government ownership of public utilities and transportation, the member so bold as to mention this section stood a good chance of being expelled. William Hutcheson logically enough defended and supported the Republican Party. The more reactionary that Party of open shop employers became, the more Hutcheson approved. Even the timid, backward A.F. of L. executive council endorsed the thirty hour week and President Roosevelt's plan to reform the Supreme Court. Not Republican Hutcheson. That, he contended, was "going too far afield."

In 1936, the Republican Party lauded Hutcheson's "experience in the labor field and his liberal views and fairness to all parties concerned"; the president of the carpenters in return resigned from the executive council to avoid association with the council's report approving the Roosevelt administration. His understudy, Frank Duffy, remained on the council so that the carpenters could keep a finger in the pie. (It was Frank Duffy who declaimed to the carpenters' convention: "Before Sam Gompers died he said 'Carry on.' I am one of those who want to carry on. I want to hand down the principles of true trade unionism.") Yet Hutcheson's resignation did not weaken his bitter fight against the C.I.O.; more than any other individual, he had caused the council to suspend the eight original C.I.O. unions under threat of taking the Brotherhood out of the Federation, and with it, as many of the other building-trades unions as he could influence. With the United Mine Workers suspended for C.I.O. affiliation, the carpenters were the dominant union in the A.F. of L. Without them, the Federation would be a labor organization in name alone. So Hutcheson's word carried more weight than that of any other single member of the executive council. Through Frank Duffy, Hutcheson dictated to the council, which had no other choice than to abide by his demands. No doubt that explained the high praises bestowed on him by the Liberty League, whose spokesman proclaimed that Hutcheson "represents the forward progressive element in the ranks of organized labor in America."

The spectacle of a major labor leader officially linked to the Republican Party and the Liberty League, the record of extreme reaction and corruption, the autocracy which surrendered workers to the most extreme exploitation with cynical disregard did not add faith in the official labor movement. That William Hutcheson could retain power and influence for almost a quarter of a century was bad enough. But that he could have a commanding voice in the A.F. of L., and that such influential Federation officials as John P. Frey, Matthew Woll, Frank Morrison, Daniel Tobin and others considered Hutcheson a respected colleague indicated the depths to which Gompersism had dragged the A.F. of L. The bitter open shop employers who backed the Liberty League could justly be proud of William Hutcheson's record of "sane unionism." The rule of the whip had helped to split the labor movement and to demoralize the workers. Hutcheson had done more than his share to lay the groundwork for Fascism in America.

III. EDWARD F. McGRADY

Salesman of "Industrial Peace"

EDWARD FRANCIS McGRADY, best dressed of labor leaders, flying salesman of "industrial peace," and careerist who overcame the handicap of poverty, was born in 1872 in Jersey City, New Jersey. Like the hero of an Horatio Alger novel his life was a triumphant ascent to prestige and power — the story of a printer who grew up in the slums of South Boston and became President Roosevelt's Assistant Secretary of Labor and the nation's ace "trouble shooter."

Two attributes helped Edward F. McGrady in his climb to high estate: an appreciation of what publicity could do for him and an almost sixth sense of how to get it. A bit of straight-from-the-shoulder talk (at the right moment), a dramatic gesture (when such a gesture could not be overlooked), a touch of becoming modesty (with all eyes upon him), a dash of courage (properly exhibited), a defiant mien, a display of what passed for integrity, an unalterable will (so long as he was in no way committed) — such qualities McGrady brought to the business of impressing others. In all its fifty years, the American Federation of Labor produced no more skillful diplomat — including even the "old fox" Gompers.

Yet estimates of Ed McGrady varied. Employers rather liked him and found him reasonable enough to deal with. The A.F. of L. executive council regarded him as a worthy representative of its dignity and respectability. The Roosevelt administration depended on him as "peacemaker" between capital and labor. Still, workers distrusted McGrady, frequently denounced him as a "sell-out artist" and "strikebreaker," accused him of tricking them with slick words or of attempting to hamstring their unions. Of himself, McGrady said, "When I was a young boy, she [his mother] did her best to guide my thoughts and footsteps. Approximately fifty years ago she taught me the following:

When I am dead, if men can say,
'He helped the world upon its way,
His ways were straight, his soul was clean,
His failings not unkind or mean.
He loved his fellowmen, and tried
To help them' — then I'm satisfied.

I have tried to live up to this."

Both Edward's father James, and his mother Jane, were of Irish stock and devout Roman Catholics. They managed to put their son through grammar and high school, and in spare moments Edward helped the family income by taking odd jobs. After the family moved to Boston where James became an assistant foreman in the street department, young Edward, well aware of the value of an education, attended night courses on economics and business management at the English High School. On the side, he took up boxing and was known in the neighborhood as a first class ringman. Once a priest told Edward that the number of saloons in the South Boston slums set a record, and that the tuberculosis rate in those sections surrounding the saloons was the highest in the country. Edward joined the St. Peter and St. Paul Abstinence Society and from then on remained a member — and a teetotaller.

In 1894 McGrady took a job as pressman with the Boston *Traveler*, and soon rose to foremanship. He was also interested in the printers' union and in politics. Known among his associates as an expert "spieler," he was elected organizer of the union, and subsequently, in 1907, president of the Webb Pressmen.

There was no stopping Ed McGrady. Ambitious, self-confident, a convincing and incessant talker, the slim, eager, shrewd printer held one union and political office after another, making friends in high circles and enemies only of those who had little or no influence. He held in turn the position of superintendent of the U. S. Employment Service in Massachusetts, acting federal director of this same service, secretary of his union, president of the Boston Central Labor Union, president of the Massachusetts Federation of Labor. At the Mobile Pressmen's convention he met George L. Berry, international president, who admired McGrady's easy energy and appointed him a national organizer of the union. He served two years as representative of Ward 13 in the Boston Common Council; and he sat for a like term in the Massachusetts House of Representatives.

But it was the war that elicited all McGrady's zest for public service. No one defended democracy more vociferously, or hated the "Huns" more wholeheartedly, than he. No one outdid his passionate hawking of Liberty Bonds, or surpassed his bitter denunciations of slackers, aliens and pacifists, or equalled his sentimental rhapsodies over the nobility of the drafted heroes. And it was natural that Edward McGrady be given charge of the organized labor division of the Liberty Loan drive in Massachusetts, to be followed by a place on the Industrial Priorities Commission for facilitating war business. In those frenzied days, McGrady, the patriot, completely obscured McGrady, the labor official, and McGrady, the politician. Almost any noon the veteran office holder could be seen shouldering his way through the crowd in Boston Common to the Parkman Bandstand. Usually dapper, Ed McGrady was on these occasions anxious to impress other workers that he was one of them. Dressed in ink-stained work clothes, he would lash his listeners into an ecstasy of national pride, and later he would sell great quantities of bonds. Even then, McGrady was not one to rest content. As president of the Boston Labor Council, he urged that body to expel all members who were non-citizens, unless those members immediately took out their first papers. Edward F. McGrady did a good deal more than his bit to make the world safe for democracy.

The U. S. Treasury Department valued his devotion. During the coast-to-coast Liberty Loan campaign, billboards and posters depicted a brawny overalled worker — none other than Ed McGrady whose physique had been somewhat remodelled and enhanced by an unknown artist — assuring America: "Sure, we'll finish the job!"

Following the war, Samuel Gompers, always on the lookout for aggressive, personable labor leaders whom employers would respect and whom the executive council could control, dubbed Edward McGrady the official A.F. of L. lobbyist. "That's a man who can be useful to any cause," Gompers commented on his new representative. So in 1919 Ed McGrady set himself up in Washington, D. C. His new job put him in contact with the right people and he was a good mixer. From George L. Berry he had learned to dress stylishly, in neat double-breasted suits, with a hat jauntily perched on one side of his slightly bald head, and with a pearl tiepin holding his cravat tastefully in place. From Gompers, he learned to be thankful for any plum thrown the A.F. of L. by Congress.

As legislative agent, McGrady gained only two significant successes in fourteen years at Washington. He lobbied for the Norris-LaGuardia Anti-Injunction Act passed in 1932. Yet McGrady could never have wheedled Congress to approve the bill without the pressure of labor and liberal opinion. He also conducted labor's campaign to block the appointment of Judge John J. Parker of North Carolina to the U. S. Supreme Court, since it was Parker who had handed down a notorious decision upholding the yellow-dog contract.

Though McGrady's Washington record was hardly impressive, he made good use of the chance to form personal friendships. Meanwhile, he laid the foundations of his career as New Deal "trouble shooter" by serving in a similar capacity for the Federation. Polished and adroit, McGrady resorted when necessary to what he considered rank and file language. "Listen, you bastards," he once screamed at recalcitrant strikers, his usually affable face grim and the clipped, military moustache bristling, "I went to jail myself. I'm one of you! Haven't you sons-of-bitches any gratitude?" And he pounded the table in front of him, threw his arms wide, and chewed viciously on his cigar.

Despite dramatics and self-proclaimed integrity, McGrady cautiously trod the line laid down for him by the A.F. of L. executive council. When Gompers died and William Green was abruptly pushed into the presidency, Federation officials continued to chorus the stale refrains of Gompersism in which they had been schooled. McGrady hummed along, altering not one note of the A.F. of L.'s hymn celebrating class collaboration, craft unionism, and renunciation of independent political action. An excellent hired man, McGrady knew better than to criticize; rather he sang bravely the tunes approved by the executive council.

During the fourteen years of lobbying, McGrady was sometimes summoned to represent the executive council as a special or emergency ambassador. His best known exploit, discreetly publicized, occurred in April 1929, when William Green dispatched McGrady to Elizabethton, Tennessee, to take charge of a strike of rayon workers. One night, employers' gunmen and vigilantes dragged McGrady out of bed and rode him to the state line at Bristol, Virginia. "If you ever come back to Elizabethton," they warned, "you will go out wearing a wooden jacket." Three hours later McGrady was in a hired car riding back to Elizabethton where he remained until the end of the strike. Efforts to prosecute the kidnappers failed. But the episode won McGrady the Loyal Legion's medal as the outstanding labor figure of the year.

Physical courage McGrady undoubtedly displayed. But toughness of mind was a different matter. Toward progressives and radicals in the labor movement, McGrady nursed an unreasoning hate. The aims and methods of the independent or progressive unions, so long as they had any hope of success, riled McGrady and he fought them automatically. He had neither the interest nor the integrity necessary to judge their merit and importance. Instinctively he resented their challenge to the mold in which his trade union principles were cast.

For example, in 1926, the New York furriers under the leadership of Ben Gold, a Communist, struck for a forty hour week. For seventeen weeks the strikers resisted gangsters and professional scabs hired by the employers, and the sabotage of the international union officials. The membership rejected a settlement made with the employers by William Green who had dashed to New York and, in an attempt to get rid of the union's rank and file leadership, had accepted an agreement specifying a forty-two hour week. The workers defied Green's strikebreaking, kept the strike alive, and finally won a forty-hour week. Green then handed over the task of breaking the militants to McGrady who for six years headed the pack that yapped noisily at the left-wingers. "We have the fullest coöperation of the New York police," McGrady bragged, "in our work of cleaning up the Furriers' Union." McGrady and his group accused Gold of mishandling union funds, bribing the police, using violence in strikes, and violating the union constitution. Eventually, the rank and file turned the accusations against the Federation officials and proved, much to McGrady's discomfiture, that the fur union officers whom the Federation supported were actually guilty of the very crimes falsely laid to Gold.

Nevertheless, the Federation empowered an "investigating committee," composed of Matthew Woll, Joseph P. Ryan, Hugh Frayne, J. Sullivan (most of this group were able to handle such matters in none too gentle fashion as a result of abundant experience in the past), and Edward McGrady, to expel Ben Gold and hundreds of other fur union militants. In addition, the committee dissolved four locals and arbitrarily replaced them with groups of their own making. The expelled members joined the Fur Workers Industrial Union affiliated with the Trade Union Unity League. The Industrial Union recruited most of the industry's workers. Seven years later, in 1933, the union, with Ben Gold president of the powerful New York local, was admitted to the A.F. of L. By that time, Gold had become one of the most respected and forceful union leaders in America.

McGrady never forgave Ben Gold. When Gold was arrested in Wilmington, Delaware, for leading the Hunger March of 1932, another chance fell McGrady's way to injure the fur leader. On a false charge of "rioting," Gold was sentenced to sixty days in jail. It was suggested that the Department of Labor should point out to the Wilmington authorities that Gold was needed in New York to help formulate the N.R.A. fur codes. General Johnson and Secretary Perkins sidestepped the issue and referred the question to McGrady. The "trouble shooter" (who wanted everyone to say of him, "his soul was clean") could not resist the opportunity to hit out at Gold. He urged the judge to enforce the sentence with the result that the president of the furriers, whom McGrady described as "a menace to society," served forty days in the workhouse.

Still, if left-wingers were not involved, McGrady could be splendidly generous. "He loved his fellowmen, and tried to help them," read the little poem he had learned in his youth. When three years after the Elizabethton kidnapping, the leader of the vigilante-employer gang was indicted for misappropriation of funds, McGrady interceded with the attorney general on the terrorist's behalf. Only against progressives did the lobbyist show no quarter. He zealously aided the employers in their fight against the National Miners Union, affiliated with the T.U.U.L., when miners struck in Gallup, New Mexico. On two occasions, he urged owners not to sign agreements with left-wing unions.

Even after his appointment to the Labor Department, McGrady sniped against progressives: during the 1934 West Coast maritime strike, he used all his ingenuity to turn workers against Harry Bridges, militant rank and file leader of the longshoremen. He failed miserably. For a year thereafter, McGrady threw whatever weight he had behind Joseph P. Ryan, president of the International Longshoremen's Association, who both feared and resisted Bridges' influence. Only after Bridges had established his leadership on the Pacific Coast so unshakeably that it could no longer be questioned, did McGrady soften his public attacks and grudgingly refrain from openly flaunting his hostility.

Thus McGrady, professional patriot and labor official, spent long years at Washington flattering the powerful, slapping the backs of the mighty, and fighting union progressives. After Roosevelt's victory in 1932, many thought that the incoming president would appoint his friend, Ed McGrady — whom he had met immediately after the war — to the post of Secretary of Labor. The A.F. of L. favored Daniel Tobin, president of the teamsters, for the position, but had no objection to McGrady who bustled about Washington while his admirers hailed him as "Mr. Secretary." Much to the lobbyist's chagrin, Roosevelt selected as secretary the sociologist Frances Perkins. It was suggested to Madam Perkins, a timorous crusader, that she name McGrady her assistant. She refused with a good deal of indignation, since the Federation had opposed her appointment.

General Johnson came to Ed McGrady's rescue, taking him into the National Recovery Administration as deputy administrator. Only later, after McGrady had become the man of the hour by talking captive coal miners in Pennsylvania into abandoning their strike, did Madam Perkins invite McGrady into her department. To Postmaster-General Farley, who had also urged McGrady's appointment to the Department of Labor, she admitted, "I was mistaken about that Mr. McGrady." Nevertheless, she resented her subordinate's genius for publicizing himself and spent a good deal of thought and energy to keep him in second place.

WHEN EDWARD F. McGRADY left the A.F. of L. to enter the national administration, he was no less convinced that Gompersism was the fountain head of all trade union wisdom than he had been when he arrived in Washington fourteen years before. In all that time, Congress had passed only two measures of importance to labor — the Norris-LaGuardia Anti-Injunction Act, which he had supported, and the deceptive Railroad Labor Act of 1926, which had been under the wing of the Railroad Brotherhoods' lobby. McGrady had, however, witnessed countless legislative defeats administered to the

unions: child labor laws declared unconstitutional; the dismissal
without serious consideration of legislation backed by the United
Mine Workers and designed to stabilize the coal industry; the right
to strike and picket attacked from all sides; and legislation dealing
with hours of work, minimum wages, old age security, unemployment insurance, and countless other problems affecting labor completely disregarded by the federal government. Never once did
McGrady bother to analyze what it was in Federation methods that
discouraged rather than induced legislative concessions. Except for
an address to a labor party conference in Chicago in 1923 (which
frightened poor Gompers almost witless), McGrady remained
oblivious to the issue of independent political action. He was a lobbyist: as such, he coaxed and flattered the powerful. Now and then a
crumb fell his way, for which he expressed surprised and effusive
gratitude.

McGrady certainly did not possess the vision to realize that the
Federation's refusal to enter independent politics with a realistic
program amounted to relinquishing any hope of legislative protection, just as other A.F. of L. policies abandoned the majority of
American workers to the open shop. True, the A.F. of L. accepted,
when it could get them, laws that restrained government agencies
from interfering with union activities. But labor's political efforts, so
the blind men on the executive council contended, should be directed
not toward building a labor party but to the support of "good"
candidates and the defeat of "bad" ones. Consequently, there was
nothing unusual in the spectacle of William Hutcheson campaigning
for the Republican Party during a national election while Daniel
Tobin orated for the Democrats.

The remaining labor officials lined up on one side or the other, or
like William Green made a pretense of "neutrality." The attendant
confusion and the splitting of the labor vote enabled anti-labor
judges and legislators to slip into office. And as a result, reinforced by
no independent political unity, McGrady's labors in Washington
were of necessity largely fruitless. He fought this bill, supported that,
but he offered Congress no guidance and too often was not sure which
measure to favor, which to oppose.

The legislation affecting labor that did pass federal and state bodies
fell into two categories: that which attempted to alleviate the worst

abuses of a highly industrialized system of production and that which sought to protect the right to organize and through collective action to force concessions from the owning class in labor disputes. The inclination of the courts over the years was to invalidate any legislation favorable to workers. Just as during the C.I.O. campaign the reactionaries clamored for legislative and judicial decisions outlawing the sit-down strike, so in the past employer groups attempted with great success to nullify labor's every gain. Only when pressure from workers, liberals, and their sympathizers became too explosive did the courts experience a sudden change of heart and reverse former unfavorable decisions.

Because the A.F. of L. repudiated independent political activity, social legislation in the United States not surprisingly lagged when compared to legislative advances in other industrial nations. Thus, though mechanization of industry resulted in a decided increase of injuries and deaths among workers engaged in manufacturing, for years the only recourse open to an injured worker was through common law. The courts found innumerable excuses for refusing compensation. Laws holding employers liable for certain mishaps proved worthless, since to establish employer responsibility, workers were forced to take their cases to court. The attendant delay and expense, the inability in a majority of cases to prove employer negligence to the satisfaction of the courts discouraged suits.

To rectify this abuse, some states framed workmen's compensation laws. Maryland enacted the first compensation law in 1902. The United States Supreme Court promptly declared it unconstitutional, and did not reverse its decision until 1917. By 1934, all but four southern states had adopted compensation legislation; in far too many states, however, payments were inadequate and excluded important categories of workers. The intensity of the problem can be judged by the annual number of accidents estimated by Dr. I. M. Rubinow: 30,000 men were killed, 74,777 suffered dismemberments of one or more parts of the body; 3,540 were permanently disabled; 78,608 suffered partial permanent disability; 6,888 were disabled for over six months; and 3,032,072 were disabled for less than six months.

Moreover, workers received hardly any protection against occupational diseases — bends, anthrax, silicosis, scores of other maladies.

In addition, safety legislation, varying widely from state to state, failed on the whole to achieve its end because of inadequate inspection staffs, and improper and corrupt methods of enforcement.

Bitter struggles also accompanied attempts to limit work hours. Though in 1840, President Van Buren fixed the ten hour day for government employees, and later this maximum was reduced to eight hours, these rulings signified little for the great body of workers. Toward the turn of the century, some years after the struggle for the eight hour day was dramatized by the Haymarket massacre and the hanging of labor leaders, Utah limited workers in smelters, refineries, and the ore reduction industry to an eight hour day. The Supreme Court allowed the statute to stand, but in 1905 weakened this precedent by declaring discriminatory a New York law which limited the work day of bakers to ten hours. In 1917, the Supreme Court sanctioned the Oregon statute which pruned the work day in certain industries, where health was endangered, to ten hours — partly because just a year before railroad workers had threatened to strike unless Congress passed the Adamson Act establishing an eight hour day for certain groups in the transportation industry.

The Supreme Court, always loathe to uphold legislation affecting the work day, winked at laws protecting women against excessive hours, since long hours endangered women's health and since the Court refused to allow "mothers of the race" to be endangered. On the other hand, in 1907, the Supreme Court would not tolerate legislation forbidding night work for women and only reversed itself in 1915.

Similarly, legislation providing for one day's rest in seven, old age pension plans, the inadequate and tricky Railroad Pension Act which provided small annuities for aged railroad workers (largely paid for by the workers) were all rejected by the Court. Indignation eventually forced the Court to reverse all its original rulings except for the Railroad Pension Act. Minimum wage laws for women and minors (the Federation at times opposed minimum wage legislation for men on the fallacious grounds that such laws would injure the labor movement by encouraging workers to look to the government for help), were granted first by Massachusetts in 1912 and in the following fifteen years, by fourteen other states.

While originally sustaining these laws, the Supreme Court turned on itself in 1923 in the famous *Adkins* v. *Children's Hospital* case, in which the court held that since the Nineteenth Amendment had granted women the right to vote, women were presumably equal to men and therefore should not be discriminated against through legislation hampering their freedom to work for any remuneration they wished to accept. Moreover, the Court added — indicating its bias — the law took no account of the employers' position. The *Adkins* case successfully abolished minimum wage laws for women. Renewed attempts were made to control women's pay, laws were formulated and reënacted, but again in 1936 they were found unconstitutional. Once more general anger aroused by the Court's reactionary decision forced the eminent justices to scamper for shelter. In less than a year they had changed their minds and had approved minimum wage legislation.

The eagerness with which the Court invalidated social legislation made for confusion, delay, discouragement, and suffering. But never did the Court so defy public sentiment as in its consistent refusal to permit legislation outlawing child labor. Both in 1916 and in 1919, Congress banned child labor in interstate commerce. The Supreme Court canceled each bill. In 1924, Congress approved a child labor amendment to the Constitution which by the middle of 1937 had not yet received the endorsement of the required number of states. During the first part of 1937, the New York legislature rejected the amendment: opposition from large employers, from most of the newspaper publishers, and from the hierarchy of the Catholic Church, who contended that the banning of child labor robbed the child of his "liberty," defeated the measure. Many states endorsed child labor statutes; but in the South and in agricultural regions where child labor was most extensive, such legislation either did not exist or was inadequately enforced.

Likewise, the federal and state legislatures neglected almost completely the problem of social insurance, defined by Grace M. Burnham as "a system of government support to give workers financial assistance, thus affording them a measure of security in case of accident, sickness, death of the wage earner, unemployment, child bearing, or dependent old age." Only one state, Wisconsin, had passed by 1932 a compulsory unemployment insurance law. The Wisconsin act provided for no contribution by the state to the fund which was sup-

ported entirely by the employers. The plan provided negligible payments to applicants and when severe unemployment occurred, reserves seemed sure to be speedily exhausted, leaving the unemployed
without insurance when they needed it most. More recently, several
states passed unemployment insurance bills, but all consistently excluded large categories of workers and provided for infinitesimal payments in the future. Unemployment insurance plans set up by several large corporations during the 1920's broke down after 1929
under the strain of mass unemployment and were either discon-
tinued or drastically curtailed.

The federal Social Security Act, passed in 1936, failed to provide
direct unemployment insurance, and granted such low scale old age
pensions (paid for almost entirely by the workers) as to be almost
worthless. Yet even the recognition such legislation gave to the need
for social insurance met immediate opposition from the judiciary; a
federal district court in the spring of 1937 pronounced the Social
Security Act unconstitutional, and the case was referred to the
Supreme Court, where it was declared valid.

Consistently enough in view of its anti-political attitude, the
American Federation of Labor for many years opposed rather than
advocated unemployment insurance. Only recently, the executive
council reversed its policy. But the shift did not affect Matthew Woll,
president of the Photo-Engravers and member of the executive
council, who continued to oppose unemployment insurance — although Woll did not abandon his own private and thriving insurance
business.

The backing of social insurance legislation by the A.F. of L. proved
to be both grudging and nominal. Among the rank and file, however,
pressure increased for all types of insurance, particularly for the
revised Workers Unemployment and Social Insurance Act, known as
the Frazier-Lundeen Bill, as a first step toward social insurance for
workers and farmers. To the mass of workers it became increasingly
evident that social insurance, like any other beneficial measure, was
in the end dependent on the power labor could muster to support such
legislation. And once they had won legislation, workers must also
defend it from attack by the courts. The A.F. of L.'s refusal to enter
the political arena with a party of its own served only to delay and
defeat labor's efforts to gain greater security: in essence, the executive

council reinforced the owners' resolve to withhold even a modicum of protection from the majority of wage and salary workers.

OF ALL labor's rights, recognition of its claim to organize and bargain collectively met the severest resistance. Whenever labor attempted to increase its power through united action, the class bias of the entire state mechanism became glaringly evident. If all measures to improve workers' conditions through social legislation met opposition — since such legislation cut into the profits of the dominant class — it could hardly be expected that the state would be more inclined to tolerate unions through which workers could compel employer concessions. Big business ruled the legislatures and the courts, both local and national. A.F. of L. labor groups which were content passively to wait for consideration from the government found that because labor's needs ran counter to the interests of employers, workers could expect few gifts. The strike and the picket line, weapons designed to force better conditions, failed of course to win approval from judges and legislators who reflected the views of the owning class from which they were either drawn or to which they aspired. Not surprisingly in a government administered by men counting for support, reëlection, and advancement from bankers and industrialists, respect for property outweighed all other considerations. The vested interest of property ownership, not the vested interest of workers in their jobs, became the first concern of legislation affecting the working class. Labor found itself no match for capital in the legal contest for safeguards and recognition.

At each step in the painful journey to attain economic protection through organization, labor encountered new barriers. At first, even trade unions were considered criminal conspiracies designed to rob employers of their property. Then, in 1842, a Massachusetts court ruled that combinations of workers to withhold their labor for higher pay were lawful. Thereafter, unions slowly established their legality — but the recognition of strike action, essential if collective bargaining were to have meaning, remained under constant attack. Even in 1937, court decrees forbade railroad unions to strike if by so doing they interfered with interstate commerce and the mails. While the courts in the past few years were more or less inclined to permit strikes intended to achieve economic improvement for workers, the legality of strikes to obtain the closed shop was never fully conceded. Precedents still existed for outlawing any strike which in the court's judgment attempted to injure an employer and had not as its primary objective the betterment of the workers. Similarly, the sympathy strike, called in support of beleaguered workers, had a doubtful legality never wholly clarified. Only one state, California, legalized all strikes, with the exception of those led by progressives or radicals who were in constant danger of prosecution under the state's criminal syndicalism law.

Even with the right to strike granted, workers had to make their struggles known and prevent strikebreakers from taking their jobs. Picketing was ever under attack: three states — Alabama, Colorado, and Washington — prohibited picketing, and in many other states court interpretations resulted in similar bans. The attitude of the federal courts, always averse to picketing, was picturesquely summed up by a judge who answered a brief upholding peaceful picketing: "There is and can be no such thing as peaceful picketing any more than there can be chaste vulgarity, or peaceful mobbing, or lawful lynching." In 1921, the Supreme Court finally sanctioned "missionary" pickets, so long as they were peaceful, and ruled that one picket at each entrance to an industrial plant was the maximum that could be tolerated. But mass picket lines continued to appear wherever workers militantly resisted exploitation. More workers were fined and imprisoned for picketing — often under such vague, misleading charges as "blocking traffic," "rioting," "inciting to riot," or "resisting an officer" — than for any other activity. Whether the courts frowned or not, workers defied restrictions in order to preserve one of their most effective weapons.

Not so successful was the struggle to preserve the boycott weapon. Whereas formerly the boycott was an important and useful labor tactic, the growth of mass-production industries, the tendency of manufacturers to brand their products under a dozen or more different labels, and the national character of industry made boycotts increasingly difficult to enforce. Yet, in the early 1900's, the offensive against labor's boycott became exceedingly vicious and far-reaching. Two cases dealt the unions particularly staggering blows. In the Danbury Hatters case, in 1908, the Sherman Anti-Trust Act was tortured to include labor unions, and the union which had called the boycott was crippled by a fine amounting to three times the estimated damage to the company, or over $200,000. About the same time, the A.F. of L. defied an injunction and issued a "we don't patronize list" naming as unfair the Bucks Stove and Range Company. The courts handed out jail sentences (never served) to high Federation officials, including Samuel Gompers. These decisions completely forbade the secondary boycott, in which parties other than the union directly involved were called upon to ostracize the offending employers. The boycott fell partially into disuse — though union labels and publicity given to strikes in some degree achieved the purpose of the boycott.

Employers, nevertheless, themselves utilized the boycott without restraint. The blacklist, which prevented individual workers from obtaining employment, flourished without interference from the courts. Those laws that sought to forbid blacklists failed to protect the workers, inasmuch as no means existed to prevent a company from volunteering information to another company concerning a worker's union activity. Yellow-dog contracts, binding workers not to strike or join a union as a condition of employment, constituted a form of boycott that became increasingly popular among industrialists. Those workers who violated yellow-dog agreements were immediately blacklisted and at times even prosecuted. Although in 1898 Congress declared yellow-dog contracts illegal, the Supreme Court ten years later invalidated the act. Previously it had declared unconstitutional the Kansas law of 1903 which made it a crime to force a worker to sign a yellow-dog contract. In support of such agreements, the courts went so far as to enjoin unions from organizing among employees who had been forced to sign yellow-dog contracts — as the United Mine Workers discovered in 1917 — and invariably the Supreme Court upheld the lower courts. Not until 1929, when the Wisconsin legislature took the lead by proclaiming the yellow-dog contract against public policy, and in 1932 when Congress approved the Norris-LaGuardia Act forbidding the use of yellow-dog agreements as grounds for granting federal injunctions, were the unions offered any relief.

Hostile as the courts were to legislation favoring labor, court interpretations of legislation not originally intended to apply to unions hampered workers even more. Thus the Sherman Anti-Trust Act, passed in 1890 supposedly to restrain monopolies and huge industrial combinations in interstate commerce, was used to smash the railroad strike of 1894 and to jail the brilliant leader, Eugene Debs. With the Sherman Act as justification, the courts argued that strikes restrained interstate trade. They inundated the unions with injunctions, orders issued by judges forbidding activities which in the opinion of the courts should be forbidden. No adequate refuge from these orders existed; even a temporary injunction usually proved sufficient to end a strike prematurely. By the time the case came up for final decision the employers' need for the injunction had in the majority of instances ended. No proof that an existing statute had been violated was demanded by the judges before issuing temporary restraining orders. Defiance of the injunction meant imprisonment without jury trial.

The Arizona legislature in 1913 forbade the use of injunctions against strikes, boycotts, and picketing, and was immediately overruled by the Supreme Court. The following year, Congress approved the Clayton Act, ostensibly abolishing the use of injunctions in disputes over terms or conditions of employment so long as the methods of the disputants remained peaceful and lawful. The delight of Samuel Gompers and the other high A.F. of L. officials over the Clayton Act and its declaration that "the labor of a human being is not a commodity or article of commerce" proved premature. Gompers burbled that the Act was "the Industrial Magna Charta upon which the working people will rear their constructions of industrial freedom." The courts thought otherwise: on the principle that property must not be endangered, the courts continued to deluge unions with restraining orders and Gompers discovered that his Magna Charta offered no more protection than a badly tattered umbrella in a cloudburst.

The Norris-LaGuardia Act, passed by Congress in 1932, was designed to halt the epidemic of anti-labor injunctions in federal courts. But a great number of state courts retained their enjoining power. The extent to which courts indulged in anti-union actions was indicated by the 300-odd orders reported delivered by federal courts against the railroad shopmen during the 1922 strike. From 1914 to 1933, over 800 injunctions were directed against labor organizations by New York state courts alone.

With the entry of the United States into the World War, the federal government for the first time established what passed for a visible labor policy. The War made essential the task of raising production to the highest possible level. To keep it there, it was imperative that strikes disrupting the flow of war supplies be prevented. Samuel Gompers and other A.F. of L. officials willingly coöperated with the government. While the war period saw more strikes than any other previous period of American labor history, these strikes rarely occurred in basic industries. Gompers accepted a hampering "peace-in-industry" policy, refusing to take advantage of the war to organize workers in the mass-production industries.

The War Labor Conference Board, supplanted by the National War Labor Board, granted workers the right in theory to organize and to bargain collectively. The National Board, in addition, vaguely approved the basic eight hour day, the principle of a living wage (never adequately defined), safeguards for workers' health and safety; and opposed lockouts, discrimination against workers for union activity, and the use of coercion against unions. In return, the administration demanded — and received from the A.F. of L. officialdom — the pledge not to strike for the duration of the war. Newly formed mediation boards in various industries were intended to act as courts of last resort, and assumed no jurisdiction in disputes between employers and workers where agreements already existed or federal statutes provided a means of settlement. Actually the mediation boards often urged and at times came dangerously near to compelling arbitration.

Nevertheless, unions increased their memberships during the war though by no means to the size that potentialities warranted. A.F. of L. officials were too busy being honored by the government to organize the workers. Whenever rank and file leaders reflected the militancy of the masses — as William Z. Foster did in the meat-packing industry — the old line office holders joined the government and the employers to oppose strikes and union expansion. Deceived by a war time administration, the A.F. of L. executive council expected the government's superficial tolerance of the Federation to outlast the war. Immediately the war ended, labor found the courts fully as hostile as they had been prior to the war, and perhaps more so. Injunctions again shattered the unions; the government lent the workers no aid in their attempts to win collective bargaining. Rather than advancing the labor movement, as many had predicted it would, the war only ushered in a more severe open shop campaign. With weak and defeatist leadership, the unions lost members and experienced a disastrous series of reversals.

Particularly did the "American Plan" of anti-unionism and non-unionism gain headway. By 1922, some 2,000 employers' associations existed throughout the country, almost all pledged to "discourage" union growth. Spies, undercover agents, provocateurs were employed by corporations to report union talk and "agitators." Owners set up "employee representation plans," a more appealing label for company unions, to destroy real organization. Throughout the arrogant, open shop campaign, the A.F. of L. officials became more cautious than ever. Green preached sonorous sermons on what labor's task must be, intoning against the "Reds" and the progressives, while the prelates of the executive council passed the dues plate among the rapidly thinning parishioners and later solaced themselves by digging into the collection.

In consequence, when the depression throttled America in 1929, the unions were too small and too powerless to resist wage cuts, speedup, longer hours, the shattering of work standards. The Federation had refused to organize the majority of American workers. Now the rapidly growing army of unemployed lacked union consciousness or allegiance; the jobless flooded the labor market with desperate, unorganized men and women willing to work for almost any wage. Appalled and bankrupt, the executive council attempted neither to revive the labor movement by organizing mass-production industries, nor to protect the craft unions by organizing the unemployed. Instead, the officials swallowed President Hoover's non-strike policy in return for guarantees against wage cuts — worthless guarantees violated almost at the moment of their granting.

Yet the A.F. of L.'s leadership could not check the rising resentment of the working class. Progressive and radical workers led hunger marches, organized demonstrations for unemployment relief, provided militant leadership to the independent unions and to the Federation's rank and file. The Communist Party and other radical groups successfully guided the struggle to compel higher relief payments. Whether or not the A.F. of L. officials approved — and more often than not they didn't — workers began militantly to resist the ravages of economic breakdown.

The inauguration of the Roosevelt administration was greeted by an unprecedented restlessness. With the banks closed and the financial structure of the nation tottering, President Roosevelt realized that he must placate the workers if he was to gain their support for a "recovery" program. As occurred during the War, the government bid for labor coöperation by granting certain minimum concessions. Codes of fair competition, aiming to stabilize industry by regulating production and sales competition, also prohibited some of the most repressive employer practices in interstate commerce. A "partnership" between capital and labor, always trotted out by the government in times of crisis, was announced as the basis of the National Recovery Act. Codes also ostensibly granted minimum wages, maximum hour restrictions, and the regulation of child labor. Section 7-A seemingly guaranteed the right of workers to organize for the purposes of collective bargaining.

At first glance, it appeared that labor had finally won a definite status under the law. But Section 7-A was merely a statement of policy, and had no legal weight. In practice, when workers attempted to enforce the minimum wage provisions, the maximum hour and collective bargaining grants, they met firm resistance. Often the N.R.A. proved unenforceable — as in the case of the Weirton Steel Company and the Ford Motor Company. To enjoy benefits supposedly proffered labor by an enlightened government, workers were forced to strike to establish their claims, as they had always had to do before. In 1934, strikes flared in almost every industry: particularly bitter were employer efforts to prevent organization of maritime workers on the West Coast, of teamsters in Minneapolis, of Electric Auto-Lite workers in Toledo, and of textile workers throughout the East. The National Labor Board, created to "consider, adjust, and settle differences and controversies," engaged mostly in mediation and was unable to enforce its decisions on stubborn industrialists. During the six months ending December 1934, regional labor boards decided 566 cases and disposed of 2,509 additional cases. Yet the Boards did not succeed in avoiding strikes; almost all important disputes resulted in walkouts, and workers learned that they benefited in exact proportion to the strength of their organizations and their ability to force industry to yield to their demands.

During the War, in return for paper concessions, the federal government sought to outlaw strikes. And with the New Deal under way, General Johnson, head of the N.R.A., told the A.F. of L. that strikes were illegal. Edward F. McGrady blustered in 1934, "No doubt that the public sentiment of the country is almost unanimously behind the president. Unnecessary strikes will turn that sentiment against organized labor." But in contradistinction to its wartime experience, the A.F. of L. executive council was unable to restrain the workers. Only by disregarding such warnings as those broadcast by Johnson and McGrady did the workers manage to give the N.R.A. any meaning at all. And therefore, as soon as the most severe economic emergency had passed, the Supreme Court rallied to the aid of hard-pressed industrialists: a barrage of decisions canceled the N.R.A., the Railroad Pensions Act, the Guffey Bill, and other New Deal legislation. The slate was hastily wiped clean of disconcerting declarations even vaguely hinting at labor's rights.

One thing the N.R.A. had accomplished: it had encouraged the growth of company unions and employee representation plans. To prevent genuine unions from encroaching in mass-production industries, employers instituted elaborate schemes that gave the workers "organization" carefully supervised and controlled by the management. In steel, in automobile, glass and rubber, in every important industry company unions flourished. The Supreme Court had on one occasion declared against this form of organization: in 1930, it had stopped the Texas and New Orleans Railroad from discharging union men and from paying other employees to build a company union. The decision upheld the 1926 Railroad Labor Act (expanded in 1934), which in exchange for collective bargaining virtually forbade strikes among railroad employees by providing elaborate mediation machinery and fact finding boards, and thereby delaying strike action indefinitely. But this anti-company union decision applied only to one industry.

Still, even though canceled, Section 7-A had established a precedent, at least in the minds of workers. Its substitute, the Wagner Labor Relations Act, made a gesture to eliminate company unions and to prohibit certain employer practices in interstate commerce. Here again loopholes remained which allowed company unions to continue. The act, however, encouraged labor to organize in opposition to employee representation plans. The Supreme Court, facing mass revolt against its usurpation of legislative power, and after much delay, finally upheld the Wagner Act. Until this decision, the provisions of the Act had remained unenforced. For as Earl F. Reed, Liberty League counsel of the Weirton Steel Company, remarked: "When a lawyer tells a client that a law is unconstitutional, it is then a nullity and need no longer obey that law." And the Liberty League lawyers unanimously condemned the Wagner Act.

The Supreme Court's favorable decision, wrung from it by Roosevelt's threatened reform of the federal courts, was undoubtedly an important victory for labor. Recognition of the right of unions to organize and the provision demanding that corporations deal collectively with their employees came at a time when the Committee for Industrial Organization had achieved its first victories in the automobile and steel industries, and served to stimulate further unionizing campaigns. Like all legislation, however, the Wagner Act remained open to Supreme Court emasculation and to the limitations placed upon it by judicial interpretations.

Moreover, some employers attempted to evade the intent of the Wagner Act by agreeing to endless and inconclusive negotiations and even verbal understandings, but steadfastly refusing to sign contracts with the unions. The Act, they protested, provided only for the forms of collective bargaining and was powerless to compel employers to reach an agreement in writing. And though its constitutionality aided labor, the Act in practice meant only what the militancy of the workers could make it mean. In the light of Gompers' joy over the Clayton Act, William Green's declaration that the Wagner Act represented "the Magna Charta of labor" had an ominous sound. But then, William Green and his associates fortunately had no voice in the direction of the C.I.O.

As could have been anticipated, when the C.I.O. swept into the mass-production industries the reactionaries insisted that Congress and state legislatures respond with Red-baiting and anti-labor bills. With the Wagner Act upheld by the courts, the offensive augmented tenfold. It was only necessary to recall two acts passed by state legislatures in the past to realize the menace of the new drive. In the wake of a mine strike, Colorado in 1915 enacted an industrial disputes bill forbidding strikes and lockouts in industries "affected with a public interest" until elaborate investigations had been made.

Following the coal miners' strike in 1919, Kansas approved compulsory arbitration and outlawed strikes, boycotts, and picketing, though the bill was later found unconstitutional because it contained a wage-fixing clause. And as the wave of sit-down strikes crippled the automobile industry early in 1937, similar legislation was proposed — and was actually passed in Vermont and Tennessee.

Attempts to incorporate unions seriously menaced the right to organize and strike. For incorporation denied unions their status as voluntary associations of individuals, and made it mandatory that they beg permission from the government to exist. Furthermore, once the state was granted the power to license unions, it would have the right of "visitation and inspection" — a power which allowed a judge to send any agent, however reactionary, into any union to examine all records, membership books, accounts, etc., if such an examination was demanded by even one member of a union. Since there was nothing to prevent the one member from being a company spy, such inspection would help build employer blacklists. In addition, if the judge decided that a union was not "living up to the purposes of its charter," he could dissolve it, appoint a receiver, attach union funds, and cripple the organization. Hand in hand with agitation for incorporation went proposals to make arbitration compulsory, to forbid sit-down strikes, and to outlaw pickets — all reinforced by opposition to reforming the Supreme Court.

To meet such threats, labor needed more than indignation. Labor's Non-Partisan League took the first steps toward mobilizing the political power of the working class. It supported the plan to overhaul the Supreme Court. It campaigned for state legislation similar to the Wagner Act and the Norris-LaGuardia Act. It demanded broader guarantees of civil liberties. The League's progressive program endorsed the Black-Connery bill to institute minimum wages and maximum hours, and legislation to force the licensing of all private police, guards, and detectives. Through this campaign, the Non-Partisan League did much to arouse the workers' political consciousness.

But the history of labor legislation taught that to advocate legislation and to fight for it through non-partisan organizations were insufficient to assure labor's freedom from coercion. Significantly, beneficial legislation in the past had been won primarily through the political efforts of partisan groups. In the twenties, the Trade Union Educational League, and subsequently the Trade Union Unity League, with their emphasis on independent political action, did more than any other labor agencies to publicize and mobilize resistance against repressive legislation as well as to win the few legislative concessions obtained. Progressives in the recent campaigns for industrial unionism stressed that only through a broad Farmer-Labor Party, enlisting union support and the participation of farmers, middle class elements, and white collar and professional employees, could labor consolidate economic victories. Certainly the "nonpolitical" policy of the A.F. of L. executive council too clearly proved not only an obstacle to labor's influence on the government but also an ever-present danger to the security and continued existence of the unions.

Moreover, the rank and file of the unions began to understand that local gains were transitory unless backed by independent political action. It was all very well for maritime workers on the West Coast, coal miners in the Tri-State area, or automobile workers in the Middle West to organize powerful unions and improve their conditions. But to preserve their gains, to supplement and spread them to new groups of workers depended on labor's ability to prevent anti-union legislation no less than on the continued militancy of workers' organizations. In order to heighten the struggle and guard the labor movement against Fascism, large numbers of workers joined local political movements — the Commonwealth Federation in Washington, the Farmer-Labor Party of Minnesota, the Progressives in Wisconsin, the American Labor Party in New York.

Actually workers were becoming disinclined to accept the government's traditional hostility to strikes that sought to improve the standard of living and the security of the majority. Nor was a national Farmer-Labor Party either visionary or unattainable. Through it, progressives in the rank and file pointed out that workers could guarantee their right to organize, strike, and picket; to win the thirty-hour week; to gain unemployment and social insurance, and old age pensions; to preserve civil liberties and abolish criminal syndicalism laws. Moreover, a Farmer-Labor Party could inaugurate legislation assuring economic equality to women, Negroes, and other minorities. A campaign to abolish sweatshops and to curb speedup would aid in eliminating industrial accidents and would also protect minimum wages. Labor's political power, by no means an impossible achievement or necessarily remote, could end anti-labor injunctions and company unions. It could assure freedom of the press and radio, could release political prisoners, could eliminate such terrorist organizations as the Ku Klux Klan, the Black Legion, the vigilante groups, company spy systems and private police forces whose ravages were so graphically revealed by the LaFollette senatorial investigations.

In advocating a broad Farmer-Labor Party, the rank and file progressives stressed that the government had hitherto always been the property of a reactionary minority. The bankers, industrialists, and large landowners controlled the courts and at the same time they held the state legislatures and even the national Congress under their thumbs. In contrast, with labor a political force, the government would evolve into a democratic instrument of the majority. The American people as a whole would finally gain the means of controlling their own destiny.

EDWARD F. McGRADY, however, was too concerned with the problem of preserving peace between employers and employees to worry about the benefits that the working class would enjoy from independent political action. As a member of the Roosevelt administration, he took on the protective coloring of an "impartial conciliator." His interests centered wholly in ending labor disputes. It was not his business to ascertain which group, employer or worker, received the greater advantages from his services.

For the first few months of the New Deal, workers took Ed McGrady at his word when he thundered, "The government has pledged its good faith to industry and the workers, and we are going to see that the faith is kept." Such assurances persuaded bituminous miners in the Monongahela Valley to call off their strike in August 1933. McGrady's stock rose sharply in administration circles as a result: a week later, miners protested that the company refused to re-employ strikers, in violation of the truce. McGrady counseled patience and let the matter stand.

Soon, whenever the Assistant Secretary of Labor arrived in a strike area to "help" settle a dispute, workers warned, "Beware of the strikebreaker." For McGrady's prestige rested not on the terms of a settlement but on the speed with which he could herd men back to their jobs. He "impartially" attacked the side which refused to end a walkout; and since industrialists willingly agreed to resume production if the men would only return to work and forget their demands, the unions aroused McGrady's ire by their insistence on recognition and concessions before they returned to work.

It was Mr. McGrady who conceived the idea of importing Joseph P. Ryan, president of the International Longshoremen's Association, to San Francisco to break the 1934 maritime strike. Ryan cooperated with McGrady wholeheartedly, but unfortunately for the alliance, it turned out that the international president lacked jurisdiction over the autonomous West Coast district of the I.L.A. Even more unfortunate for McGrady's scheme was the failure of Ryan's secret settlement with the shipowners. The maritime workers almost unanimously rejected the terms of the agreement which they called an undisguised "sell out." McGrady fumed and called names while Ryan scurried for cover.

It was also McGrady who ended the Toledo Chevrolet strike leaving the workers' wage demands to go begging. It was McGrady who mediated the 1935 rayon dispute in Cleveland after which fifty-nine strikers were refused reëmployment. The great conciliator had the number of workers discriminated against reduced to eighteen, and tacitly sanctioned the blacklisting of these militants who incidentally formed almost the entire leadership of the union. It was McGrady in 1935 who attempted to split the solidarity of the Maritime Federation of the Pacific by Red-baiting "in the name of the United States government."

It was McGrady who did yeoman's service in helping Governor Paul V. McNutt of Indiana break the Terre Haute general strike of 1935, though employees of the Columbian Enameling and Stamping Company did not receive a settlement. It was McGrady who flew to New York during the 1936 elevator strike, and again by Red-baiting attempted to force operators back to work before they won concessions. It was McGrady who advocated "arbitration" in San Francisco late the same year, though the maritime unions had already arbitrated the dispute two years before (McGrady had been a member of the Arbitration Board) and the employers were merely trying to find some means of canceling the previous award.

By November, 1936, McGrady had traveled over 145,000 miles by air alone in the cause of industrial peace. He shuttled from one labor dispute to the next, suavely smoothing things over. Always fearful — and not without reason — that his presence might not produce a settlement, Ed McGrady played safe. His invariable response to inquiries as to what hope he had of ending a conflict was a gloomy "Well, brother, it looks bad." Chewing his cigar, he stalked into conference rooms where he proceeded to belabor the workers' representatives only interrupting himself to dash from the room to issue press bulletins predicting an early agreement. Despite his reputation as conciliator, he failed to achieve lasting settlements in almost every important dispute. Sometimes he emerged with a truce; but the terms were usually so disadvantageous to labor that in a brief time the strike was resumed.

McGrady's most ballyhooed contribution to the machinery of settling strikes was evolved in the early autumn of 1935. The "Toledo Peace Plan", as McGrady christened his scheme, was designed to postpone strikes indefinitely and to dissipate workers' militancy through protracted discussions, mediation, and arbitration. Not so original as McGrady liked to make out, the Toledo Plan had much in common with the 1915 Colorado industrial disputes bill and the 1926 Railway Labor Act. McGrady's scheme, based on its trial in Toledo, operated through eighteen citizens, important in community affairs and therefore according to McGrady, "neutral." They constituted a permanent mediation board, with a chairman and vice chairman elected from their numbers. When an industrial dispute arose, but prior to the outbreak of a strike or lockout, the vice chairman was instructed to summon a few members of the board to form a consulting panel which then met with representatives of the employers and the union. Should the attempt to conciliate prove fruitless, the vice chairman thereupon reported to the chairman and the remaining board members. If the chairman wished, he could summon the entire board and initiate an elaborate and slow process of mediation and arbitration that could stretch out for months.

Meanwhile, workers were forbidden to strike though the company involved could shift production to another plant during the maze of inquiries, consultations, depositions, and deliberations. If a strike eventually resulted despite the committee, the company was so fully prepared and the workers were so demoralized by the delay that the employer could sit back confidently and wait for the recalcitrant employees to starve themselves into submission. The Toledo Plan was a little too crude even for William Green to stomach. The A.F. of L. president denounced it. On the other hand employers showered McGrady with praise, and General Hugh S. Johnson was moved to write several newspaper columns extolling the genius of his former assistant. The Plan, of course, failed to hoodwink the unions and McGrady was soon compelled to eliminate it from his bag of tricks.

The failure of the Plan did not prevent McGrady from continuing to chase about America and from intervening in most major strikes. But as months passed, as workers grew more wary of his promises and suspected his good faith, the effectiveness of labor's leading politician waned. Prophets remained, however, who predicted that Roosevelt's election victory of 1936 meant McGrady's elevation to the position of Secretary of Labor. But Frances Perkins remained at her post, and McGrady served on as her assistant.

With his inability to avert the 1936 maritime strike on the West Coast, with the advent of the C.I.O., McGrady temporarily slipped from the headlines. He did not participate in the highly important negotiations to end the General Motors or Chrysler strikes. Some explained his absence by recalling McGrady's rôle two years before when he helped to create the Auto Labor Board which the workers had neither forgotten nor forgiven. Whatever truth this rumor contained, McGrady spent his time hailing the Supreme Court's decision upholding the Wagner Act, predicting an unprecedented era of industrial goodwill, and tactfully deploring the C.I.O. — A.F. of L. split, though just as tactfully did he avoid taking sides. Early in the conflict, he offered to conciliate between the craft and industrial unionists, but his offer was ignored. Rumors also circulated that McGrady would welcome a job in private business — he needed, the explanation went, a larger salary than he received as assistant secretary. But McGrady shook his head when questioned about his plans, hedging patriotically: "I will work for Frank Roosevelt in any capacity he wants me to, from office boy up, as long as he wants me to."

Though Edward McGrady brought an exhibitionistic fervor to his job as assistant secretary, his conduct in office had been no different from that of former labor department officials. James J. Davis, once an iron puddler, and Edward Nuckles Doak, once a railway worker, forgot the needs of the labor movement once they took a government portfolio. Edward F. McGrady followed the same pattern. As a government official, he was ostensibly "above the battle," which meant that he played his part the way it had always been played before. For labor could look for support and sympathy from government officials only when it had a real voice in the composition of the legislature and the courts. To assure itself an even more strategic position, labor had also to develop its independence in politics. By the middle of 1937 workers were beginning to take these lessons to heart.

IV. JOHN L. LEWIS

Samson of Labor

IT TOOK TIME for John L. Lewis to learn: he distrusted theory and depended on experience. For ten years, he won repeated victories over the employers — on paper; only after ten years, in 1933, did he seem to appreciate that too often these victories obscured retreats which would lead to ultimate rout. The more this Samson of labor, as he liked to represent himself, lashed out at the coal operators, the more they sheared his power. He enjoyed struggle, believed in it. "They are smiting me hip and thigh," he exulted, and "Right merrily I shall return their blows." Yet from 1925 to 1933 the United Mine Workers lost over two-thirds of its membership. And it apparently dawned on John L. Lewis that for all his shrewdness and energy, he was sinking to the level of just another A.F. of L. official, heading a handful of workers while the mine operators manacled them to yellow-dog contracts.

Then came 1933 and the N.R.A. Lewis, the modern Samson, struck out with Section 7-A. In a few months he recruited most of the coal miners into the United Mine Workers of America. This time, he resolved, victory would not blind him to reality. John L. Lewis had Red-baited with the best of them, had voted the Republican ticket, and had been undismayed by the Federation's refusal to organize the unorganized. But in the end, Lewis understood that it was necessary for the survival of the labor movement to bring the thirty million workers outside the A.F. of L. into industrial unions. As he stated to the 1935 A.F. of L. convention, the Federation had "a record of twenty-five years of constant, unbroken failure." It was imperative that the A.F. of L. "condemn itself for its own shortsighted policy and for creating gratuitously a situation that permits an enemy to come over its walls and wage destruction in its internal affairs."

William Green, William Hutcheson, all the petty bureaucrats on the executive council tried to prevent the impending drive. Furiously

Hutcheson denounced Lewis at the 1935 A.F. of L. convention, and in his rage called the mine leader a "big bastard." Lewis' deep-set eyes under the shaggy brows shone with hard anger as he knocked Hutcheson down. Within a fortnight, Lewis and the presidents of seven other A.F. of L. unions formed the Committee for Industrial Organization. Within a month, Lewis dramatically resigned from the A.F. of L. executive council. Within a year, William Green was wailing that his old friend John had turned traitor ("Alas, poor Green," mocked Lewis, "I knew him well.") and William Hutcheson, campaigning for the Liberty League, was venomously denouncing Lewis as a "Red" and warning that "A vote for Roosevelt is a vote for Lewis." Within a year and a half, inspired by the C.I.O., workers began their victorious march. Employees in the flat-glass industry struck and won a blanket pay increase; rubber workers gained higher wages and improved conditions; the Amalgamated Clothing Workers negotiated a twelve percent wage rise for all employees in the tailoring branch of the industry; the United Automobile Workers forced the huge General Motors Corporation to recognize their union as the bargaining agent in twenty plants; and, most important of all, the traditionally open shop United States Steel Corporation signed an agreement with the C.I.O.'s Steel Workers' Organizing Committee recognizing the Amalgamated Association of Iron, Steel & Tin Workers, granting improved wages, the forty hour week and pay for overtime. Behind the historic success of John L. Lewis and the C.I.O. was the eagerness of workers to join and support labor organizations based on logic, prosecuted with energy, and promising a new era of genuine achievement for the American labor movement.

JOHN LLEWELLYN LEWIS, who at fifty-five turned on his past, was born in 1880 at Lucas, Iowa. His Welsh parents had left mining communities in the old country; they met in Lucas, married, and raised a large family. John's father, Thomas, was a member of the Knights of Labor. Active in a mine strike, his name appeared before long on the company blacklist. He moved with his family to another town, where he again found employment in the pits until the blacklist caught up with him. From then on, he welcomed any job he could get.

John received the usual upbringing of a boy in a small mining

town. He attended elementary school, entered the mines at the age of twelve, organized a baseball team, fought hard and enthusiastically with his ham-like fists, and later made public addresses whenever anyone would listen. He was a self-possessed youth, with a poker face, a pugnacious chin, and heavy, bulldog features. He liked to wag impressively the leonine head with its unruly shock of red-brown hair. He dramatized himself, puckering his thick and bristly brows, pouting his full lips, jutting his jaw forward belligerently. Wherever John Lewis went, from his youngest days, he attempted to dominate, and he usually succeeded. Above all, he had curiosity, a desire to know for himself — perhaps because knowledge added to his self-assurance. He read carefully the Bible, Shakespeare, the books that his future wife, a young school teacher, chose for him.

At twenty-one, John had grown restive, cramped by the small town. He wanted to see the country, to try his luck elsewhere. Moreover, mining was a dangerous, difficult occupation, and John felt no great urge to stick to it. Accordingly, he roamed through the West. But mining was what he knew and he invariably ended up in the pits. He dug copper in Colorado, silver and coal in Montana, gold, soft coal, hard coal here and there. He witnessed strikes and took part in them. He helped dig out 400 miners killed in the 1905 mine explosion at Hannah, Wyoming. He drove mules, and displayed his peculiar audacity when a vicious animal called Spanish Pete attacked him in a mine corridor. John brained the mule with the sprag of a coal car, covered its wounds with clay, and told the foreman that Spanish Pete had died of heart failure.

By 1906, John Lewis had drifted back to Lucas. He persuaded the local union members to elect him delegate to the United Mine Workers convention. The following year he married the school teacher, Myrta Edith Bell, who had helped him educate himself and who in the future was to polish off his thunderous rhetoric.

Once again, in 1909, he moved, this time to the coal fields of Panama, Illinois. Here his career in union circles got seriously under way. Unable to quit the mines during his wanderings, he decided to get out of the pits by rising in union circles. Elected president of the Panama local which he and his brothers dominated, he acted as a one man grievance committee, and in a few months had talked himself into the position of state legislative agent for the union. At the state capital, his dramatic presentation of the horrors of the Cherry mine explosion won safety measures for the miners.

John Lewis enjoyed haranguing the legislature. He spoke his ornate sentences from puffed cheeks, lowered his voice to a tense stage whisper, shook the furniture with his deep-throated roar. His eyes flashed under brows drawn frowningly together. He pounded tables, stretched his arms wide as he beseeched the heavens to hear him. But often the revivalist declamation, so full of bombast, grew trenchantly brilliant, and then the tub-thumper was transformed into a caustic phrase maker.

At thirty-one, Lewis' prodigious and noisy energy impressed Samuel Gompers, who appointed him field and legislative representative of the A.F. of L. Lewis welcomed the chance to act as Gompers' personal emissary; the job took him all over America: into the glass, lumber, rubber, and other industries. He participated in the Calumet copper strike. He attempted to organize steel, and saw the craft officials wrangling in jurisdictional disputes that kept the campaign from making any headway. He appeared before legislatures in several states, before the national Congress, and in 1916 served as a member of the Interstate Scale Committee. That same year he acted as president pro tem at the United Mine Workers' Convention. When John P. White, president of the U.M.W., appointed him chief statistician of the union, he quit his job as Gompers' special representative. High time, Lewis felt, to get back into his own union, for there lay his future — power in the United Mine Workers and through it, power in the Federation.

Industrial in form, the largest union in the A.F. of L., the United Mine Workers had survived twenty years of harsh struggle. The rank and file knew the meaning of blacklists, terror, protracted strikes, harassing pressure from the coal operators. The union had joined the Federation in 1890; seven years later the miners, under the then militant John Mitchell, won their first national strike. But John Mitchell fell easy prey to Gompers' policy of collaboration; by 1902, he was deferring to J. P. Morgan, and when the anthracite miners struck that year, he refused to permit the bituminous miners to strike in support — on the ground that they were bound by contracts signed with the operators. Mitchell considered a contract sacred above all things — even when the operators violated it, the miners must continue to observe it. And John Mitchell bequeathed this principle to the officialdom of the U.M.W., which reverently conformed to the tradition. Mitchell left the union for business and died with a fortune of $250,000.

Tom Lewis (no relation to John L.), who followed Mitchell to the presidency, later went South, where he bought and operated a non-union mine. John P. White, his successor, allowed John D. Rockefeller, through terror and massacre, to institute company unionism in Colorado. He ended his career by taking a job as permanent arbitrator. While patrioteering during the War, White evolved the philosophy that high profits were the only guarantee that could assure the maintenance of full production, and therefore the first concern of the miners must be for the earnings of their employers. After White came Frank Hayes, a friendly, ineffectual man who drank too much and who let John L. Lewis, whom Hayes appointed first vice president, take full charge of the union.

With this advancement, John L. Lewis plunged into years of turbulent activity. The War, just over, had offered unprecedented opportunity for organization. But the officials of the United Mine Workers had been too busy selling Liberty Bonds to find time to build the union. Obligingly, it had signed an agreement with the Federal Fuel Administration pledging the union to ask for no change in the wage scale for the duration of the War. The scale had been raised in 1916 from $3 a day to $5; and on that basis the union relinquished all struggle for better conditions while international hostilities lasted. But by 1919, with the armistice a year old, rank and file miners were clamoring for higher pay and a stabilized work week. Mining was hazardous, and the conditions under which miners worked were far worse than even the shameful conditions existing in most American industries. When the delegates met at the 1919 convention, over which John L. Lewis presided in Frank Hayes' place, the overwhelming majority supported demands for a sixty percent raise in pay, a six hour day, and a five day week.

No alternative remained but for Lewis to inform the operators that unless they granted the miners' terms, the U.M.W. would strike. Negotiations got nowhere; coal operators had a fixed principle never to yield to the miners until no other way out remained. The government suggested arbitration. Lewis snorted at the idea: "In the language of Elbert H. Gary," he proclaimed, "I cannot discuss arbitration at this time."

The owners flocked to Washington, insistent that the government put down the threatened "insurrection." They were greeted with ready sympathy by officials who in turn confided their political ambitions to the understanding operators. President Wilson, from his sick bed, once again rallied to the defense of democracy by warning that no peace treaty had yet been signed with the Central Powers, and consequently the United States was still technically at war. He recalled the wartime agreement between the miners and the government, though the Fuel Administration had long since been disbanded. The strike, Wilson concluded, "is not only unjustifiable, but is unlawful." To prove it, the notorious attorney general, A. Mitchell Palmer, obtained a temporary injunction from a federal court in Indiana which forbade the strike.

John L. Lewis was equal to the battle of words. "Today, when the coal miners of the country, in a justified attempt to improve their conditions, undertake a wage move, we find our efforts strangled by the President of the United States. . . ." The rank and file applauded; on November 1, 1919, the date set for the walkout, seventy percent of the bituminous miners, about 411,000 in all, stayed away from the pits.

Victory seemed certain. Europe faced a coal shortage: in England, coal miners were on the verge of a strike; the Austrian government, desperately in need of coal, was planning to buy from America; many French mines had been ruined by the German invasion; elsewhere, the war had dislocated production. No possibility existed of breaking the U.M.W.'s strike by providing the American market with imported coal. The miners, firm in their demands, held a strategically impregnable position.

The only flaw was the government's determination to smash the strike. Less than a week after the miners had stopped work, the attorney-general received a permanent injunction from a willing court, which ordered the cancellation of the strike by November 11. Lewis, although he had been defiant just a few days before, was still under the sway of the ruinous Gompers tradition of complete coöperation with the employers, and was inexperienced in negotiations of such complexity. He called a secret conference of coal union heads, and they advised him to stop the strike. Accordingly, Lewis announced the strike's termination and ordered the workers to return to the pits. "We cannot fight the government," he apologized. He held no referendum, made no attempt to resist the injunction, and neglected to announce the terms under which the miners were to resume work.

During the next few weeks, the miners straggled back to their jobs — except in Illinois, where they refused to abide by Lewis' order and where they remained on strike until December. Their insubordination gained them better terms than those obtained by the miners who had returned to work. The majority, when months later they finally learned the results of arbitration, discovered that they had received less than half their demands: a 27 percent increase in the wage scale and no change in the basic eight hour day. Even with the new scale, miners earned at best from $900 to $1000 a year. Yet Lewis claimed a victory.

Lewis bluffed through the 1920 convention of his union, masking his capitulation with ponderous speeches, overruling the disgruntled delegates with iron arrogance. By 1920 Lewis had been officially elected to the presidency of the U.M.W. by a vote conducted through the mail and counted by friends at union headquarters. Because of his retreat during the 1919 strike he faced dissension in the union. The militant Alexander Howat, president of the Kansas District, defied Lewis by leading a strike against a newly passed state law instituting compulsory arbitration. When Howat was jailed, he continued to conduct the strike from his cell. Lewis "outlawed" the strike on the grounds that it violated a contract between the union and the operators. But Lewis' real reason stemmed from Howat's open opposition to the manner in which Lewis ran the United Mine Workers and from a growing fear that Howat's influence might weaken his hold on the presidency of the U.M.W. Without trial, Lewis expelled Howat and the Kansan's supporters from the union and replaced the insurgents with his own machine appointees. The struggle between Howat and Lewis stretched over many years; Lewis, however, managed to retain his original victory though the running fight split, and so weakened, the union.

Likewise, he quarreled with the Illinois district president, Frank Farrington, a far different man from Howat. Farrington, a confirmed reactionary, was building a strong place for himself on the discontent that Lewis' tactics aroused among the rank and file. Lewis feared Farrington's power in the Middle West; he had sparred cautiously with Farrington for years, waiting for an opening which would allow him to demolish the Illinois clique. Finally, in 1925, with Farrington in Europe, Lewis disclosed with much fanfare that the district president was receiving $25,000 a year from the Peabody Coal Co. Farrington admitted the charge and countered by accusing Lewis of similar deals. Mutual recrimination did not add prestige to the U.M.W. leadership; in the end Lewis came out on top, expelled Farrington and watched the membership of the U.M.W. diminish as a result of this internecine war. Nor had Howat's and Farrington's opposition to him in 1924 when he attempted to capture the A.F. of L. presidency from Samuel Gompers made Lewis less bitter or less anxious to break both rivals.

Again, in the 1922 strike of all coal miners to retain the 1920 wage level, Lewis pursued a short-sighted policy. On the first day of the strike he made a bargain with the employers in western Kentucky whereby he ordered resumption of work in that district in return for an agreement extending the old terms until the following year. A few days later, he signed two-year contracts for southeastern Kentucky and Tennessee. The flow of coal from these sections weakened the nationwide strike.

Unfortunately, Lewis' lack of vision did not end here. He greeted the spontaneous walkout of nearly 100,000 non-union miners in southern Pennsylvania with fulsome delight — but when it came to signing contracts at the strike's conclusion, Lewis abandoned them to the mercy of the operators. His excuse was that the industry included "twice too many mines and twice too many miners." To preserve the bargaining strength and jobs of the U.M.W. membership in the face of an oversupply of miners, Lewis paid no attention to the non-union mines which were begging for organization, and further shattered whatever trust the rank and file retained in his leadership. Lacking organization, the miners were unable to resist disastrous wage cuts. The competitive advantage thus gained by the non-union operators over those operators who had signed wage contracts with the U.M.W. provided an excuse for the owners of union mines to violate contracts. And Lewis discovered that his attempt to save the U.M.W. by excluding the "surplus" workers from the United Mine Workers not only did not help the union, but seriously threatened its very existence. Partial unionization failed; it was a lesson that later caused Lewis to realize the necessity of organizing not only all the mines but also all industry.

The 1922 strike ended with another victory that in reality was another setback. Membership in the U.M.W. dwindled. The union was forced by terror and injunction to withdraw from one district after the other. Gone were Alabama and West Virginia. Union control vanished in Colorado, Utah, Texas, Maryland, Virginia. When Lewis extended the bituminous contract in 1924 for three more years — the famous Jacksonville agreement — he achieved this agreement only by paying a stiff price for it: he relinquished western Kentucky, and maintained only nominal control over less than one quarter of the mines and miners in Oklahoma, less than two-thirds of the miners in Arkansas. Within a year of his so-called triumph at Jacksonville, the operators were violating the agreement; 110 mines in Pennsylvania alone shifted to open shop.

Failure did not alter Lewis's approach. To preserve the Jacksonville agreement, he called another strike in 1927. By now he had given up the pretense of pushing ahead for improved conditions, and had substituted the defeatist slogan, "No Backward Step!" Years of negotiations, the method Lewis had learned from Gompers, had so undermined the principle of blanket agreements covering all union mines that Lewis instructed each district to settle on whatever terms it could obtain from the operators.

The inevitable result was loss of membership. The United Mine Workers decreased from 402,700 members in 1924 to approximately 150,000 members in 1932. For all the blustering defiance, Lewis closed his twelfth year as president of the U.M.W. with the union disintegrated and the operators more secure in their oppressive power than they had been for thirty years.

THE BLAME did not rest solely with Lewis. During the War, the coal industry had expanded; by 1923, the capacity of bituminous mines alone surpassed one billion tons. Production never exceeded half this tonnage. Oil, gas, electric power, improved combustion methods, rationalization of processes in the railway and iron and steel industries restricted still further the already oversupplied market. The price of coal sank; operators speeded up the workers, mechanized the mines, chiseled wages. In three years, 200,000 miners were squeezed out of the industry; those still able to find employment averaged 171 work days a year. The disparity between the labor supply and the falling demand helped shatter union standards and union strength. In the space of twelve months, the number of non-union mines increased from 40 percent to 60 percent. The southern coal fields, 50 percent organized during the war, by 1927 had completely succumbed to the open shop. Moreover, the output of non-union districts soared; the unorganized fields in West Virginia and Kentucky produced 23 percent of the nation's coal in 1920; by 1927, they supplied 41 percent. In these open shop districts, wages remained at a depressed level of $3 a day or lower, contrasted to the wages of $7.50 a day supposedly maintained in the union mines. The consequence was a shifting of orders to those mines where the low price of coal reflected the starvation wages. To complete the gloomy picture, union mine operators met this competition by violating wage contracts.

The federal government, moreover, added to Lewis's discomfort by coöperating wholeheartedly with the anti-union offensive. Not only did the Coolidge administration grant open shop operators preferential freight rates, thus penalizing those owners still abiding by their union contracts, but in addition the courts willingly responded to employers' demands for strikebreaking injunctions. Typical was Judge Langham's order in 1927 banning all meetings and songs on a lot more than a quarter of a mile from a struck Pennsylvania mine, and prohibiting any demonstration within hearing of scabs. (The judge had $6,000 invested in the coal company to which the injunction was granted, but he assured the miners that his financial interests in no way influenced his decision.) Another judge upheld a coal corporation's wholesale eviction of 450 striking miners. A third ruled that pickets must be English-speaking American citizens. Still another forbade the Wheeling, Pa., Ladies' Auxiliary of the local union to hold meetings. Mass picketing was declared illegal repeatedly. The courts, along with the state police, proved invaluable to the operators in mopping up the remaining outposts of the U.M.W.

John Lewis, who had long ago fooled a foreman by stuffing clay into a dead mule's wounds, attempted to conceal the rout by thundering "No Backward Step!" This hardly disguised the fact, which

Lewis himself could not deny, that something was wrong and it was only a matter of time before the U.M.W. would be composed of a high salaried officialdom and no membership.

No matter how anxiously John L. Lewis, protégé of Gompers, scratched his massive head, he was unable to scratch up a solution. For ten years he had been bargaining in the name of the U.M.W.; each time the employers contracted with the union, he boasted another victory. Invariably, the owners violated the terms. When the operators in one section backed down on their obligations, Lewis fought them only in that section, holding the other districts in check, outlawing sympathetic strikes. He maintained a rigid separation between bituminous and anthracite workers. His conciliatory tactics destroyed unity of action and threw away all advantages accruing from industrial organization.

Above all, Lewis had no ultimate objective. Like the craft officials who influenced him, he stressed immediate economic gains, pursuing a day-to-day, hand-to-mouth program that he increasingly modified into non-existence. His stiff-necked refusal to acknowledge class relationships prevented him from perceiving that unenforceable contracts between employers and workers offered no solution to the struggle between capital and labor. More vital still, he failed to realize that while the great majority of American workers remained unorganized, the U.M.W. or any other organized segment of the working class was isolated and predestined to failure.

Lewis was finally forced to seek a way out through legislation, and thereby partly broke from the strict non-political position of the craft unions. From 1920 on, the economist of the U.M.W., W. Jett Lauck, had been drawing up legislation designed to control the coal industry. None of these proposals ever passed Congress. Nor could Lewis quite make up his mind what legislative course he favored: in 1919, he opposed nationalization of the mines; in 1922, he advocated some sort of federal regulation; three years later, in his book *The Miners' Fight for American Standards*, he defended the free play of economic law. It was only in 1933, after America had experienced over four years of depression and unemployment and after Lewis had seen the United Mine Workers unable to resist the powerful monopolies unified by interlocking directorates that he reached a tentative decision. Still thinking purely as a unionist, he concluded that not only must wages be fixed and employment guaranteed in the coal industry, but in all other industry as well. For these concessions, he was willing to strike bargains with the employers.

As Lewis floundered and the union retreated, resentment in the U.M.W. found expression in revolt. Lewis had consistently turned thumbs down on any attempt by the rank and file to democratize the U.M.W., fearing union democracy as a menace to his reign. Since 1920, in six of the union's nine presidential elections, only Lewis' name had appeared on the ballot. At conventions he steadfastly refused the floor to opponents, disregarded or overruled adverse decisions, terrorized opponents. He expelled progressive John Brophy, president of a western Pennsylvania district, and the Socialist, Powers Hapgood, after having them beaten by thugs.

He revoked the charter of the entire Illinois district, overruled a referendum which had defeated by a 5–2 vote a new wage agreement, and saw to it that the second ballot was "stolen," which allowed him to announce that the scale rejected by the majority was in effect. He perfected Red-baiting, denounced all critics as Communist agents, and bludgeoned the 1927 convention into barring Communists from membership in the U.M.W. He suspected that "Reds" dominated the Nova Scotia district, and withdrew the charter. Not given to modesty, he demanded and got a fifty percent increase which swelled his salary from $8000 to $12,000 a year, though the union was financially exhausted by internal struggle and unsuccessful strikes. He showered critics with abuse; he wriggled out of difficult situations by bewildering the delegates with words none of them understood. With the fight in the Kansas district at its height, he talked long and loud of the "imbroglio" and tricked the convention into voting his way. He had the grand manner: in response to a question by a delegate who formerly owned a saloon, Lewis puffed himself up like a bullfrog and berated the unfortunate man as a "damnéd publican." Astonished, the delegate slumped down in his seat. After the session, he sidled up to Lewis. "Why, John," he protested, "I thought you were a Republican yourself."

So far as union philosophy, or lack of it, went, Lewis did not differ, in his first years as president of the U.M.W., from Green or Hutcheson. Unconscious of the anomaly presented by an industrial union being guided by craft prejudices, Lewis conducted the United Mine

Workers in much the same manner as the other members of the executive council ran their unions. As a consequence opposition grew in the union. His contradictory, high-handed leadership forced the opposition out of the United Mine Workers, and spurred it to forming the militant National Miners Union, affiliated with the Trade Union Unity League. While the U.M.W. lost membership and throughout the coal fields the miners raised the cry: "Lewis must go!", the new union, controlled by the rank and file, and based on the policy of class struggle, grew steadily from 1927 on, and led strikes that involved as many as 40,000 workers. In Illinois, too, secession spread, but here Frank Farrington, who looked upon the labor movement as a lucrative racket, captured the union and gave the Illinois district much the same rule that Hutcheson gave the carpenters.

By 1932, it looked as though John L. Lewis, self-proclaimed Samson of labor, had not only been clipped by the employers, but had had his head shaved as well. Lewis took stock. First, he concluded, it was imperative to stabilize the coal industry. He made little progress; the Davis-Kelley bill (a revision of the former Watson bill), which sought to make it mandatory on the government to license interstate coal corporations while guaranteeing the right of labor to organize into authentic rather than company unions, failed to pass Congress. A year later, Lewis expanded this plan, envisaging legal guarantees of wages and working conditions to include the nation's entire productive mechanism. He proposed to the Senate Commission on Finance that the Sherman Anti-Trust Law be suspended and that labor be granted strict protection. He still lacked any definite suggestion as to how labor's rights could be safeguarded while the anti-labor industrialists and bankers controlled the government. And Congress still ignored his proposed legislation.

While Lewis wrestled painfully with his legislative program, Congress passed the N.R.A. which included Section 7-A, embodying most of the labor provisions Lewis had advocated in the Davis-Kelley bill. The N.R.A. expressly acknowledged the right of workers "to organize and bargain collectively through representatives of their own choosing." But legal permission to organize meant nothing unless workers were brought into strong, aggressive unions. Wherever the A.F. of L. craft officials attempted to take advantage of the N.R.A., as they half-heartedly did in the rubber and automotive industries,

they were hampered by craft divisions and by the growth of company unions, which thrived under the vague wording of the Act.

Lewis saw the danger of delay. He swept into the coal fields; the U.M.W. shot up from 150,000 members to triple its size in four months, recaptured the South, the Middle West, all the districts lost in the preceding decade. The National Miners' Union, along with the other affiliates of the Trade Union Unity League, voluntarily disbanded for the sake of greater unity in the labor movement, throwing its strength into the revived U.M.W. and other forward-moving unions. For now there was emerging a group of leaders within the A.F. of L., who, like Lewis, were beginning to launch realistic organizing campaigns.

The operators, caught napping, retaliated by disregarding wage contracts. This time Lewis thought he was ready for them; he demanded the passage of the Guffey bill, written by him and establishing the National Coal Commission with powers to fix prices and allot production. The bill also created a Coal Control Board designed to settle disputes between operators and the union. The labor provisions of the Guffey bill were vague. The U.M.W., so strongly organized, was in the position to force through Congress a bill embodying stronger guarantees for higher wages and granting workers greater protection against the employers. But Lewis learned slowly. When the bill passed Congress, he called the much-postponed strike and through it raised wages to $5.50 for a seven hour day, $5.10 in the South, thus proving that labor's economic power alone, in the last analysis, assured the attainment of those gains conceded by law.

Lewis had brought the U.M.W. back into the sun. But in 1920, when he had first become president of the union, the United Mine Workers had been strong, yet within ten years it had been on the verge of collapse. Lewis resolved not to repeat the mistakes of former years. He could see now that it was insufficient to rebuild the U.M.W.; without a strong labor movement to support them, the miners suffered the brunt of the owners' attack and lacked strength to withstand it. Coal was only a link in the vast industrial chain; so long as steel remained open shop, so long as auto, aluminum, rubber, and similar industries lacked strong organizations, the isolated U.M.W., with only a tiny segment of the working class, was attempting to withstand the full virulence of the anti-labor drive. Barely one-tenth of the

working class had been enlisted into the A.F. of L. Lewis concluded that the only course left was to stake out a far larger field than the coal industry for unionization.

Lewis reached a further conclusion. While the N.R.A. had given the coal miners the opportunity to organize the industry, the craft unions had met with no such success. Wherever they had attempted to follow the example of the U.M.W., jurisdictional disputes had reduced their campaign to inter-union squabbles. Craft separatism meant defeat. Moreover, the majority of the A.F. of L. executive council continued to disregard the mass-production industries which employed the majority of workers. By concentrating on the organization of a handful of highly skilled workers (largely displaced through mechanization and technological advance by the semi-skilled), the executive council displayed its real desire to exclude the bulk of the working class from the Federation rather than to bring it in. Obviously, effective action could be achieved only through industrial organization which "combined the workers on the basis of the product made or material used, regardless of skill or craft."

Throughout America, the standard of living for most wage earners (which never approached the glowing picture of comfort and security over which after-dinner speakers rhapsodized before chambers of commerce) sank during the depression to a bare subsistence level or worse. Unemployment had reached the incredible figure of almost twenty million. Agricultural workers, Negroes, employees in most mass-production industries had experienced ever-increasing exploitation long before 1929. For example, workers in steel, as John L. Lewis pointed out in 1936 when he began publicly to explain the campaign to organize the industry, were "never throughout the last thirty-five years paid a bare subsistence wage, not to mention a living wage." Steel profits mounted dizzily, he continued, but "greater payments have not been made to wage and salary workers because the large monopoly earnings have been used to pay dividends on fictitious capital stock . . ."

What was true for the steel workers held good for those engaged in all mass-production industries. The discontent arising from the need for increased earnings, diminished speedup, shortened hours and improved working conditions, presented the A.F. of L. with the opportunity to recruit great numbers of the unorganized. Of their own accord, searching hopefully for strength through organization, workers throughout the nation flocked into the A.F. of L.'s federal unions wherever these were set up or authorized. The craft officials, instead of capitalizing on this trend, quarreled over the distribution of dues and jurisdiction, while denying the newcomers' votes at the convention, and endeavoring to stifle rank and file militancy. Discouragement and disillusion followed in the wake of mismanagement: with a gain of 352 federal unions in 1934, the Federation suffered a net loss of 110 federal unions by the next convention. Workers searching for leadership found themselves in the same old inert Federation and quickly dropped out again in disgust.

Furthermore, John L. Lewis was not oblivious to the growth of reaction throughout the world. Fascism in Europe, it was plain to anyone who would examine it, had doomed even the most conservative labor leaders. If Fascism were to be prevented in America — and there were alarming indications, which Lewis could not dismiss, that the large financial and industrial interests were anxious to institute Fascism in this country — Lewis realized that only a firmly established, unified labor movement could provide an adequate defense. Such a movement necessarily demanded industrial organization. It was not until several years later that Lewis crystallized what was at first a vague fear of reaction into a firm anti-fascist position. Then he declared:

> "The establishment of a fascist dictatorship in the United States, would undoubtedly assure a retrogression from which civilization might not recover for ages and from which it would certainly not recover for many years. I know of only one means of insuring our safety — the workers of America must find self-expression in economic, in social, and in political matters . . . Labor to us extends from the unskilled industrial and agricultural workers throughout the so-called white-collar groups, including technicians, teachers, professional groups, newspaper employees, and others . . . If the fate of Germany is to be averted from this nation, we must and we shall secure a strong, well-organized, disciplined, and articulate labor movement."

But even in 1934, John L. Lewis was sufficiently aware of the fascist menace to realize that industrial organization should not be delayed. At the convention held that year in San Francisco, Lewis urged the inauguration of a strong campaign to unionize industrially. The convention yielded so far as to vote unanimously that:

". . . the executive council is directed to issue charters for national and international unions in the automotive, cement, aluminum, and such other mass-production and miscellaneous industries as in the judgment of the executive council may be necessary to meet the situation."

During the ensuing year, the craft officialdom controlling the executive council disregarded this mandate. To be sure, it granted international charters to automobile and rubber workers; but the United Automobile Workers was denied jurisdiction over the skilled workers in the industry, and the rubber workers were refused an industrial charter. Applications by groups of federal unions for international charters were also rejected in the radio, cement, aluminum, oil, public utility, gas, and by-product coke industries.

John L. Lewis raged at this betrayal and resolved to push organization whether the executive council liked it or not. Earnestly, at the 1935 Atlantic City convention, he defended the minority report of the resolutions committee on organization policies. As he urged industrial unionism, he utilized all the tricks of oratory he knew so well: now cajoling, now flattering, now defiant. He clinched each paragraph with clear logic, and from beneath the well known histrionics rang a passionate convictior that only industrial unionism would save the official labor movement. So far, he told the tense convention, organizational progress had been obstructed

"by reason of the fact that the American Federation of Labor has not organized the steel industry and the few industries similarly situated. . . . We are assured the way is now open for an aggressive campaign of organization in the steel industry. What kind of a campaign — a campaign to organize them in fifty-seven varieties of organization? . . . If you go in there with your craft unions, they will mow you down like the Italian machine gunners mow down the Ethiopians. . . . The proponents of this minority report are asking that the convention adopt a policy designed to meet modern requirements under modern conditions in this industrial nation of ours. If we fail to have this convention adopt this policy, then, of course, the responsibility falls upon the American Federation of Labor, and

the world and the workers will believe now and for the future
that the American Federation of Labor cannot and will not
make a contribution toward the obvious need of our present
economic conditions in this country of ours."

The craft officials listened. They thought of what Lewis' "aggressive campaign" entailed, the threat it carried to their sinecures, the
break with tradition. They voted Lewis down.

But Lewis had determined what his course must be. A week or so
after the convention, he met with seven other presidents of A.F. of L.
unions to form the Committee for Industrial Organization

"for the purpose of encouraging and promoting the organization
of the unorganized workers in mass-production and other industries upon an industrial basis. . . ."

Among those participating were David Dubinsky of the International Ladies Garment Workers with 210,000 members, and Sidney
Hillman of the Amalgamated Clothing Workers with 125,000 members, both semi-industrial unions. Charles P. Howard of the International Typographical Union was designated secretary, Lewis was
chairman. As a start, the Committee, which also included the United
Textile Workers, the Oil Field, Gas Well, & Refinery Workers, the
International Union of Mine, Mill, & Smelter Workers, and Max
Zaritsky of the Cap & Millinery Workers, voted $500,000 for the
steel campaign. These unions affiliated with the C.I.O. had all under-
gone experiences similar to those of the U.M.W.: the weakness of the
Federation, with the resultant lack of organization among the workers, had handicapped them and often endangered their existence.
The formation of the C.I.O. testified to their resolution to change all
this by unifying workers into effective unions.

Stormy abuse from the executive council greeted the C.I.O. William Green demanded its dissolution. Unable to resist a dramatic —
if precipitous — gesture, Lewis resigned from the council. William
Hutcheson, smarting from the blow Lewis had given him at the previous convention, immediately insisted that the unions affiliated with
the C.I.O. be expelled from the A.F. of L. Bespectacled Colonel John
P. Frey, who because of his ability to use large words in an abstruse
way was conceded the title of A.F. of L. theoretician, "prosecuted"
the C.I.O. unions with unbounded rancor before the executive

council. The remainder of the council led by Matthew Woll and Arthur O. Wharton, president of the International Association of Machinists, vied among themselves in abusing Lewis and the offending unions. "I would rather see the labor movement go under and myself in hell," remarked Wharton, "than have John L. Lewis get away with it." Surpassing them all, William Green fumed that the C.I.O. had "thwarted an organizing campaign in the steel industry."

As the C.I.O. gained headway, the members of the executive council became more frantic. By the fall of 1936, after raising the Red scare, they hastened to suspend those unions directly affiliated with the C.I.O. — about forty percent of the Federation. For though it lacked any legal power under the A.F. of L. constitution to suspend international and national unions except by a vote at the annual convention, the executive council dared not wait. It feared that if the C.I.O. unions had a voice in the next convention, the bureaucracy was in danger of defeat. After the suspension order, the executive council offered "unity" — on condition that the C.I.O. disband. But for all their pleas for "unity," which their suspension order had shattered, the council indignantly refused Lewis' proposal that the suspended unions be allowed full participation at the coming Tampa convention in return for a pledge by both factions to abide by a majority decision.

The 1936 Tampa convention, controlled as it was by the craft officials, rubber-stamped the suspension order. The vote of 21,679 to 2,043 no more represented the majority opinion of the rank and file than the members of the executive council represented the workers in their respective unions. By not allowing the C.I.O. unions a voice in the convention, the council had ruled out 12,000 adverse votes. Typical was the action of Hutcheson who cast the carpenters' 3,000 votes in favor of suspension although 70,000 members in Northwest locals supported the C.I.O., and numerous other carpenters' locals had gone on record against suspension. Similarly, a number of the federal unions and central labor bodies with one vote each (completely disproportionate to their large membership) and many of the smaller unions, dared not oppose the executive council for fear of reprisals. In other cases, reactionary officials disregarded definite instructions by their unions and cast their bloc of votes against the C.I.O. Twenty-two state federations of labor, with two-thirds of the membership in the A.F. of L., protested the suspensions. But that did not deter the executive council. The net effect achieved by the executive council at the Tampa convention was to hamper unity. The executive council openly declared war upon all who sought to bring progressive and vigorous development to organized labor.

INDUSTRIAL UNIONISM was nothing new in America. Even before the formation of the A.F. of L. in 1886, the Knights of Labor had advocated organization on an industrial basis. Mistakes of leadership and the admission by the Knights of small merchants and farmers in what was supposed to be a trade union organization confused the movement and laid it open to attacks from the church, the state, and the employers.

Though Samuel Gompers joyfully participated in the ceremonies that finally laid the Knights to rest, and though he rejoiced that the labor movement was safe at last for craft separatism, agitation for industrial organization cropped up continually, so that in 1901 the A.F. of L. was forced to adopt the so-called Scranton Declaration. The declaration recognized that in exceptional cases (such as the United Mine Workers), industrial organization should be tolerated by the Federation. It further suggested amalgamations which permitted unions to organize an entire industry or major branch of it, while preserving craft lines among the component sections of the union (for example, the International Ladies Garment Workers' Union).

Throughout the succeeding years, the Federation was faced by opposition labor movements advocating industrial organization — the Industrial Workers of the World and the Workers International Industrial Union before the war, the affiliates of the Trade Union Unity League in the late twenties. For over a decade, the League, with its predecessor the Trade Union Educational League, founded by William Z. Foster, had steadfastly promoted industrial unionism as the only realistic way of organizing American labor. It was Foster, the leader of the 1919 steel strike, who demonstrated that the A.F. of L.'s craft philosophy prevented the successful unionization of workers in mass-production industries.

Each attempt to introduce industrial organization met opposition from the A.F. of L. When the Committee for Industrial Organization announced plans for unionizing the thirty million still outside the labor unions, the craft officials responded as they had done for forty years — smash the progressives! Ironically enough, William Green, before he had become president of the A.F. of L. had written in 1917:

"The organization of men by industry rather than by craft brings about a more perfect organization, closer coöperation, and tends to develop the highest form of organization. The causes of jurisdictional disputes are considerably decreased, and in many industries can be eliminated altogether. . . . It is becoming more and more evident that if unskilled workers are forced to work long hours and for low wages, the interests and welfare of the skilled workers are constantly menaced thereby. . . . Some of the advantages resulting from an industrial form of organization are the reduction of opportunities or causes for jurisdictional disputes, the concentration of all men employed in industry, and the advancement and protection of the unskilled laborer in the same proportion as that of the skilled worker."

Green had long since abandoned this convincing line of argument. Yet the records of the few industrial unions in the Federation, when compared to those of the craft unions, bore out his 1917 statement. From 1920 to 1935, industrial unions increased their memberships by 6 percent while craft unions diminished by 32 percent. Significantly, those semi-industrial unions that endorsed Lewis' position at the 1935 convention, gained five percent in numbers; the semi-industrial unions opposing him lost 60 percent. Moreover, strike offensives during this fifteen year period were almost completely restricted to those industries where organization along industrial and semi-industrial lines existed: marine, needle and garment trades, and mining.

Backed as it was by well established unions with substantial resources, and coming as it did at a time when workers welcomed organization, the C.I.O. got off to a quick start. Attacks by the executive council failed to dismay Lewis. "I fear his threats," he remarked of Green, "as much as I believe his promises." While Lewis lacked a clear perspective of the profound implications of the C.I.O. program, he pushed it forward with the same fury that had attracted Samuel Gompers' admiration twenty years before.

One thing Lewis insisted upon: the C.I.O. must enlist as many able labor leaders and organizers as possible. Philip Murray, resourceful vice president of the U.M.W., was appointed chairman of the Steel Workers Organizing Committee. When John Brophy, whom Lewis had formerly expelled from the United Mine Workers, offered his services to the drive, Lewis accepted and appointed him director of the C.I.O. No one could doubt Brophy's firm integrity, his ability and his devotion to the labor movement, nor challenge his progressive outlook. With Brophy came other men of the same calibre — Powers Hapgood, Clarence Irwin, the long list of rebels many of whom had fought Lewis' reactionary policies years before. Socialists and Communists organized intensively for the C.I.O. "It's a pretty good rule to work with anyone who will work with you," Lewis replied to those who puzzled over his change from the Red-baiting days.

And by early summer, 1936, organizers invaded for the first time in over a decade the small shanty towns along the Monongahela, flocked into Youngstown, Aliquippa, Gary, into the Middle West and South, wherever the furnaces of the great steel trust flamed and smoked to the sky. The steel drive was on. Unless the steel barons recognized the union and bargained collectively with it, John L. Lewis and the C.I.O. threatened to strike the mills. Contracts between the United Mine Workers and the coal operators expired in the spring of 1937. By that time steel would be organized. If the coal operators refused to yield to the union, veteran miners would unite with the aggressive steel workers (as they did when the C.I.O. in June 1937 struck the captive mines of Youngstown and Bethlehem Steel Corporation in support of striking steel workers) and the owners of the two basic industries would be faced with a closely knit labor movement, ably directed and financed.

Steel was the key to the mass-production industries, the fortress, till then unconquered, of the open shop. But while steel was the concentration point, the C.I.O. campaign spread to other fronts as well. Rubber workers, supported financially and organizationally by the Committee, consolidated their union and made substantial gains in wages and conditions. Their weapon, the sit-down strike, later proved of vital importance to the C.I.O.-supported glass-workers, and to the strike that crippled the General Motors Corporation for over a month. Under the leadership of their president, the young ex-minister, Homer Martin, in coöperation with Wyndham Mortimer, George Addes, Edward Hall, and the host of other progressives who headed the United Automobile Union, the workers occupied the auto plants and challenged J. P. Morgan and the du Ponts. The auto union won exclusive bargaining power in twenty of the corporation's plants; it cracked the anti-labor mass-production industries' front that bulwarked the open shop. But most important, for the first time in the history of American unionism, a national labor organization supported the strike of an affiliate, and became the determining factor in the struggle. The C.I.O. threw its weight and resources behind the automobile workers. Arrayed against the Committee and the strikers were William Green and the A.F. of L. executive council who in their spleen tried to dismiss the victory as a "surrender." The success of the auto strike gave heart and incentive to the still more ambitious steel campaign. As Lewis declared, "This struggle now in the automobile industry is only the first engagement between labor and finance." He added, in his vibrant, dramatic way, "Mr. Morgan and Mr. du Pont might as well know that collective bargaining is coming soon in their own steel industry."

Come it did, in less than a month after the automobile workers ended their sit-down. The steady advance of steel organization, the success of the West Coast maritime strike, and the victory of the United Automobile Workers convinced the steel trust, particularly the United States Steel Corporation, that the Amalgamated Association of Iron, Steel and Tin Workers, backed by the C.I.O., had the economic strength to force recognition and collective bargaining. By February 1937, 200,000 steel workers had flocked into the Amalgamated Association, and every week brought thousands of new recruits. The company unions, originally set up by the steel corporation to block real unionism, either had gone over en masse to the Amalgamated, or had indicated their intention of following C.I.O. leadership. Nor had the half million dollars in advertising distributed to 375 newspapers by the American Iron and Steel Institute, composed of corporations pledged to combat organized labor, turned the trick for the trust. The average newspaper reader had little sympathy for the steel owners who in the preceding year had amassed fantastic profits and yet wailed that collective bargaining would raise wages and so decrease the size of extra dividends.

The significance of the steel trust's capitulation could hardly be exaggerated. After fifty years, organized labor had finally gained recognition from the most bitter and powerful combination of anti-union corporations in America. The sacrifices of Homestead, the experiences gained from the 1919 steel strike led by William Z. Foster (who more than any other man had carried on the struggle for industrial organization) were at last productive. Recognition of the Amalgamated Association was the turning point in labor's ceaseless war, the Antietam that preceded emancipation. When General Motors and U. S. Steel were forced to yield, the other mass-production corporations retreated: for example, General Electric agreed to discuss collective bargaining, and drives to organize the Chrysler Corporation, Packard Motor Company, Hudson Motor Company, Jones and Laughlin Steel Company, were launched and the corporations forced into line.

Not that the war was won. The policies of William Green and the A.F. of L. executive council dovetailed more closely than ever with those of big business, deepening the split in labor's ranks by ordering C.I.O. unions excluded from central trades and labor bodies and state federations. John P. Frey rushed to the aid of the company unions set up by the Carnegie-Illinois Steel Corporation (owned by U. S. Steel), in the hope of thwarting the C.I.O. The moribund metal trades department of the A.F. of L. announced plans to "organize the steel fabricating plants — to block further the successes in bringing these workers into industrial unions." The executive council attempted to prevent the C.I.O.'s progress in the textile, oil, and shoe industries.

Moreover, the C.I.O. gains had yet to be consolidated. The majority of workers still remained outside unions. But the C.I.O., with its ability to penetrate company unions, with its insistence on unity between Negro and white, foreign born and native workers, with its purposeful leadership and tactic of throwing its entire strength behind organizational campaigns and strikes, gave new courage and resource to all wage and salary workers, whom the executive council of the A.F. of L. had refused to draw into the labor movement. And to those unions and labor bodies that the council expelled, the C.I.O. offered affiliation and support so that these groups would not stand alone.

The C.I.O. was a powerful force for progress. But the open shop corporations had by no means exhausted their resources; espionage, intimidation, reactionary legislation, injunctions, Red-baiting, vigilante terror were still at their disposal. The leaders of the C.I.O. did not have to be clairvoyant to predict that the large interests, even those which had already signed agreements, would band together and employ every ruse to prevent future gains. By the middle of 1937, the signals of a fresh offensive against the C.I.O. were reflected in the Memorial Day massacre of Republic Steel pickets, the attack by Ford's "service men" on auto organizers, and the systematic violation of the Wagner Act quietly sponsored by the Chamber of Commerce of the United States and the National Association of Manufacturers. Yet labor had tasted power; above all, workers had seen what unity of action and unity of organization could accomplish.

The impulse given by the C.I.O. promised also to be of great importance in the fashioning of a political influence which could turn back the threat of Fascism and assure greater security, a higher standard of living, the preservation and extension of civil rights, the increased freedom of the masses, whether industrial or agricultural workers, professional or white collar employees. The C.I.O. was changing the face of America.

JOHN L. LEWIS, no longer a young man, still found as great joy in a fight as he did in [the old Lucas days. The new drive, however, implied a fresh perspective foreign to the Gompers tradition. Painstakingly deliberate when it came to reorienting his approach, Lewis clung to many of his old ideas, grudgingly discarding them only after he was positive they had become a dead weight. Nevertheless, objective forces exercised increasing pressure. The U. S. Supreme Court decisions declaring the N.R.A. and the Guffey bill unconstitutional momentarily staggered Lewis, then led him to revise his conception of labor's rôle in politics. Economic strength, he began to concede, was not enough. To preserve what labor won through its economic power, he found it imperative to invade the political field. The financial and industrial barons still controlled the political machine and, through it and the courts, they violated labor's rights, nullified progressive legislation, bound the labor movement at every turn. Only if labor could exert political influence could it expect more than transitory gains.

Lewis was not yet ready for the full step of independent political action. With hesitation he helped form Labor's Non-Partisan League to resist the toryism of the Republican Party and the Liberty League in the 1936 national presidential campaign. The Non-Partisan League endorsed Franklin D. Roosevelt. Lewis made clear that the League did not support the Democratic Party, but only the candidate. Of himself he stated, "I am not a Republican. I am not a Democrat" — a step forward from his former allegiance to the two party system. But he insisted that as yet he had no other political ties.

The disastrous defeat of the Republican Party revealed the antipathy in America to open reaction. Yet whatever Lewis' hopes in Roosevelt, they were soon severely strained. Curtailment of unemployment relief, the rebuke to Lewis when he demanded support for the thousands of workers in the General Motors strike (though because of the public sympathy for the strikers the President later softened this rebuke so that it lost effectiveness), the gigantic war budget, Roosevelt's refusal to enforce the Wagner Act in the strike against Little Steel, all indicated that the backing given Roosevelt during the election would be of no assistance to labor unless the workers had the strength to squeeze concessions from the administration.

Lewis wisely agreed with other leaders not to disband Labor's Non-Partisan League after the election. The League at first remained passive, and Lewis postponed committing himself once and for all to independent political action. Instead of pressing forward, the Non-Partisan League showed an initial inclination to mark time. Instead of expanding itself into a Farmer-Labor Party on a broad platform that would win the confidence of workers, farmers, and their allies among the middle classes, instead of preparing for the future when it would be imperative to fight on the political front, the leaders of the Non-Partisan League, Lewis among them, delayed, and so, for a period, endangered the League's effectiveness.

But when President Roosevelt proposed to reform the Supreme Court, the Non-Partisan League exerted its full power in support of the plan. And with this willingness to take sides on the political front came a new resolution to carry the battle for progressive legislation into all states, to mold the Non-Partisan League into a decisive political instrument. In the Declaration of Purpose, the League stated: "This organization will be used, in election campaigns of the future, to insure the nomination and election to public office of men and women who are not only pledged to support labor and other progressive measures, but whose record also justified the belief that these pledges will be kept." And further, "We will work with every progressive group whose purpose is to secure the enactment of liberal and humanitarian legislation." The League thus repudiated the "nonpolitical" premise of the A.F. of L. Lewis, in his own name, strongly advocated a legislative program, though the C.I.O. officially made no demands. Lewis called for an amendment to the federal constitution that would limit the jurisdiction of the federal courts, and vigorously backed President Roosevelt's plan to reform immediately the Supreme Court. For the rest, except for his support of the new Guffey Bill, the child labor amendment and the Black-Connery wages and hours bill, Lewis' legislative program remained somewhat hazy, indicating that Lewis himself was not yet fully certain what further steps Congress should take to prevent the mounting exploitation of workers.

Lewis' political activities advanced the rumor that he wanted the presidency in 1940. Whatever political ambitions he harbored, Lewis did not let them blind him to the first task of organization. He saw plainly that his future as a labor leader or as a political figure was linked to the success or failure of the C.I.O. He replied to questions concerning his presidential hopes:

"I have tried to avoid any public discussion of the idea of the presidency. I am not seeking public office. I have turned down public office. I could have been Secretary of Labor years ago.

"When the workers are organized, there will be by-products of that organization, but this is not the time to discuss them. What they will be will be up to the workers, after they are organized."

REPEATEDLY the anti-union critics of the C.I.O. pointed to Lewis' past record of failure and autocracy in the United Mine Workers, and questioned his sincerity in heading the C.I.O. They solicitously expressed fears that he would betray the campaign for industrial organization before the labor movement achieved its goal. The picture of the C.I.O. as a one man organization, however, distorted reality. Lewis never presumed to be the C.I.O., though he was the central figure in its formation. He helped create an organization which, because of its progressive character and because the need for it was great, drew into it a host of militant and able labor leaders. As the C.I.O. grew and coördinated the working class, Lewis would either have to keep pace as he had done so brilliantly during its first two years, or give way to men who would not be deterred even if he suddenly cried "halt." If Lewis kept the C.I.O. movement united, drawing in all unorganized workers regardless of political beliefs, race, or creed; if he pressed for the unification of labor in one trade union federation; if he prevented Red scares and fought against them; if he didn't slow up the pace at which the C.I.O. had begun, and continued to press ahead undeterred by employer, court, government, and A.F. of L. attacks; — if, in other words, he travelled the same road that he had taken since 1935, he would undoubtedly retain the allegiance and support of the American working class and its allies.

Significantly, since the formation of the C.I.O., John L. Lewis had indicated an astounding capacity for growth and development. "I don't give a hang what happened yesterday," he told an interviewer. "I live for today and tomorrow. I will say only this: It takes every man some time to find himself in this world, to decide what he wants to do with his life. It took me longer than most people."

V. HEYWOOD BROUN

It Seemed To Him

THE PUBLISHERS greeted the formation of the American Newspaper Guild with sad shakes of their heads, predicting that newswriters could never successfully be organized. As Roy Howard, president of the Scripps-Howard chain of newspapers, complained to his
employee, Heywood Broun, "You're doing a very silly and evil thing
in trying to get reporters into a union. That would rob them of their
initiative and take the romance and glamour out of the newspaper
business. Still, I don't have to worry; the Guild will never get to first
base."

Roy Howard was wrong. Not only did the Newspaper Guild grow,
but it fought William Randolph Hearst, the most powerful anti-labor
publisher, and emerged from the showdown victorious. Actually
Howard, Hearst, and the rest of the prophets who scoffed at the idea
of unionizing newspaper workers overlooked the change of attitude
through which professional and white-collar workers were passing.
Loss of jobs, pay cuts, longer hours with no increase in earnings, insecurity of tenure, retrenchments that preluded dismissals did not
bolster the myth that salaried employees somehow enjoyed a favored
position in the economic structure. The dignity of profession that
accompanied the supposed romance of editorial work proved insufficient recompense when the landlord and corner grocer presented
overdue bills.

The depression spared the white-collar and professional employees
no more than the wage workers. At first, the heavy blow of "retrenchment" was delayed; once it came, the salaried groups had even
greater difficulty obtaining new jobs than the wage workers, and the
rate of reëmployment among the salaried categories proved far
slower. And just as, in the years of economic crisis, the newly formed
Committee for Industrial Organization broke away from the bankrupt Gompers tradition that ruled the American Federation of
Labor, so the salaried categories began to question the illusion that

they were "different" from wage workers. The most successful of the pioneering organizations to emerge from the depression was the American Newspaper Guild.

At the time of his election to the presidency of the Guild, Heywood Broun, like most professional and white-collar workers, had no training in union organization. Aside from a previous brief and abortive attempt to unionize newswriters, he had given the problem little thought. When the Guild came into existence, Broun was firmly established as one of the leading columnists in America. His large salary assured him far more security than that possessed by the average professional. Yet he brought to the Guild a passionate devotion, a fervor that speeded the union's growth and did much to establish the Guild as a leader in the field of white-collar and professional organization.

Certainly Samuel Gompers, with his distrust of "intellectuals," would never have countenanced Heywood Broun. Gompers disapproved of such men in the labor movement: too often they introduced new ideas, and Gompers resented new ideas, considered them dangerous. Like Gompers, William Green and William Hutcheson and the rest of the A.F. of L. executive council felt uneasy about this new type of labor leadership, heading a union of professionals and white-collar employees. But in 1933 Gompers could have done no more to end the heresy of a union electing a president who had gone to Harvard, had written novels, had been an editor and a war correspondent, than the executive council was able to do — which was nothing. Still, there was always the prospect, as the employers also pointed out, that newswriters would be easily discouraged or lacked sufficient drive to meet the obstacles in the way of organization.

The election of Heywood Broun to the Guild's presidency seemed to buoy that hope. For Broun had a reputation for being something of a dilettante, too easy going and undisciplined to solve the vexing problems that would confront a new union in a traditionally unorganized profession. Broun's career just didn't hold promise that he could stick with the Guild for long. The union, critics agreed, would start out with glowing promises and ambitious plans, but in a year or so it would peter out.

True, Heywood Broun had always shown more than casual interest in the plight of the oppressed. He had played a leading rôle in the

fight to save Sacco and Vanzetti from legal lynching. He had even run for Congress on the Socialist ticket. But such incidents, according to those who foresaw disaster for the Guild, were for the most part the dramatic adventures in Broun's life. Building a successful and aggressive union meant hard work; the personal satisfaction of achievement was often obscured by dreary, day-by-day struggles to consolidate the union and draw in new members.

Nothing in Broun's career seemed to equip him for the task. Born in Brooklyn in 1888, he went through school and to Harvard where his inability to pass an elementary French examination kept him from receiving a degree. He began to work on newspapers while still an undergraduate. At the time of the Guild's inception, he was in his twenty-sixth year of newspaper work, having acted as reporter, rewrite man, sports editor, dramatic and literary critic, and columnist. He painted a little "for the fun of it."

Large, loosely built, with a diffident, amiable smile and a genial manner, Heywood Broun prided himself on his sloppy dress, his membership in the Thanatopsis Literary and Inside Straight Club, and his ability to make others like him. He talked well and fluently, whether to a select group in a drawing room or to a mass meeting at Madison Square Garden, and what he had to say was distinguished by a goodnatured directness, a sharp wit tempered by a disarming candor, and an impatience with hypocrisy. During the years following the War, when America basked in prohibition and a business boom, when the professional and white-collar workers enjoyed a deceptive security, Broun was looked upon as the playboy of the newspaper industry, sought after by the financially mighty who were amused by his humor, and who chuckled tolerantly at his light, persuasive prods to their smug contentment. In the days when prosperity arrived in America supposedly never to depart, when economic alchemists declared that American industry and finance had discovered the formula that forever abolished depression, the big publishers and theatrical producers, the wealthy patrons of art and the socially élite could afford to indulge themselves by enjoying Broun's jovial irony. At times, the columnist felt vaguely uncomfortable, for he was conscious of the relationship existing between himself and his hosts, the relationship of employee to employer. In the New York *Tribune* office, and later at the New York *World*, he was aware that other newspapermen and women, who worked harder than he did and whose ability he admired, received salaries that were far too low and worked hours that were far too long. The inequality bothered Broun, but he had no clear idea what he could do about it. Besides, he was paid a large salary; he was secure, exceptional, able to write what he pleased.

Broun had always been troubled by injustice. He went to France in 1917 as correspondent for the American Expeditionary Forces and found that he did not like war and could work up no enthusiasm for the murder that was to preserve democracy. Instead Broun gibed at the inefficiency of the War Department, and George Creel of the Bureau of Public Information sent him home. The correspondent came out of the War with a dislike for Creel, a vague annoyance at himself for his incapacity to express a proper patriotism, and a belief in disarmament. A confirmed pacifist, he remarked, "Of all cleaning fluids, blood is the least effective." Nor did he succumb to the Red scare that followed the War. He derided it, resisted it. Later as a columnist for the *World* he lashed out at injustice, discrimination against Negroes, the Ku Klux Klan. But it was the Sacco-Vanzetti case that opened Broun's eyes to the insecurity of the professional's job in general and his own in particular, and enlightened him on the true meaning of the phrase sacred to all publishers, "freedom of the press."

When the Italian anarchists, Nicola Sacco and Bartolomeo Vanzetti, were condemned to the electric chair as blood sacrifice to the Red scare, Broun became thoroughly aroused. He used his column in the *World* to fight the frame-up, to expose it. Of the men who had condemned Sacco and Vanzetti, he wrote:

"I've said that these men have slept, but from now on it is our business to make them toss and turn a little, for a cry should go up from many million voices before the day set for Sacco and Vanzetti to die. We have a right to beat against tight minds with our fists and shout a word into the ears of the old men. We want to know, we will know, 'Why'?"

For two successive days Broun's emphatic attacks appeared in the *World*. But two later columns were excluded. The *World* refused to print them. Broun resigned from the newspaper. In his letter to Ralph Pulitzer, the publisher, he wrote:

"By now, I am willing to admit that I am too violent, too ill-disciplined, too indiscreet to fit pleasantly into the *World's* philosophy of daily journalism. And since I cannot hit it off with the *World*, I would be wise to look for work more alluring. . . . In farewell to the paper, I can only say that in its relations to me it was fair, generous and gallant. But that doesn't go for the Sacco-Vanzetti case."

It was not a final farewell. With Sacco and Vanzetti executed, Broun patched up his difference with Pulitzer in January 1928. The reconciliation lasted four months. In April, Broun wrote an article for the *Nation* in which he declared that New York had no liberal newspaper. Perhaps, he went on, the *World* most nearly approximated the liberal position, but it did not truly attain it. The same night that the article appeared, Broun read in the *World* that he was no longer in the newspaper's employ.

The incident impressed on Broun that despite his reputation, his popularity as a columnist, his large salary, his friendly relations with the publisher, he was in the last analysis only another paid employee. So long as he conformed, he would get his salary and be "free" to do as he pleased, and he could also enjoy Pulitzer's warm regard. But once he ran counter to the interests of his employer, the management dropped him precipitously, just as it fired any other recalcitrant worker. The press, boasting its freedom and liberality, would not permit such license as the expression of ideas that in any way endangered or embarrassed the ruling class.

Broun soon had another column, on the Scripps-Howard chain, where his contract specified that his opinions would appear "without regard to the paper's editorial policy." But even with this guarantee, Broun was not free of all restriction. In 1934, his comments on the San Francisco general strike failed to appear in the San Francisco Scripps-Howard paper. Editorial censorship continued. Broun, however, had come to realize that he alone could not fight even his own battles with the publishers. He was by that time deep in the task of building the American Newspaper Guild.

For one brief moment before this, in 1930, Broun had entered politics to run for Congress on the Socialist platform. He could never quite explain how he happened to campaign for office. "I might lose my job on the *Telegram*," he remarked, "and then the radio people might not like my socialism either, and I might get fired by them too." But he campaigned — and was defeated.

He left the Socialist Party soon afterward — dissension within the Party discouraged him. Yet he wanted to help the underdog. His interest in the theatre prompted him to write, produce, and act in "Shoot the Works," a coöperative venture to provide employment for actors and stage hands who had been unable to find work during the depression. The venture had some success, but Broun remained at loose ends.

In 1933, when the newspaper code was being formulated — by the publishers — in compliance with the N.R.A., spontaneous organization sprang up in several newspaper offices in different parts of the country. The first unit was formed in Cleveland. New York followed, and groups appeared in Tulsa, Minneapolis, St. Paul, Toledo and elsewhere. Heywood Broun, whose lazy energy until this time had lacked direction, showed immediate interest in the new organization. "The fact that newspaper editors are genial folk," he pointed out in his column, "should hardly stand in the way of organization of a newspaper writers' union. There should be one. Beginning at 9 o'clock on the morning of October 1, I am going to do the best I can to help in getting one up."

He did not have to wait that long. September saw the formation of the New York Guild. In December the local guilds called a convention in Washington, D. C., and launched the American Newspaper Guild with Heywood Broun as president.

THE ECONOMIC PRESSURE that led to the organization of newspaper workers likewise affected all other salaried employees. For forty years, as industry throughout the world underwent basic changes, a new category of workers had been rapidly emerging: it was a vast army of salaried employees that steadfastly blinded itself to the economic bonds which linked it to the working class. Instead, these salaried groups clung to the self-deception that their economic interests more nearly coincided with those of their employers. They cherished unfounded hopes that some day they could break into the owning class. Actually their propertyless, insecure position forced them, like the wage workers, to sell their labor power: it doomed them to mounting exploitation and, with the coming of the post-war depression, to unemployment.

Yet the majority of salaried workers rejected reality. Their thinking was not unlike that of the executive council of the American Federation of Labor which refused to acknowledge the basic shift in the American industrial setup and which concentrated on organizing skilled workers at a time when the composition of the working class had become overwhelmingly semi-skilled. Similarly, the salaried groups failed to comprehend economic changes brought about by the intense concentration of capital and affecting their relationships both to the owning and working classes.

In 1870, salaried employees constituted about three percent of the gainfully employed; by 1930, this proportion had risen to twenty-two percent. From approximately 670,000 white-collar and professional employees in 1870, the number had shot up to almost 12,000,000 in 1930. Gone was the opportunity to serve a salaried apprenticeship in preparation for a more lucrative and responsible job of manager or supervisor. As the consolidation of industry progressed, monopolistic corporations replaced the small, individually owned enterprises, and simultaneously altered the function and composition of the salaried groups. On the one hand, mechanization and expansion transformed the clerk from a more or less trusted managerial assistant with a knowledge of the problems and needs of his employer, into a low-paid, unskilled employee working in a huge office. On the other hand, professionals and technicians found themselves unable to exist as self-employed individuals, and forced to accept salaried jobs from corporations.

Salaried employees (as a rule paid by the month and not by the hour or according to the job performed) could be conveniently classified as either white-collar employees, or salaried professionals and technicians. The white-collar category included all manner of clerks, office workers, transport and express agents, promotion and sales agents, assistants to professionals and technicians; anyone of the network of inspectors, salesmen, messengers, recorders, accountants, and civil service workers, which the complicated superstructure of modern industry required and the frenzied efforts to boom sales for all kinds of necessary, as well as useless, products entailed. The category of professionals and technicians embraced those employees whose "occupation is based on specialized intellectual study and training, the purpose of which is to supply skilled service or advice to others"

— the architects, engineers, chemists, teachers, social workers, musicians, artists, actors, writers, economists, doctors, lawyers, and others, all highly trained and highly specialized men and women who were employed by the state, by public and private institutions, and by manufacturing and commercial enterprises.

Of the two categories, the white-collar group was by far the larger. In composition it was overwhelmingly native born and white: only 9.2 percent of the white-collar workers were of foreign birth, one percent was Negro, and .4 percent other races. In 1930, at least 8,000,-000 of the 52,000,000 gainfully employed in America were engaged in white-collar pursuits, an increase of over 2,067 percent since 1870. This phenomenal rise took place as capital accelerated its concentration, which allowed vigorous corporations to swallow smaller manufacturers and merchants, or to press them out of business. As Karl Marx had predicted, the former owners became "overseers and underlings."

The growth of large scale enterprise and constantly rising productive capacity demanded ever expanding promotion and sales forces to raise consumption and to overcome public resistance to the flood of new products. Manufacturers of "luxury" goods, makers of gadgets, owners of "service" organizations swelled their staffs of salesmen, clerks, and promotion men. Large, centralized offices required a host of clerks to perform the numerous functions of billing, accounting, stenography, circularizing, tabulating. With the technical perfection of the telegraph, telephone, and radio; with the growth of transportation facilities; with the mass use of automobiles and the accompanying chains of filling stations; with the thousands of new devices arising from mechanization and electrification, the demand for salesmen, canvassers, demonstrators, messengers, and clerks seemed unlimited.

These white-collar employees thought of themselves as part of the middle class — which unlike the working and owning classes had no common economic interest. Instead, the middle class fell between the two fundamentally opposed classes of capitalists and workers, a group in constant flux without economic homogeneity, and therefore without any possibility of class allegiance within itself. Vague middle class ambitions inspired the white-collar workers. Many came from middle class homes; those with worker backgrounds fervently desired to enter into what they considered the socially more desirable middle class. Almost without exception, white-collar employees, no matter what salary they received, looked down upon wage workers, considered themselves superior. The "new middle class" of salaried employees dazzled itself with dreams of economic "independence," too proud to accept any theory of action that admitted the existence of the class struggle, fortifying its pride by denying class antagonisms.

As a rule, each salaried employee harbored a fantasy of owning his own business, or some property, or of rising to managerial station, though such hopes, because of the restrictions accompanying the intensification of monopoly capitalism, were impossible of fulfillment. White-collar workers depended on large capital for employment. Supervisory and managerial posts were few, and if anything the demand was contracting as industry became more centralized. Certainly the number of highly paid positions was infinitesimal compared to the supply of white-collar workers, while the aggregate of small enterprises was diminishing rather than growing. Opportunities to earn sufficient to buy property or to achieve any sort of economic independence became increasingly slim. Actually, those of the middle class who still owned houses or small businesses or a little property found the struggle to retain these possessions growing yearly more bitter. Small owners who formed a large part of the middle class were cruelly pressed from above, and were rapidly losing their holdings. Their former limited security gave way to despair as they saw themselves dispossessed, bankrupt, declassed.

Of course, the high salaried overseers and directors shared the economic interests of their employers. Those who were paid well for serving in a supervisory or executive capacity had a stake in the successful working of the capitalist system; their jobs depended on their ability to increase the owners' profits. Their alliance with the big owners had economic justification. This was not true of the average salaried employee. While most white-collar workers were slow to comprehend what was happening to them, the process of proletarianization continued just the same. White-collar employees could anticipate no greater opportunity to improve their status than factory workers could to improve theirs. They enjoyed no greater security of employment. They sold their labor power to the owning class which exploited them just as it exploited the industrial and agricultural workers. The difference in clothes worn to work in no way altered the white-collar employees' economic relationship to the employers.

Nor did the failure of white-collar workers to realize that they were members of the working class prevent them from experiencing harsher oppression as financial monopoly spread. Mechanization and expansion, which in the beginning had intensified the demand for white-collar workers, also lowered salaries. Machines simplified the jobs; on the whole, white-collar jobs demanded little skill and paid the employee less than skilled wage work and often less than manual work. Moreover, machines and speedup cut down the demand for office workers.

The economic depression which followed the post-war boom tended to bring home to white-collar workers their relationships both to the employers and to the wage workers. They found that like the wage workers, their jobs were insecure. While the first year of depression did not affect white-collar employees so drastically as it did workers in industry and agriculture, unemployment set in soon afterward, and with it, wage cuts. In many instances salaries sank far more drastically than wage rates. In New York City, for example, salaries of women clerical workers diminished from twenty-five to forty percent, to the depressed average of $11.39 per week. On the basis of a 1932 survey of 218 companies with 111,700 clerical workers, *Business Week* concluded that 19.4 percent of the 4,000,000 clerical workers were unemployed; the remainder had experienced salary cuts averaging 14 percent. While in certain industries wages rose in 1933 with the passage of the N.R.A. (largely in those industries where effective union organization existed), salaries for the most part fell, and salary minimums tended to become the maximums. Thus, the New York University Employment Bureau pointed out that "the $20 and $22 job is now about a $15 job."

What was true of the white-collar workers also held for professional and technical employees. The same economic forces drove this category into the "new middle class"; once they assumed a salaried post, they became economically a part of the working class. Formerly, professionals and technicians were able to support themselves through individual practices; but like the small merchants and manufacturers they could not resist the pressure of an expanding monopoly capitalism and the majority accepted employment from corporations or their varied subsidiary institutions. Others, particularly among the "free professions" of medicine and law, maintained a status of semi-employment; part of their income came from private practices and the remainder from some form of salaried professional employment. In other words, many doctors and lawyers struggled to keep their badly paying practices by propping low incomes with clinical, institutional, or corporation work. Even so, approximately two-thirds of the professionals and technicians were crowded out of the self-employed field and into salaried posts.

Once this process began, professionals and technicians found that because they lacked organization and therefore the power to resist exploitation, their salaries in no way reflected the responsibility or quality of their work. Technological improvements and the over-supply of professional men forced salaries not infrequently to the level of wages for unskilled work. In addition, with the economic depression, unemployment among professionals and technicians reached staggering proportions. In 1933, it was estimated that ninety-eight percent of the architects were unemployed, eighty-five percent of the engineers, sixty-five percent of the chemists. Per capita earnings in the same year for public school teachers, including supervisors and principals, averaged only $1,414 annually; physicians and surgeons averaged $3,079; dentists, $2,413. Inasmuch as these averages included the well paid and successful "top" professionals, the earnings of large numbers were below even a subsistence level. Technical employees in 1933 received as low as thirty-five cents to forty-five cents an hour. Salaries of qualified chemists fell to $14 a week. And since in 1930 four out of five of the 3,500,000 or so professionals and technicians were salaried employees, these men and women began to understand that their lot was if anything more calamitous than that of the average worker.

The smashing of all standards proved that without union organization neither the white-collar nor the professional and technical employees could hope for improvement or relief. Psychological resistance to unions impeded the action of both groups. Unions meant struggles against employers which led to strikes and all the methods which duplicated the wage workers' opposition to exploitation. And members of the "new middle class" found it difficult to relinquish all their illusions by finally admitting that they were in the same foundering boat as the wage workers and must use the same methods to bail it out or sink. After the first three years of depression it was clear to many more that only unionization could protect the mutual interests of salaried and wage workers. And it also began to dawn on both the professionals and technicians, as well as on the white-collar employees, that unions designed to impose just claims on the exploiting class could hardly be considered undignified.

UNIONS were not altogether unknown to either white-collar or professional employees. Among professionals, the American Federation of Musicians, which grew out of twenty-seven local unions of musicians and a number of branches of a professional society, joined the A.F. of L. in 1896 and successfully organized most of the profession in the succeeding years. By 1936, the A.F. of M. included 110,000 members and virtually controlled the commercial field. In 1930, the union had jurisdiction over ninety percent of all musicians in New York City. But technological developments had taken a drastic toll among musicians, so that 50 percent of those who worked in motion picture theaters had been displaced by the introduction of sound films. The union also suffered from most of the diseases that Gompersism bred: racketeering, failure adequately to protect unemployed members, the granting of exorbitant salaries to the officialdom while earnings of the membership steadily diminished. Craft barriers kept the musicians from successful joint action with other unions. During the 1937 sit-down strikes in Detroit and Flint, for example, members of the A.F. of M. continued to play over the radio for the General Motors Corporation, while industrial workers were struggling to gain recognition of their union and collective bargaining.

Another important professional union, the Associated Actors and Artistes of America, affiliated with the A.F. of L. in 1919. Composed of several units, the largest being the Actors Equity Association, it maintained independent affiliates among chorus dancers, opera singers and choruses, vaudeville actors, screen actors, and other groups. With 14,000 members, the 4 A's enforced a virtual closed shop in the legitimate theater. Yet the Association was hesitant to demand unemployment relief for its membership, and was riddled with craft snobbery. In the early days of the Association when it was necessary to strike to obtain recognition and contractual agreements with the employers, organized electricians, stage hands, and other theater workers aided the Association. Unfortunately, once it was firmly established, the Association often refused to support the wage workers, considering them on a plane "below" salaried professionals.

On the whole, however, the A.F. of L. took even less interest in professional employees than it did in unskilled workers. The fear of "intellectuals," the resistance of professionals themselves to organization, the narrow craft outlook and do-nothing policy of the executive council with its reluctance to invade new fields, blocked extensive organizational work. Moreover, professionals and technicians, believing that they had little in common with wage workers, formed associations which were soon dominated by the very wealthy doctors or lawyers or professors or architects, whose economic interests coincided with those of the owning class. Such associations, instead of improving the lot of the membership, actually impeded progress by fostering misconceptions concerning economic relationships between professionals and technicians and their employers by obscuring the main issue of economic security with vague ethical generalizations. Too often these associations fought any advance that smacked of liberalism. The American Bar Association endorsed reactionary legislation, and thereby actually sacrificed the economic interests of the majority of lawyers. The American Medical Association, ruled by a highly conservative leadership, resisted popular health insurance and socialized medicine. The American Association of University Professors, with 12,000 members, while concerned with problems arising from the violation of academic freedom, "investigated" and made reports of abuses but seldom took steps to enforce its decisions.

In 1916, the A.F. of L. chartered the American Federation of Teachers. The union had an early history of militancy, but later became dormant until revived by the depression. Thereafter, despite dissension within the union caused by reactionary cliques which utilized the Red scare to impede organization, the A.F. of T. raised its membership to 25,000 in 1936, and with a newly elected leadership took an active rôle in the fight for higher salaries, academic freedom, and relief for their unemployed. Teachers suffered severely from unemployment; those with jobs experienced the highest degree of speedup, salary cuts which reduced pay to a vanishing point, or in many cases delays in pay which stretched over many months.

On the other hand, the International Federation of Technical Engineers, Architects, and Draftsmen (A.F. of L.) chartered in 1918, never succeeded in gaining a foothold in the profession. Its membership dropped steadily during the depression until in 1936 it claimed 1,800 members and actually had less than 1,000. Significantly, the independent and militant Federation of Architects, Engineers, Chemists and Technicians, formed in 1933, grew in three years to 7,000 members, largely because of its all-inclusive character which allowed workers employed by W.P.A. professional projects, the unemployed, and those engaged in civil service and private industry to join. The Federation's realistic struggle for adequate relief, higher salaries, and improved standards met with astonishing success and attracted new members steadily. It was also the first professional union to affiliate with the C.I.O.

Since 1930, organization of the professional groups received a strong impetus. The Air Line Pilots (A.F. of L.) and the independent American Radio Telegraphists Association, both formed in 1931, expanded rapidly in their respective spheres. Particularly did the Radio Telegraphists (affiliated with the C.I.O. in 1937) play a part in the successful West Coast maritime strikes of 1934 and 1936, and continued to coöperate with wage workers and other groups of licensed personnel. The depression fostered scores of other professional unions, many independent, and a few affiliated with the A.F. of L. and some with the C.I.O. Artists, cartoonists, nurses, physicians, pharmacists, dental and laboratory technicians, authors, dramatists, screen writers, librarians, research workers, clergymen, social workers formed unions which for the most part were progressive in their leadership, controlled by the rank and file, and militant. And almost all of these young unions waged struggles of the utmost importance for more adequate unemployment relief and against curtailment of W.P.A.

Similarly, in the white-collar field, organization proceeded rapidly during the depression. Here too A.F. of L. unions existed, but on the whole they played a static, ultra-conservative rôle. The largest white-collar union, the Brotherhood of Railway and Steamship Clerks, Freight Handlers, Express and Station Employees, founded in

1898, closed its ranks to Negro workers, and though it enrolled 135,000 members, it relied on lobbying to achieve concessions, and failed to resist severe salary cuts. In the same way, the National Federation of Post Office Clerks (A.F. of L.) with 40,000 members, based its policy on recognition "that legislation and not strike is the last resort in the adjustment of our grievances, and therefore we oppose strikes in the Postal Service." Among the postal groups, the A.F. of L. maintained two other unions with a total membership of 55,345. Likewise, three independent unions of postal employees with a combined membership of 83,519 remained largely conservative in outlook.

The A.F. of L.'s policy of neglecting white-collar workers was reflected in the low memberships of such organizations as the Retail Clerks International Protective Association, and the Bookkeepers, Stenographers and Accountants Union (the B.S. & A.U.). After 1890, the Retail Clerks managed to enroll only 15,000 of the half million or so eligible to membership. Recently, in San Francisco, the Retail Clerks received encouragement from the success of the maritime unions. And in the beginning of 1937, the sit-down strikes in the automobile industry served as an example to clerks in such stores as Woolworth's and H. L. Green's in New York City who adopted similar methods, and won new members, higher wages, and better working conditions. In protest against the reactionary, racketeering leadership of the International, many locals of the Retail Clerks joined the C.I.O. and established the United Retail Employees of America. The B.S. & A.U., formerly a federal union, was organized in New York City in 1910; while the New York union was the largest of over fifty similar federal unions, the total membership of these unions was approximately 10,000, with nearly 5,000 in New York and with over 2,000,000 eligible for membership. In New York City, the disbanding of the militant and independent Office Workers Union and the entry of its progressive membership into the B.S. & A.U. helped to activize the older union. It was the Office Workers Union that conducted the successful strike against the Macaulay Publishing Company in 1934, one of the first white-collar strikes to rally professionals to assist clerical workers, and it served to encourage union organization among salaried employees generally. Recently, the B.S. & A.U. elected progressive rank and file candidates to office and under young Lewis

Merrill, president, the union immediately showed a more aggressive and active interest in spreading its organization. In May 1937, this and other federal locals broke all ties with the A.F. of L. and affiliated with the C.I.O., a necessary step that initiated for the first time in fifty years a nationwide organizing campaign of all office and professional employees into one industrial group, the United Office and Professional Workers of America.

Among government and civil service employees, the American Federation of Government Employees (A.F. of L.) with 22,000 members was the most progressive. In 1932, the more conservative group quit the Federation and formed an independent union which retained control of 64,000 employees, the largest union of civil service workers. The A.F.G.E. also split in June 1937 when 3,200 members affiliated with the C.I.O. under the title of the United Federal Workers of America. Altogether, approximately eighteen unions existed in this field, almost all conservative and largely working at cross-purposes. Again the C.I.O. stepped in, forming one union for government employees which would bring order out of chaos.

Other white-collar unions embraced substantial numbers of workers but, as a whole, organization within the white-collar and professional groups still lagged even in 1936. Of the 8,000,000 in the white-collar category, less than 1,000,000 belonged to unions. Less than 300,000 of the 3,500,000 professionals and technicians were organized. The lack of adequate organization not only exposed salaried workers to even more intensified exploitation but also threatened them and the rest of the working class with the danger of Fascism. At the mercy of the employers, retaining illusions as to their class relationships, the "new middle class" could easily be misled and used as a foil against organized industrial and agricultural workers. Monopoly capitalism, raising its own contradictions that necessitated more stringent exploitation of the working class, could still in the future hope to utilize the insecurity and false conceptions of the "new middle class" to reinforce reaction.

The precedent for such a manoeuver was only too clear. In Germany, lack of coöperation between the "new middle class" and the wage workers immensely aided Hitler's rise. Not that white-collar and professional groups alone enabled Hitler to achieve power: the split in the working class, the collaborationist policies of the Social-

Democratic leadership, the inability of working class political parties to arrive at a common program of action, contributed largely to the victory of the fascist National Socialist Party. But the disillusioned, hard pressed, unattached white-collar and professional employees were easily deceived by the spurious promises of the Nazis. Still believing that they were in some way "different" from wage workers, the white-collar and professional employees flocked into Storm Troop and other Nazi organizations, and so became a powerful weapon in the hands of the extreme reaction. Though the "new middle class" groups were fighting against their own best interests, they lacked an understanding of class relationships and therefore a comprehension of their rôle. Middle class psychology and the false dream of white-collar workers that some day they could slip into the ranks of the capitalist class aided the Fascists in victimizing the salaried groups.

So long as the "new middle class" preserved similar misconceptions, they would run the same danger of serving reaction in America. Certain sections of the salaried groups in this country had already been seduced by the Huey Longs, the Father Coughlins, the Gerald K. Smiths; had already shown their willingness to grasp at such panaceas as the Townsend Plan, the Social Credit Plan, the Utopian Plan, the Share-the-Wealth Plan. However, once organized into strong, progressive unions, white-collar and professional employees soon learned that no real chasm separated them from the wage workers. Both were constantly subject to the same oppression. Both were ruled by the same economic laws. And salaried employees began to perceive that they had as much to lose under Fascism as their wage earning brothers.

"Small fry are no longer small when they begin to organize," Heywood Broun remarked. "They take on purpose and power." Organization of white-collar and professional employees, no less important, was no more impractical than organization of wage workers in basic industries. Governed by identical laws, both salaried and wage workers could become effective in their fight for better wages, better working conditions, and in their common stand against reaction if they organized, as Heywood Broun insisted, into unions industrial in form. The C.I.O., comprehending that white-collar and professional employees were an important section of the working class, laid plans for organizing them into solid united unions and so implementing them toward the struggle against Fascism and in defense of democratic rights.

IN THE SPRING OF 1935, Heywood Broun wrote:

> "The snobbishness of the white-collar groups is on the whole exaggerated. If clerks, newspapermen, accountants, and professional men have been slow in organizing, it has not been altogether because of reluctance. It is rather an inability. We have neither the tradition nor the training. . . . A very considerable proportion of white-collar workers are ready now to join the parade of organization if only space is assigned to them."

The experience of the American Newspaper Guild served to encourage unionization among other groups within the "new middle class." Newspapermen met every form of opposition from legalistic red tape to intimidation and violence. The success of the Guild illustrated the ability of professionals and white-collar workers to overcome the powerful hostility of the employers, and in the face of it to achieve unity.

The Newspaper Guild was by no means the first attempt to organize newswriters. In 1900 William Randolph Hearst smashed a small pioneering union in Chicago. During the War, when unionization advanced in all fields, Boston reporters and editorial workers organized into the International Typographical Union. The I.T.U.'s jurisdictional claim over editorial workers was recognized by the A.F. of L., and with the help of the printers, reporters succeeded in raising their salaries. Other attempts in New York City and elsewhere did not fare so well. The pension and insurance benefits carried by I.T.U. members necessitated high dues which proved prohibitive for most editorial workers. The union refused to make an exception for the newcomers. The result was that the Boston group lagged, the New York reporters were defeated, and the I.T.U. soon gave up the project of organizing editorial staffs as a bad job. By 1923 the I.T.U. went so far as to relinquish jurisdiction over editorial workers. Newspaper unions continued in Milwaukee, Wis., and Scranton, Pa., but as a whole editorial workers remained unorganized.

With the depression, salaries of newspaper employees were cut from 10 to 40 percent: earnings of reporters with twenty-years' experience averaged $38 a week. Speedup, discharge, longer hours ruled the industry. Yet when the publishers drew up a so-called newspaper code under the N.R.A., they saw to it that the code did not interfere with their right to hire child labor, and did not include any section guaranteeing editorial employees a shorter work week and minimum wages. Furthermore, in order to protect "freedom of the press," the code specifically provided that no provision could be altered without the consent of the nation's 1,200 publishers. To be doubly certain that the code would in no way benefit editorial workers, the publishers carefully classified members of editorial staffs as "professionals," and thus excluded them from wage and hour provisions.

Newswriters balked: spontaneously they formed local unions and by December 1933 the locals had called a conference which formed the national Guild. Jonathan Eddy was elected executive secretary, and Heywood Broun president. All officers served without salary.

Broun at first conceived of the Guild both as a professional organization, a sort of liberalized American Medical Association of newswriters, and a bargaining group to raise economic standards for editorial workers. Of himself he said, "As one of the early leaders of the guild I saw my job to be that of a kind of ballyhoo man and advance agent." Like most of the first members to join the Guild, Broun was reluctant to consider the relationship between the salaried newspaper employees and the publishers as one of "boss and his wage slave. All my bosses," he declared, "have been editors and not a single Legree in the lot."

But Broun soon lost his confidence in the publishers' reasonableness. The American Newspaper Publishers Association, formed in 1887 "to protect newspaper publishers against labor," took an immediate and violent dislike to the Guild. The Association had little patience with labor organizations. Guildsmen, and especially local leaders, were dismissed — for reasons of "economy" — and replaced at the same salaries by non-Guildsmen. Heading the offensive was William Randolph Hearst, who admired the labor policies of Hitler and Mussolini. Accordingly, when R. L. Burgess of the San Francisco *Examiner* joined the Guild and was elected chairman of the local unit, Hearst fired Burgess without delay. Redfern Mason, music critic on the *Examiner* for over twenty years and active in the

Guild, was demoted and forced to resign. Dean Jennings of Hearst's
San Francisco *Call-Bulletin* planned to use his vacation to attend the
1934 Guild convention at St. Paul; Hearst shifted the vacation
period at the last moment and obtained Jennings' resignation.

The Jennings case more than any other event in the early days of
the Guild revealed to the membership what it could expect from the
publishers. Appeal to the San Francisco Regional Labor Board
resulted in delay and postponement; after months, the case was
shunted to the National Labor Relations Board, then to the Newspaper Industrial Board (composed of four publishers and four labor
leaders who split on every important issue and were unable to reach
any decision), back to the San Francisco Regional Board, and
finally to the National Labor Relations Board in Washington. In the
end, the N.L.R.B. ordered the *Call-Bulletin* to reinstate Jennings.
The publishers, acting as a man, threatened to withdraw from the
N.R.A. Donald Richberg thereupon persuaded the Board to reopen
the case. Once more the N.L.R.B. decided in favor of Jennings, and
when Hearst disregarded the reinstatement order, the Board demanded that he relinquish the Blue Eagle insignia. The American
Newspaper Publishers Association retaliated by calling a meeting of
all publishers to consider resignation as a body from the N.R.A. In a
panic, the National Recovery Administration referred the Jennings
case to President Roosevelt who voided the twice given decision and
reprimanded the N.L.R.B. for its presumption. Hereafter, the
President decreed, matters involving publishers would be left to the
Newspaper Industrial Board — which the publishers controlled, or
at least could hamstring. The Guild had previously been refused
representation on this "impartial" board; only the voluntary with-
drawal of a labor member made room for the appointment of a
Guild delegate.

As Heywood Broun remarked, in the Jennings case "the publishers
cracked down and the President cracked up." To Broun it was plain
that "the government of the United States has been held up by the
publishers of the United States. The President surrendered at the
point of a wooden gun." Guild members began to realize that a
polite professional organization would not get very far. Open opposition from the publishers compelled the Guild to undertake traditional union tactics, and relegate to a less harassed future the original
Guild plans to improve professional standards, institute sick benefits,

open schools for copy boys, and start employment offices for those out of jobs. Obviously the Guild's existence rested on its success or failure on the economic front. Above all, the Guild must establish its right to bargain collectively; it must gain sufficient strength to win better hours and working conditions, higher pay and a minimum wage.

> "I am proud of the fact that when organized newspapermen made their first articulate demands [Broun declared], I did make a short speech in which I said that if we could not get those things which we needed through the N.R.A. and through a guild type of organization, we would seek them through trade unionism . . . I based my prophecy on the distinct feeling that the newspaper publishers would not meet us half-way, one-third of the way, or even one-hundredth of the way."

But the publishers considered themselves prepared for the attack. They had what they considered an all powerful joker up their sleeves: "Freedom of the press." And after the care with which they had written the newspaper code, after the meticulous manner in which they had guarded freedom of the press by making sure that the code in no way supervised or restricted their anti-labor policies and that it assured them the liberty of firing Guildsmen, the publishers continued the fight for their precious "freedom" by practicing any and all repressive measures against the young newspaper union. Purely in the interests of this mythical free press, the publishers objected to the unionization of reporters because, they protested, once newspapers were organized all labor news would thereafter reflect an undue sympathy to organized workers — an interference with "free press" which to that time had been consistently hostile to labor. Still more, the publishers worried lest Guildsmen would lose their devil-may-care attitude, and might even become politically minded. Then their reporting would be colored by personal beliefs. Formerly, of course, even before the Guild was formed, newspapermen had voted and held political beliefs without endangering the editorial policies of the papers for which they had worked. Somehow, objected the publishers, that was different. The practice that publishers had of reflecting the political and labor views of their large advertisers also did not interfere with the press' freedom. And the employers refused to be comforted by the Guild's constitution which stated that no one, under any circumstance, could be excluded from

the Guild because of his political opinions, or because of any views
he expressed in his writing.

Furthermore, the owners would not admit that the experience of
English publishers was valid, even though in England a powerful
reporters' union had in no way impeded the presentation of news in
accordance with the individual paper's editorial policy. Instead,
American publishers clung to their slogan, "freedom of the press";
it was the guillotine by which they hoped to decapitate the Guild.
The weapon had a general usefulness, too, whenever publishers were
hard pressed: a Boston publisher whose plant had been condemned
as a firetrap howled that "freedom of the press" was being trampled
upon; the same cry sanctified opposition to child labor laws interfering with the right of newspapers to employ children. Unfortunately,
the too ardent repetition of the slogan dulled its edge. It began to
bore the public, especially when William Randolph Hearst, the
Guild's bitterest enemy, aired it daily in his papers which continued
"freely" to falsify and censor news.

For the first eighteen months, organized newspapermen met with
discouraging defeats. Yet in the face of the Jennings case, widespread
dismissals of Guild leaders, and two small unsuccessful strikes, the
Guild's membership grew. The one bright spot of those months was
the strike against the Newark *Ledger*, the owner of which refused even
to meet Guild representatives. He displayed his determination by firing eight of the more active unit leaders before leaving for Florida on
his vacation. Forty-five Guildsmen on the editorial staff responded to
the strike call. The walkout dragged along for over four months. The
usual mass arrests, intimidation, police brutality, instead of discouraging the Guildsmen, rallied numerous professional and working
class organizations to their support. In the end, the strikers were rein-
stated. Broun estimated the strike as a substantial victory:

> "I do not think that anybody can question the success of the
> settlement achieved by the white-collar union [he said] even
> though it did not gain its entire list of objectives. There may be
> some criticism of the fact that the fate of the employees, who
> were originally discharged, was left to arbitration, but any agree-
> ment which provides for the return of all strikers and the dis-
> charge of strikebreakers deserves to stand as a labor triumph
> . . . In Newark, an effective part of the public could and did
> stop buying the *Ledger* while the hostilities were on . . . P. W.

Chappell, the federal mediator, forced me to nibble a few of my words in which I maintained that no good thing could come out of Washington. The principle remains the same, however. The strength of a labor group remains within its own hands. No sort of legislation will work for weak unions. 'Them as has gets.'"

Members of the Guild knew that they could only survive if they built the union's economic power. The former resistance characteristic of white-collar and professional workers to straightforward union methods disappeared. The Guild adopted a militant policy. In the strike against the *Amsterdam News* in New York City, the Guild won all its basic demands. Moreover, the strike found white and Negro employees side by side; equality, guaranteed by the Guild's constitution, was (unlike the practice in many A.F. of L. unions) accepted as a matter of course.

Meanwhile the employers continued their attacks on newswriters who joined the Guild. The Associated Press discharged Morris Watson, veteran employee and vice-president of the Guild. The National Labor Relations Board, petitioned by Watson, ordered the Associated Press to reinstate him and to pay his salary for the time he was out of work. The A.P., however, refused to comply with the decision: it appealed to the Federal District Court, which ruled against the corporation. Next, it took the case to the Circuit Court which also upheld the N.L.R.B.'s finding. Finally, the case, upon which hinged the constitutionality of the Wagner Labor Relations Act, was appealed to the United States Supreme Court where the decision of the N.L.R.B. was upheld.

By the spring of 1936, the Guild was strong enough to strike Hearst's *Wisconsin News* in Milwaukee. Broun led the picket line and with other strikers was arrested and jailed. The public and the rank and file of the unions supported the Guild. Again the young union emerged triumphant, with all strikers returned to work, and winning substantial gains that granted a minimum wage, hours of work, dismissal notices, overtime, and vacations with pay. The Guild had fought Hearst and, to the astonishment of most publishers, had forced him to capitulate.

Still, Broun realized that the union needed more powerful support than could accrue from the union's own membership. It needed roots in the organized labor movement; to obtain these roots, the Guild must affiliate with the A.F. of L. A certain section of the

Guild's membership revived all its white-collar pride and snobbish-
ness to block affiliation when it was proposed in 1935. Yet in the
space of a year, even the formerly backward Guild members had
changed their opinion. Publishers' overeager advice to shun the
A.F. of L. rang suspiciously offkey. As Broun remarked, "The very
same publishers who talk of the Guild's not seeking counsel from
experienced labor leaders are the very ones who say, 'Don't you
realize that it would be fatal for you boys to go into the American
Federation of Labor?' " In the fall of 1936, the national convention of
the Newspaper Guild voted overwhelmingly to join the A.F. of L.
The Guild had come of age. Struggle and necessity had blasted its
original vague aspirations to build another professional organization;
the old suspicion of unionism had disappeared, and in its place had
arisen an acceptance of the urgency for realistic organization. "The
publishers," Broun admitted, "had convinced them of the necessity," and had encouraged the union to affiliate with the Federation
"not by words but by deeds."

Late in the summer of 1936 occurred the strike against Hearst's
Seattle *Post-Intelligencer*. This strike taught the Guild its most valuable
lesson. With the dismissal of two veteran members of the editorial
staff for "inefficiency," the staff walked out. Because the Northwest
labor unions had learned the value of solidarity during the 1934
maritime strike, because the Guild had been attacked by Hearst who
had consistently advocated the destruction of all unions, teamsters,
teachers, longshoremen, sailors, lumber and metal workers, hundreds of union members joined the Guild in picketing. Typographical
workers refused to pass through the line. Hearst's powerful newspaper closed down and Seattle was without a morning newspaper
except for the *Guild Daily*. The Central Trades and Labor Council
endorsed the strike; Mayor Dore spoke in its favor. Naturally, the
publishers of rival newspapers lined up with Hearst against the
Guild, screaming violation of "freedom of the press."

The *Post-Intelligencer*, however, did not appear. Hearst's elaborate
plans to import thugs and strikebreakers, to organize vigilantes and
launch a reign of terror, failed in face of the iron unity of all Seattle
labor. The strike ended with another victory for the Guild, the second
against Hearst in three months. In its wake came agreements with
all the major San Francisco and Bay Region newspapers (including
three Hearst papers, two of which, the *Examiner* and *Call-Bulletin*, had

so strenuously opposed the Guild in its early days). By the middle of 1937 membership had risen to 11,000. Seventy-eight newspapers had signed contracts recognizing the Guild, including the New York *Daily News* with the largest daily circulation of any newspaper in America. In three years the Guild, Roy Howard's predictions notwithstanding, had quite noticeably succeeded in worrying the publishers. A number of papers in the Scripps-Howard chain signed Guild contracts.

It was the *Post-Intelligencer* strike that finally convinced most Guild members that solidarity with, and mutual support of, all other labor organizations, whether these organizations were composed of wage or salary workers, meant the success of any single union. It was the *Post-Intelligencer* strike that strengthened Heywood Broun's determination to fight for industrial organization in the American labor movement. He joined, as an individual, the Committee for Industrial Organization. "Labor's job and labor's obligation are perfectly plain no matter who sits in the White House," he insisted. "It must develop large and aggressive organizations. It must organize not only the mass-production industries but also the white-collar workers and the unemployed. And it must organize along industrial lines."

The false distinction between salaried employees and wage workers was breaking down. The Guild, more than any other union of white-collar and professional men and women, blazed the trail. Significantly, the importance of organizing white-collar and professional groups was also recognized by John L. Lewis. In his 1937 New Year's Day speech, Lewis as chairman of the C.I.O. emphasized that the Committee

"is urging the American workers to a great appreciation of the value of organization and its influence is extending into the ranks of the technical, professional and white-collar workers in a manner which indicates that they too will avail themselves of the opportunities to participate in the benefits of modern collective bargaining. . . . Employers have treated them with the same ruthless lack of consideration universally extended to the workers in the mass-production industries. . . . Labor demands collective bargaining and greater participation by the individual worker, whether by hand or brain — in the fruits of the genius of its inventors or technicians."

The sympathy with which Guild members watched the drive for industrial unionism, the Guild's real inner democracy that gave the rank and file members a dominant voice in the conduct of the union, its militant and clear cut program distinguished it as one of the most progressive unions in the A.F. of L. The Guild threw its weight behind most progressive legislative proposals, such as the Workers' Unemployment Insurance Bill, the extension of W.P.A., reform of the federal courts. But it was the outline of policy in relation to the A.F. of L. — C.I.O. controversy that showed the real maturity of the Guild. Fully supporting and coöperating "with the progressive movement in American labor," the Guild at first demanded "the return of autonomy and democracy in the American Federation of Labor," and deplored splits in state and central labor bodies — splits engineered by the A.F. of L. executive council. In June 1937, when it was clear that the Federation executive council was determined to smash the C.I.O. even if that meant the end of the American labor movement, the Guild's fourth annual convention at St. Louis voted overwhelmingly to affiliate with the C.I.O. and give all support to the organization of the mass-production industries, extending the union's jurisdiction to include business, circulation, and advertising workers in newspaper offices. In addition, the convention called for the building of independent political action and full support to the Spanish People's Front.

HEYWOOD BROUN, dramatic critic, novelist, columnist, had become a far-sighted labor leader, who understood the threat of Fascism. With him, the majority of Guild members grasped the importance of immediate and continued resistance to reaction in this country. Broun stressed the need to politicalize the labor movement, to build a Farmer-Labor Party that would rally all liberals and progressives in the middle classes to the support of a militant working class. "I think there is small question that Franklin D. Roosevelt's labor policy will be very much governed by labor's own strength," he predicted. By pointing out that industrial unionism in conjunction with a progressive political program alone could protect workers — white-collar as well as industrial, professional as well as agricultural — Heywood Broun took his place among those progressive labor leaders pledged to prevent the horror of Fascism from overwhelming America.

VI. A. PHILIP RANDOLPH

Negro Labor's Champion

LATE IN THE EVENING, during the closing session of the 1935 American Federation of Labor convention in Atlantic City, a delegate from Seattle proposed that the meeting be hurried to an end. "I offer an amendment," he cried, "that we continue in session until midnight in an effort to finish the business of the convention, and at that time any unfinished business be referred to the Executive Council."

A second delegate objected. "I rise to oppose the motion," he remarked in a firm, deliberate voice, "because the Sleeping Car Porters are interested in the report by the Executive Council on the matter of discrimination against Negroes. This report has been so handled as to delay its presentation at this convention until the time when it will not be possible to have a full discussion. I think that that smacks of a very questionable procedure . . ."

The Negro delegate's calm tone contrasted with his challenging words and perceptible bitterness. President Green blinked, pressed his lips together, and sighed. It would hardly look well if he refused to let the delegate have his say. Rapping resignedly with the gavel, he recognized A. Philip Randolph, president of the Brotherhood of Sleeping Car Porters, and then eased himself into a chair.

At forty-six, A. Philip Randolph was accustomed to demanding the floor to address hostile or apathetic audiences. He had devoted his life to the struggle against racial discrimination, to the resistance of prejudice so frequently condoned by the simple expedient of not mentioning its existence. As he stood, tall and commanding, before the convention, Randolph's sensitive dignity exacted attention. "Why should a Negro worker be penalized for being black?" he demanded. "Why should anybody be penalized for something over which he has no control? . . . We are living in a time when there should be no division of race, religion, creed or nationality."

At the preceding A.F. of L. convention, Randolph reminded the delegates, President Green had appointed a special committee of five to investigate discrimination against Negroes in the unions. This committee had held hearings, had presented a report which four of the five had signed. Yet the executive council had suppressed the report. Was it because the special committee recommended that all international unions barring Negroes from membership or discriminating against them in any way should immediately be ordered to harmonize their constitutions and practices with the "oft-repeated declaration of A.F. of L. conventions on equality of all races within the trade union movement"? Was it because the report advocated that union charters issued by the executive council should be in conformity with the Federation's declared policy against Negro isolation? Was it because the committee urged an intensive educational drive by the A.F. of L. on the Negro problem? "The American Federation will not be able to hold its head up and face the world," Randolph insisted, "so long as it permits any section of workers in America to be discriminated against because they happen to be black."

When Randolph concluded, William Green fluttered back to the rostrum. Someone was always raising uncomfortable issues. Clearing his throat, Green restated the problem. "Has the American Federation of Labor the authority to say to an autonomous international union how it shall draft its laws?" he queried. His counsel to those organizations which did not admit colored workers — "if they would accept my advice" — was to remove the bar, for "I believe we ought to make provision for the admission of these members. But," he added hurriedly, "that is neither here nor there." What the delegates must answer, Green explained, was "Do we give national and international unions autonomous rights? Can we suspend the charter of the international union because it does not provide for the admission of colored members? Can we do that? Would you be willing to order that to be done? Are you ready to do that?" Earnestly, William Green catechized the gathering. "There is the issue," he concluded, "there are the facts presented to you in the fairest possible way that I can present them without prejudice — just the facts as they are for your consideration."

The convention upheld the democratic right of affiliated unions to ban Negroes from membership, just as southern senators preserved

states' rights by voting down national anti-lynching legislation. The delegates rejected the special committee's three recommendations outlined by Randolph, perhaps because they recalled that more than ten A.F. of L. unions prohibited the admission of Negroes, and that a host of other affiliates excluded them in practice.

Indignantly John Brophy of the United Mine Workers, who had signed the rejected report, resigned from the special committee. "The manoeuvering on the part of the Executive Council plainly indicated," protested Brophy, that the council considered the committee ". . . merely a face-saving device for the American Federation of Labor, rather than an honest attempt to find a solution of the Negro problem in the American labor movement."

The convention's rebuff neither surprised nor discouraged Randolph. It was an old story, this tale of race prejudice. He had never been content merely to plead or to protest or to attempt to reason with stubborn, often bigoted, opponents. The active struggle must continue toward the goal of eventual liberation for the Negro. This road to freedom, Randolph contended, was the same for the black workers as for the white — a steep, painful path that commenced in organization. The way merely proved a little more difficult for the Negro, a little more tortuous.

ASA PHILIP RANDOLPH, son of a Southern minister, was born on April 15, 1889, at Crescent City, Florida. Young Philip liked to read; he sensed that education was of vital importance to him. But it was not easy for the son of a poor Negro clergyman to obtain schooling. His father preached in the African Methodist Church, serving three or more parishes, with members invariably the poorest Negroes. In consequence, the salary of a minister failed to support a wife and two children. There was always the pressing need for the other members of the family to supplement the elder Randolph's miserable stipend. The family ran a small cleaning, dyeing, and tailoring shop in which all worked when no other jobs were obtainable. As a child, Philip also picked up odd jobs — his first earnings coming from a white grocer. Each day after school, Philip hurried to the man's home, called for the owner's meal and brought it to the store. Soon afterward, Philip became a clerk in a grocery shop. When he grew older and stronger, he obtained work as a section hand on a railroad, digging and shoveling dirt, loading flat-cars with sand, laying cross ties and rails. He drove a delivery wagon for a large chemical and drug company, worked for fertilizer and trucking concerns, and supplemented his earnings by selling newspapers and helping out at the little family shop.

When he had completed his high school course at the Cookman Institute in Jacksonville, Philip travelled North. He took courses at the College of the City of New York, concentrating on political science, economics, and philosophy. But always the problem of earning enough to eat interfered with his studies. He decided to try a waiter's job on a ship run by the Fall River Line: he was fired for organizing a protest against the miserable living quarters that the workers had nicknamed the "Glory Hole." He became a waiter in a Jersey City railroad restaurant, an elevator operator — any job he could land. No work paid well; only "Negro" jobs were open to Philip — heavy, menial, dirty, or irksome work. Book learning, intelligence, ambition did not overcome the handicap of a black skin.

For over five years, Philip Randolph worked as a porter for the Consolidated Edison Company of New York City. Throughout all this period, he snatched any spare time for studying. Like most Negro intellectuals he was primarily concerned with the problems of intolerance and discrimination that submerged his people. Yet Randolph had no patience with the collaborationist policy advocated by Negro reactionaries or with the extreme nationalist policy pursued by "leftists." The reactionaries preached a cringing acceptance of the white ruling class, a fawning "good nigger" sycophancy. Seizing with servile gratitude any favor carelessly bestowed by the whites, the Negro collaborationists decried all rebellion, all struggle against oppression. On the other hand, the "left wingers" advised repudiation of white standards, sneering at racial equality, and called instead for a thorough-going black nationalism.

Young Randolph was impatient of either view. In his eyes, discrimination stemmed from the economic abuses of capitalism. Demanding unconditional social, political, and economic equality for the Negro people, Randolph joined Socialists who sought the same end. This they believed could be achieved only as the exploitation of the profit system was limited, preluding the eventual abolition of capitalism. The roots of the struggle rested in the working class, black and white. When workers overcame prejudices which permitted the exploiters to pit one working class group against another, when all workers united for their common good, equality would result as a matter of course.

> "We do not accept the doctrine of old, reactionary Negroes that the Negro is satisfied to be himself . . . [Randolph wrote] We desire as much contact and intercourse — social, economic and political — as is possible between the races. This is not because of our belief in the inferiority or superiority of either race, but because of our recognition that the principle of social equality is the only sure guarantee of social progress . . ."

Randolph married in 1915. Two years later, with America's declaration of war, he and a close friend, Chandler Owen, launched *The Messenger*, a monthly magazine. The Lusk Committee later declared it "by far the most dangerous of all Negro publications." True, the editors adopted the subtitle, "The only radical Negro magazine in America." True, they argued that since the War was supposedly waged to save world democracy, such rescue work should commence at home. Since Negroes were of critical importance in mass-production industries and in the army, they should take full advantage of their position to force the government to correct the worst abuses suffered by the Negro people, even if this meant strikes and resistance to the draft.

The magazine's influence was indicated when in 1917 over twenty-five percent of the Negro voters in a New York election supported the Socialist ticket. Moreover, the editors of *The Messenger* disdained sugarcoated words:

> "Civil liberty in the United States is dead . . . [they asserted] Civil liberty for the Negro, however, was dead even before the War, killed by the combination of a hypocritical North and an unregenerate South who colluded to sweep from the Negro his last vestige of liberty. We repudiate and condemn any pretense at opposition to Jim Crowism, segregation and all forms of discrimination which does not accept the principle of social equality, since it is upon the fallacious theory of inequality and racial inferiority that all these evils are established and continued . . ."

Randolph's forthright stand led to his arrest in Cleveland in June 1918 by the same Department of Justice agent who had seized Eugene V. Debs a few days before on a similar charge of obstructing the draft. But Randolph, unlike Debs who was sentenced to ten years' imprisonment for violation of the Espionage Act, was released after a few days in the city jail. His attacks on the War continued. And when the war ended, when business patriotism burned to a savage, Red-baiting fever, it was natural that the flag wavers branded Owen and Randolph "Bolsheviki." They answered:

"If approval of the right to vote, based upon service instead of race and color, is Bolshevism, count us as Bolshevists. If our approval of the abolition of pogroms by the Bolsheviki is Bolshevism, stamp us again with that epithet. If the demand for political and social equality is Bolshevism, label us once more . . ."

Despite efforts to intimidate the editors, despite financial difficulties which occasionally forced temporary suspension of publication, *The Messenger* pursued its militant policy. And Randolph, aside from his duties as joint editor, found time to write articles for other publications in which he decried the willingness of Negroes to back the Republican Party; or exposed the hypocrisy of the church hierarchy whose aim it was to discourage the Negro people in their fight for advancement; or urged Negro workers to enter trade unions wherever possible, and to participate in the activities of progressive movements. Both Randolph and Owen became instructors at the Rand School of Social Science in New York; Randolph likewise lectured to labor, radical, and liberal schools and forums. In 1921, he ran as the Socialist candidate for New York Secretary of State, at other times for the Assembly and Congress. The masthead of *The Messenger* now read, "A Journal of Scientific Radicalism."

More and more Randolph devoted his energy to the labor movement. In 1917, he had organized a union of elevator operators and starters, the first in New York City, which later disintegrated despite the federal charter issued by the A.F. of L. Also during the War, the young Socialist attempted to organize shipyard workers in the tidewater district of Virginia, but the shipping interests proved too strong and the ruthless intimidation of Negro workers along with the opposition of Negro reactionaries prevented unionization. Randolph, however, refused to be discouraged. He participated in the post-war organizational campaigns that were launched among laundry workers, motion picture operators, and in the building and garment industries. As he familiarized himself with labor problems, he became convinced that industrial unionism must replace craft organization, since outmoded and unrealistic craft methods impeded labor's progress. He reiterated one idea, which he was still stressing in 1937: "The Negro should organize himself, because with organization he will be better able to break down the barriers and prejudices of white workers against him than he will without it . . ."

But until 1925, A. Philip Randolph remained, even in his own estimation, a writer and an editor rather than a labor organizer. Then in August of that year he and a small group of men met in a Harlem recreation hall to outline a campaign to unionize sleeping-car porters. All present except Randolph worked for the Pullman Company. Nevertheless, Randolph had studied the problems of the porters, had talked to scores of them so that he thoroughly understood their needs. The men who gathered in the bare hall that hot August day had confidence in Randolph's ability, and admired the hard, consistent fight of the thirty-six year old editor for labor unity and freedom. They elected Philip Randolph president and general organizer of the union which as yet existed only on paper.

Not long afterward the masthead of *The Messenger* changed again. Now reading "The official organ of the Brotherhood of Sleeping Car Porters" the masthead also declared that

> "*The Messenger* is the recognized mouthpiece of the most advanced section of the Negro Group in the United States. For ten years it has spoken intelligently and eloquently in behalf of organization of labor, white as well as black, believing as it does that the question of wages, hours of work, safeguards on the job and proper representation of the worker, are the most important problems confronting the majority of men and women, black as well as white, in the United States . . ."

Philip Randolph, like Heywood Broun, was a new type of labor leader, one of the "intellectuals" that Gompers warned against and had so thoroughly despised. Confronted by the same difficulties that all labor organizers must solve before they could unionize workers dominated by a company union, Randolph was further handicapped by the many other problems peculiar to Negroes. The task of organizing an oppressed minority demanded courage and resourcefulness, patience and tenacity. Randolph and the small group who worked with him managed finally to crack the barriers. They accomplished the "impossible" when they succeeded in unionizing Negro porters and in compelling the Pullman Company to recognize the organization. And they forced the apathetic A.F. of L. executive council to grant the Brotherhood of Sleeping Car Porters an international charter — the first awarded to an all-Negro union in the forty-seven years of A.F. of L. history.

PULLMAN PORTERS had attempted to organize on at least four occasions before Philip Randolph undertook to build the Brotherhood. In 1915, a few adventurous porters talked union: they were hastily and unceremoniously dismissed by the Pullman Company. During the War, when the struggle for unionism surged ahead, the porters again considered organization, but their efforts were short-lived. By 1920, low pay, interminable working hours, and other abuses prompted the porters and maids to present their grievances to the National Railway Administration. Secretary William G. McAdoo explained that the Administration was powerless to help them and advised organization — a convenient way to dismiss a highly unpleasant problem, since McAdoo was positive that no union of Negro workers could possibly succeed. But the restiveness of the porters caused several A.F. of L. and railway brotherhoods to seek jurisdiction over them. The porters rebuffed such overtures, distrusting the unions, certain that once enrolled, Negroes would be segregated into black auxiliaries where they could exercise the privilege of paying dues without being permitted a voice in the conduct of the union. The Pullman Company, however, realized that porters left to their own devices would eventually obtain genuine organization. Accordingly, the management formed the employee representation plan, known as the Pullman Porters Benefit Association, which generously offered colored employees very small sick and death benefits in return for dues payments of $26 a year.

The porters entered the employee representation plan willingly enough. "They innocently accepted it as a declaration of justice by the Pullman Company for the porters and maids," Randolph commented, "unable to realize that an organization which is handed down by the boss to wage earners is for the benefit of the boss and not the wage earner." Besides the company union made much of elaborate machinery set up to handle grievances. In practice the "impartial" Industrial Relations Bureau, as the grievance committee was named, failed to encourage workers to press complaints. A porter who trustingly used the Bureau to air his grievances against the corporation discovered that he was looked upon with suspicion and almost certain to experience retaliation. As a result, most sleeping-car employees shunned the Bureau, which only went to prove the company's contention that porters and maids were delighted with their conditions, wages, and hours. The Pullman Company's happy family of Negro workers continued to buy insurance which often they did not want, and meanwhile chafed at the low pay, and carefully concealed their resentment against company spies and stool-pigeons who rode every train and whose duty it was to report "troublemakers" and union "agitators."

Hours of work on the Pullman cars stretched out interminably — 300 to 400 hours a month. Exposed to patronizing humiliations and miserable working conditions, porters were also menaced by the threat of discharge for the slightest infraction of company rules. Wages approximated $100 a month: the Company paid $77.50 from which was deducted average monthly expenses of $33; tips averaged $54 a month (before the depression, less than half that amount since 1931). Porters received less pay for overtime than for straight work. They were required to buy their own uniforms, shoe polish, incidentals; they paid for their own meals in the dining cars (and since porters depended on tips for a large proportion of their earnings, they tipped the waiters as much as their own meager incomes would permit). Usually married, with a family to support at the home end of the run, porters had double living expenses since they had to provide themselves with board and lodging at the far end.

The weakness of all early attempts to organize Pullman employees rested in the inability of organizers to talk unionism and still retain their jobs. When in 1925, Philip Randolph led the campaign to build the Brotherhood, he had the advantage of not being dependent on the Pullman Company: no matter how bitter the struggle to enroll porters in the union became, the Company lacked means of intimidating or "disciplining" Randolph. Most of the other officers of the new union, though they had served many years as porters, no longer remained in the Company's employ. Like Randolph, Ashley L. Totten, secretary of the Brotherhood, often went without salary from the union when the struggle was most intense and funds were exhausted, moving from one back room in a Harlem tenement to another, devoting all his energy to the never-ending task of building the union. M. P. Webster, porter for eighteen years, pushed the fight with and without a job and later became vice president in Chicago. Bennie Smith, who lost his position because he refused to sign the employee representation plan promoted by the Company, acted as vice president in Omaha. C. L. Dellums agitated for the union in Oakland, California, and along the Pacific Coast, and in later years was unanimously reëlected to union office in tribute to his success in recruiting the highest proportion of dues-paying members. E. J. Bradley, another vice president of the union and a former porter, put up with extreme poverty rather than abandon the campaign he believed in so firmly.

This handful of men, scattered over America, slowly laid the foundation of the union. Many porters feared for their jobs; others signed up but kept their membership secret and refused to discuss union problems with fellow employees. The general attitude was skeptical: "If it succeeds, we are with it; if it doesn't, we are agin' it." Yet intimidation, the systematic discharge of any porter suspected of union sympathies (over 500 were dismissed for union activity during the Brotherhood's first ten years), espionage and provocation from company union officials, failed to halt the union's expansion. Randolph in vain sought help from the Railroad Labor Board. The reactionary elements of the Negro clergy attacked him as a Socialist and radical, and slandered the Brotherhood. Negro leaders were reimbursed by the Company for their denunciations of the union. Negro newspapers received monetary assistance from the Pullman Company for carrying anti-labor news, and thousands of copies of articles hostile to the Brotherhood were distributed free to the porters. Judge Woodward of Chicago denied an application by the Brotherhood for an injunction against the employee representation plan under the Railway Act of 1926, on the ground that the Pullman Benefit Association was not company controlled. The Interstate Commerce Commission refused Randolph's demand that tipping be investigated under the Interstate Commerce Act. Still the Brotherhood grew.

Throughout the discouraging first years, Randolph and the small group of devoted Brotherhood officers ignored reversals and rallied the membership to greater efforts. When the young Brotherhood began to organize, it was in the peculiar position of fighting a national carrier operating over every railroad in the country. Unlike other railway unions which fought for recognition and better conditions against one carrier at a time, the porters were forced to lock horns with the Pullman Company on all roads at once. If the union gained recruits in one locality or on one carrier, the Pullman Company fought them in another, weaker section, sapping the strength of the Brotherhood.

By 1928, the Brotherhood, with over half the porters and maids organized, was ready to threaten strike if the corporation refused to negotiate. Of course William Green "advised" against it; the union did not dare as yet defy the executive council and therefore canceled the strike. Moreover, the Order of Sleeping-Car Conductors looked suspiciously on every move the Brotherhood made. To counteract this distrust, Randolph brought forward the demand that porters performing conductors' work and employed by the Pullman Company must receive the same wage as white Pullman conductors. Since the Company would enjoy no advantage in employing Negroes at the same wage as white workers, the demand reassured the Order that their fear of Negroes displacing them was baseless.

The Pullman Company, anxious to smash the porters' organization before it grew powerful, announced a wage increase and began to replace Negroes with Filipinos, hoping thereby to raise the race issue. The Brotherhood resisted firmly, but made clear, in Randolph's words, that "the porters have absolutely no prejudice against Filipinos . . . The Brotherhood of Sleeping-Car Porters would oppose the company's using other Negroes to keep porters now working in the service from organizing a union of their own or to break down the seniority rule such as the company is using the Filipinos for."

The management's master stroke came when it announced that it would look more favorably on the Brotherhood if the membership would remove Randolph, "a known Socialist," from office. The rank and file did not fall for the Red-baiting. Randolph answered the attack with characteristic directness:

> "Of course [he wrote] labor leaders are 'outsiders' and if they were not 'outsiders' they would be as soon as the capitalists learned their identity . . . When unable to break up a union, American capitalists invariably seek to eliminate the leader of the union. The claim that they will deal with the union after the leader is gone is only a smokescreen, an opiate . . . Union men reason quite correctly that wages, hours of labor and conditions surrounding the workers on the job are the real point of issue and not who is leading the union."

Though the cancellation of the 1928 strike temporarily weakened the Brotherhood, it had become sufficiently important to compel the A.F. of L. executive council to recognize its claim for a charter. Refusing as yet to grant the porters an international charter because the Hotel and Restaurant Employees objected and demanded jurisdiction over sleeping-car workers, the council in 1929 issued federal charters to Brotherhood locals in several cities.

THE OPPOSITION experienced by the porters reflected the hostility Negroes had learned to expect from employers, from the majority of A.F. of L. unions, and from all the independent railroad brotherhoods. By relegating Negroes to an inferior position, by stirring up race prejudice, the owning class assured itself an abundant supply of cheap labor. Once Negroes left the agricultural fields to enter industry, the employers utilized this vast army of unorganized workers, separated from the whites by false barriers of color, exactly as they had utilized immigrant labor a half century before — to undermine wage standards and to prevent labor unity. Similarly, the A.F. of L. officialdom's intolerance of foreign workers was transferred to Negroes with much the same result; disunity weakened labor's ranks and proved of inestimable value to the employers.

As the legacy of the Civil War, the Negro people had supposedly been granted freedom and equality. The Thirteenth, Fourteenth, and Fifteenth Amendments "liberated" the slaves, and "guaranteed" Negroes full rights as American citizens. But Negroes discovered that with Southern landowners and industrialists administering the laws, and with the courts interpreting — and incidentally perverting —

legislation, little of the much vaunted freedom or fine sounding "guarantees" survived. Yet, in the early days enthusiasm for the new equality had not been quenched: in 1869, the National Colored Labor Convention met in Washington, D. C., and Sella Martin of Massachusetts told the eager delegates, "The interests of the laboring classes white and black on this continent are identical. We should work harmoniously together for the furtherance of the causes of labor." This wish failed to impress the only important labor organization then functioning in America, the National Labor Union. Founded in 1866 primarily as a skilled craft association the Union refused to alter its policy of Negro exclusion. Three years later, the shortlived National Union collapsed and was replaced by the Knights of Labor. Theoretically, the Knights forbade discrimination; in practice many of the organization's local groups banned Negroes. However, the Knights did organize what was for that time a creditable number of black industrial workers, largely because they feared, as a delegate stated at a Knight's convention, that "Negroes will take possession of the shops if we have not taken possession of the Negroes." The Knights' confused approach to labor problems precipitated the final crash that ended its brief career. The newly formed American Federation of Labor, struggling desperately for existence and concerned solely with protecting skilled workers, confined its activity almost exclusively to unionizing those districts and crafts where Negro labor was either non-existent or negligible. Since the A.F. of L. ignored unskilled workers, the clause in the Federation's constitution decrying discrimination had value merely as a righteous gesture.

The emptiness of this gesture was revealed in later years when Negroes commenced to filter into industrial centers. The A.F. of L. constitution did not deter affiliated unions from practicing rigid exclusion. By 1900, the Federation's discrimination could no longer be ignored. Samuel Gompers, adept at sidestepping embarrassing questions of policy, urged a compromise at the 1900 convention: the unions should encourage local unions and separate central bodies for Negroes — in plain words, Jim Crow the colored workers. The convention endorsed this proposal and matters rested there. Again in 1910, Gompers bridled at the suggestion that perhaps the Federation discriminated against Negroes. In a splendid burst of righteous bombast, Gompers proclaimed that "instead of reading the Negroes out of the labor movement, my contention and the contention of the American Federation of Labor is to try to bring them into the organized labor movement in our country."

These brave words salved the conscience of the executive council — and the problem was forgotten for a few more years. In 1916, 1917, 1918, the annual conventions of the A.F. of L. repetitiously resolved that Negroes should be organized but made very sure not to set up machinery to accomplish this end. Actually, the executive council feared to pique the majority of unions which either specifically or by subterfuge kept Negroes from membership.

Of course, the largest proportion of colored workers was concentrated in the South where Negroes engaged in agricultural labor. But with the War, which stimulated industrial production and provided employment for great numbers of new workers; with the pauperization of the small tenant farmers following the war, Negro migration to the cities accelerated. The trek from farms and plantations brought 1,200,000 Negroes from the South to the North in the period from 1915 to 1928.

The War likewise enabled Negroes to enter industries hitherto closed to them. In addition, during the post-war unrest of 1919 to 1923, when strikes broke out in almost every industry, the formerly unwanted black workers found themselves eagerly accepted as strikebreakers. Labor agents painted glamorous pictures of quick wealth, of security and opportunity. Without knowledge of industrial relations, Negro workers responded to the slick salestalk of company agents, and took jobs abandoned by steel workers in 1919, by railway employees in 1922, and by countless other white strikers.

No matter where Negroes were employed, they received lower wages than the whites for the same job, and usually were limited to the hardest and dirtiest tasks. As an Indianapolis employer remarked, "Negroes get only the left-over jobs, the hard manual work." An advertisement in a New York newspaper typified the attitude of employers: "Wanted: Factory helpers; experienced only; white $24, colored $20." Those industries that employed both black and white distinguished between Negro work which was low paid, heavy, and unpleasant, and white work which was higher paid, relatively clean, and comfortable. In the South, Negro white-collar workers were unheard of except for the few employed by members of their own race. An article appearing in *Opportunity*, 1926, stated

"There is probably not a Negro bookkeeper, stenographer, 'honest-to-goodness' clerk in the whole South employed other than by his own race; not a Negro supervisor in the Post Office, for however long the Negro may work in the Post Office and regardless of how efficient he may be, he does not get beyond the position of clerk; no street car conductors or motormen, telephone and switchboard operators."

The exclusion also prevailed in the North. Illustrative of the attitude toward Negroes was the response to a colored applicant in Philadelphia who answered an advertisement offering employment as a clerk: "What do you suppose we'd want of a Negro?" With almost no opportunity for promotion, with little chance for training, Negroes became a reserve corps of unskilled and cheap labor, often misled into strikebreaking and always a threat to wage standards.

Certain industries, however, employed Negroes in large numbers. Railroad companies hired them during strikes and later retained a great proportion of them. Whereas in 1910, five Pittsburgh steel mills and iron foundries employed less than 100 Negroes, by 1923, twenty-three plants had engaged 17,000 black workers, and by 1925, 22 percent of all steel workers in the Pittsburgh district were Negroes. The proportion of Negroes in the building, packing, and steel industries increased from 3.2 percent in 1910 to 20.7 percent in 1920. Seventeen percent of all automobile workers before 1929 were Negroes, 10,000 working for the Ford Motor Company which hired Southern whites to act as supervisors. The 13,000,000 Negroes in America composed over one tenth of the population but accounted for one eighth of the workers employed in industry.

Despite the increased importance of Negroes in mass-production industries, the unions either ignored them or actively discriminated against them. The worst offenders were the independent railway unions which unanimously drew the color line, thereby barring 115,000 black workers, exclusive of the porters, from union participation. Railroad unions did not hesitate to approve contracts similar to the one signed by the Brotherhood of Locomotive Firemen and Enginemen, which specified, according to testimony presented before a Congressional committee, "that 'at least fifty-one percent of the firemen of this line must be white' and the road agrees 'not to employ Negro firemen and in the future all vacancies will be filled by white firemen'."

The constitutions of at least twenty-two international and national unions, of which over half were affiliated with the A.F. of L., banned Negroes. Eleven of these unions had in 1935 a total membership of 436,200 workers in a field employing not less than 43,800 Negroes. In addition, a majority of the unions whose constitutions did not specifically forbid black workers from joining the union, openly discouraged Negro applicants by insisting on discriminatory initiation rituals. The electrical workers, for example, with a membership of 142,000, included only 334 Negroes though there were 13,000 colored electricians in the trade. Of the 6,000 Negro plasterers, about 100 belonged to the Union. None of the 3,500 colored plumbers were organized. The carpenters and the molders relegated Negroes to separate locals and ruled that they be represented on joint boards or central labor bodies by whites.

At the carpenters' convention in 1936, Frank Duffy, secretary of the United Brotherhood and first vice president of the A.F. of L., denounced as "Communist" a resolution demanding "Equal rights for Negro workers in the carpenter trade." "We have always tried to organize Negro carpenters," Duffy orated. "Years ago we put a Negro organizer on the road." Yet the carpenters had enrolled only 1,572 of the 34,000 Negroes eligible.

Out of 9,000 Negro painters, 718 were accepted into the union. The glass workers objected to colored glass blowers in the industry on the ground that "the pipes on which glass is blown pass from one man's mouth to another." Blacksmiths formed Negro helpers' auxiliaries but forbade promotion of colored workers to blacksmith status, banned them from shops where white helpers were employed, and frequently signed contracts with employers specifying "none but white, English speaking helpers are to be employed."

Some union constitutions went even farther than drawing the color line. The wire weavers accepted only whites and Christians. The initiation fee for foreigners was set at $1,000. The Brotherhood of Railway Carmen demanded that new members be white and "Believers in the existence of a Supreme Being." The Masters, Mates and

Pilots refused Negroes and specified that an applicant must be a "Firm believer in God the Creator of the Universe."

Those Negroes who did manage to join unions more often than not were penalized for their trouble. White members received preference of employment. Often Negro members of one local were unable to transfer because locals in other cities drew the color line. In Akron, for example, white bricklayers would not work with Negroes, though in New York the union accepted colored members. The Chicago local of the barbers' union employed a Negro organizer but in California, Negroes were discouraged from joining. In the South Atlantic and Gulf ports, Negroes organized into Jim Crow locals of the International Longshoremen's Association, found themselves assigned only the heaviest and dirtiest work for which they earned less than $200 a year. The Sheet Metal Workers allowed Negro members to work nine hours a day though the union limited other members to five hours, and also sanctioned a lower wage scale for colored metal workers than for white.

Only a few unions admitted Negroes freely. Outstanding were the United Mine Workers, the International Ladies, Garment Workers, and the Amalgamated Clothing Workers, all of which strictly prohibited discrimination and actively organized Negroes into mixed locals. On the other hand, the hod carriers and longshoremen admitted colored members into mixed or separate locals according to the locality, while the cooks and waiters, hotel and restaurant, laundry, barber, textile, and musician unions permitted only Jim Crow locals. Too frequently Negroes were organized to eliminate colored competition; once accepted by the union, Negroes found prejudice and discrimination, while the union refused to protect their jobs or their wage scales.

The policy of discrimination, the added fact that the A.F. of L. concentrated on organizing skilled workers in the North, though four-fifths of the Negroes were concentrated in the South and over three-quarters of the industrial workers were unskilled, accounted for the extremely low numbers of organized Negroes. Excluding agricultural workers, one out of every ten workers was organized in 1929, but only one out of every fifty Negro workers was unionized. A survey conducted in 1927 by the National Urban League covering 1,500,000 organized workers reported that but 65,000 of this number were Negroes and 14,500 of them were concentrated in Negro unions in New York City. The rest were distributed among longshoremen, hod carriers, musicians, garment workers, hotel and restaurant employees. In 1930, probably 100,000 colored workers had been organized: they were concentrated in the Northern industrial centers — 14,000 in New York City, 13,000 in Chicago, 2,000 in Detroit. Approximately 5,000 were members of the United Mine Workers, 3,000 had joined the musicians, 15,000 the longshoremen, 6,000 the needle trades unions, 8,000 the hod carriers and building workers, 1,000 the hotel and restaurant union. The remainder was distributed almost wholly among freight handlers, teamsters, drivers, asphalt and tobacco workers.

Not surprisingly, Negro workers eyed unions with suspicion. As a protest against the official labor movement, all-Negro unions appeared, particularly in the railroad industry. Of these, the Brotherhood of Dining-Car Employees, founded in 1920, enlisted 2,700 members; the National Brotherhood of Dining-Car Employees, established the same year, recruited another 1,100 workers for the most part on routes west of Chicago. The Association of Colored Railway Trainmen and Locomotive Firemen, formed in 1912, enrolled 3,000. The National Alliance of Postal Employees, launched in 1913, attained a membership of 4,800. None of these organizations had great significance so far as improving the working conditions of their membership went. The overwhelming majority of Negro workers shunned organization, even the all-Negro unions.

Misled by reactionaries of their own race who argued that since whites discriminated against Negroes, black workers had no responsibility to them, many colored workers accepted the theory that through strikebreaking they could enter new industries. The Negro as strikebreaker proved a boon to employers. Colored scabs helped to reinforce race prejudice among white workers, and tended to intensify resentment against all Negroes, so that union barriers against them became even more rigid. By preventing solidarity between black and white, the owners retained an invaluable weapon against the labor movement. Thus William Z. Foster characterized the refusal of union officials to organize Negroes (which directly encouraged strike-breaking) as "treason to the whole labor movement."

This treason, part and parcel of Gompersism, continued to dominate A.F. of L. leadership. As an answer to it, progressives and radicals called the Negro Labor Congress in 1925 to consider the problems of Negroes, particularly those of the colored workers. The demands of the Congress for organization, equal rights, elimination of Jim Crowism and other abuses received support from white rank and file groups. The A.F. of L. executive council, with Green galloping wildly in front, answered this plea of a minority people for democratic rights with hysterical Red-baiting. Nevertheless, the Communist Party continued to urge liberation of the black people. The Trade Union Educational League, and later, the Trade Union Unity League, conceived as one of their basic aims the wholehearted support of Negro struggles. Both Leagues attempted vigorously to enlist Negroes, and both elected colored workers to positions of leadership. Hand in hand with the insistence that the labor movement repudiate Gompersism and adopt industrial organizational methods went a firm demand that Negroes be recruited into the unions on an equal basis with whites. Only by adopting such realistic tactics, declared the progressives and radicals, could the labor movement be revitalized.

Not until 1935, when the Committee for Industrial Organization was formed, did the ideas, kept alive by a few progressives in the dark days of the twenties, find official acceptance by an important bloc of unions. The success of the C.I.O. campaign which enlisted Negroes into industrial unions, the rapid and dramatic organizational advance in the steel, rubber, auto, and glass industries, bore out the predictions made for a decade and more by Communist leaders. The C.I.O. discovered that Negro and white workers brought together in solid, militant unions could defeat even the strongest of the open shop employers.

Still more, the accusation that Negroes were strikebreakers was shown to have truth only when Negroes were systematically forced by discrimination to scab. Negroes replaced striking longshoremen in 1925; but not in 1934 and 1936 when, with union discrimination ended under the leadership of Harry Bridges and other militants, Negroes refused to pass through picket lines of the West Coast maritime workers. During the recent strikes conducted by the C.I.O. in mass-production industries, no Negro scabs were enlisted

— unlike the large scale recruiting of colored strikebreakers in the years 1919 to 1923. Wherever Negroes were accorded the opportunity to join other workers the so-called Negro menace to white workers disappeared and the Negroes proved themselves tenacious, loyal fighters.

Negroes, however, were not unionized to any large extent even by the middle of 1937. So long as they continued outside the labor movement, all organization was threatened. The task of bringing Negroes, both in the North and in the South, into strong unions remained a central obligation of the C.I.O.

THE PREDICAMENT of the Negro worker was by no means peculiar to his race. Wherever minority groups existed, employers attempted through discrimination to split and weaken the working class. In Imperial Valley, California, Mexican agricultural workers were the scapegoats. In Arizona, owners inspired race riots against Japanese field workers and so diverted white workers from the struggle to improve their conditions. In the Colorado beet fields, Spanish-Americans were pitted against the native born. Hindus and Chinese were utilized to hamper organization in the Sacramento Valley; Filipinos were played against whites in the lettuce fields of Salinas and the apple orchards of Watsonville, California. No matter what group of workers suffered discrimination, the result was the same — lower wages, the debasing of working conditions, the spreading of dissension and chaos.

Similarly, within the white working class itself, employers treated women workers as a minority who could be paid lower wages and used to displace men; child labor, too, could serve to threaten the security of both male and female workers. As could be expected, women in industry, since the great majority performed unskilled or semi-skilled labor, were neglected by the A.F. of L. executive council as completely as Negro workers. Organized women remained relatively and numerically insignificant, yet women formed 22 percent of the gainfully employed over ten years of age, and composed over half of the clerical employees and at least two million of the factory workers. At no time did the A.F. of L. recruit more than 3.5 percent of these eligible women.

And since women, like Negroes, were unorganized, they received from one-half to one-quarter less pay than men for equal work. Technological advances enabled women increasingly to replace men in many types of manufacturing processes; with the influx of these unorganized workers, wage rates were once again menaced. It was a simple matter for employers to speed up female wage workers since they lacked protection from the labor movement. Four out of ten gainfully employed women were under twenty-five years of age; over a million were from sixteen to twenty years old; and 200,000 were under sixteen. At thirty, most employers found women too old for employment: help wanted advertisements in daily papers stressed that only those female applicants between eighteen and twenty-five would be considered for jobs.

If white women suffered from low wages and insecurity, the lot of the Negro women workers was of course far worse. "Just as a woman who takes a man's job has to possess superior qualifications to make up for her lack of physical strength," reported an investigator, "so a Negro woman who goes into white woman's work has to have advantages which offset her color." In a special study, the U. S. Women's Bureau learned that wages of Negro women averaged one-third to one-half less than those of white women. In four states, a majority of Negro women made less than $300 a year; after 1929 even this meager wage diminished. The Bureau reported that in fifteen states during 1930 the weekly wage of Negro women in any branch of the textile industry ranged from a high of $8.95 a week to a low of $4.25 a week. Though the N.R.A. code for cottonmaking industries called for a weekly wage of $12, Negro women were never paid more than $9.

The differential between white and colored women workers prevailed in every occupation studied. In Louisiana, Negro elementary teachers averaged $292 a year, white $1,107. With 30,000 Negro women employed in steam laundries in the South, the Women's Bureau found that white women in Memphis averaged $9.21 a week, Negro women $5.57; in Jacksonville, $8.47 for white, $5.25 for Negro; in Savannah, $7.62 for white, $5.32 for Negro. Wages of colored laundry workers in no southern city ever rose to the low weekly minimum of $5.60 set by the N.R.A.

In like fashion, young workers, male and female, white and black, composed another huge army of underpaid, highly exploited workers, almost completely unorganized, which employers utilized to keep wages low. Including agriculture, eleven million boys and girls were gainfully employed in the United States in 1932, of which six million were between the ages of twenty and twenty-four, and five million between ten and nineteen. Two-thirds were boys, 1,400,000 under twenty worked in factories — for the most part in the textile and metal industries — and 100,000 worked in mines.

As age limits sank, young workers became of greater importance to large corporations. The Ford Motor Company doubled the number of boys between twelve and eighteen attending the River Rouge "trade school." These children worked part time for fifteen cents an hour, alternating two weeks of labor with one week in the class room. They performed duties formerly discharged by men at much higher pay. Other motor companies hired boys and girls varying in age from eighteen to twenty at one-third the wages paid to adult workers, firing older men to make way for youthful workers who combined energy with low costs.

As a result of the new importance of youth in industry, schooling of these young people was seriously impaired. Of every 1,000 children who started school, one out of ten failed to pass the fifth grade; one out of seven did not reach the eighth grade; one out of four left school before reaching high school; and only one out of every four graduated from high school. Moreover, these working boys and girls comprised a large part of the 10,000,000 physically deficient American children. They also were among the thousands maimed and killed each year in industrial accidents or ravaged by occupational diseases. Small wonder then that the Hoover investigation revealed that 1,000,000 children had weak or damaged hearts and 382,000 were tubercular.

Again, Negro youth suffered more than white. For every $100 expended to educate a white child, only $25 was spent on a Negro child. Illiteracy among Negroes rose from 26.6 percent in 1920 to 30.4 percent in 1930. Young Negroes, receiving wages of one-third to one-half lower than white workers of the same age, had less opportunity to care for their health, and the percentage of undernourished, physically deficient and handicapped youth was correspondingly higher among colored workers than among white.

Among all minority categories — Negroes, racial groups, women, youth — unemployment during the years 1929 to 1935 produced devastating effects. While minority groups naturally suffered more heavily than male, white workers, the wage standards and conditions of work for all workers were affected by the presence of hard-pressed unorganized groups that undermined union strength and depressed wages generally. Women tended to replace men at cheaper rates in many industries, youth to replace both men and women. Often the replacements were reversed: desperate heads of families took women's jobs at women's wages, Negro jobs at Negro wages, leaving the minority groups without means of support. Five to eight million young workers, many just out of schools and colleges, were unabsorbed in 1935; married women and those over twenty-five years of age could not obtain work.

As usual, Negro workers, male, female, and youth, suffered to an even greater extent; unemployment among colored workers ran four to six times as high as among the whites. In the South, where in certain cases Negro locomotive firemen managed through seniority rights to retain their jobs, they were intimidated and seven were even murdered by K.K.K. terrorists in order to create vacancies which were filled by white workers. Moreover, Negroes lost jobs earlier than any other category, the depression commencing for them in 1927; by 1929, more than 300,000 black industrial workers were without employment, and six years later this number had risen to 900,000. A survey of 106 cities disclosed that in 1931 from 20 to 30 percent of the Negro population were jobless: in Philadelphia, where Negroes constituted 11 percent of the population they accounted for 20 percent of the unemployed; in St. Louis, where they formed 11 percent of the population, 33 percent could not find work. Of the 45,000 unemployed in Washington, D. C., 30,000 were colored; in Harlem, largest Negro city in the world, three-quarters of all wage earners were unemployed. "Last to be hired, first to be fired," was the way in which colored workers expressed their dilemma. In comparatively good times, Negroes eked out a miserable, insecure, substandard existence devoid of any prospect of advancement. Dependent in depression years on public relief, they experienced heart-rending destitution. By the end of 1934 the number of Negroes in families on relief totaled 3,500,000. Colored applicants received less aid than whites: discrimination again ruled to the same extent and with the same abuses as it did in factories, mills, and mines. The Negro could be secure only in his knowledge that no matter where he turned, his needs and his desires received no consideration, that he could expect least sympathy not only from the employers, but from the government and the official labor movement.

CAPITALISM'S frenzied exploitation of all categories of workers could be combated only by a vigorous, all-inclusive labor movement. By rejecting women, youth, and racial groups, comprising great sectors of the unorganized, the A.F. of L.'s officialdom carried through the logic of its antiquated philosophy. Even the skilled aristocracy of labor could not protect its standards while ever-increasing numbers of unskilled and semi-skilled, who lacked organization, kept wages low. Negroes, excluded from unions, were compelled to work for less than the whites. Women were mobilized to replace men — once again undermining wages. And this continuous paring of incomes forced workers to send their children into factories and mines to supplement family earnings — an additional reserve of cheap labor that further depressed the general pay scale.

Conversely, when workers were organized to a degree that equal work, whether performed by Negroes, women, or children, received equal reward, when unions could compel employers to pay a living wage, the reasons for married women leaving their families or for children leaving school would be for the most part eliminated. Standards of living would rise, and with them, the general health and education of the working class. The A.F. of L. through its obsolete policies had done as much as the employers to injure and oppress the majority of Americans.

A. Philip Randolph did not accept working class wretchedness as inevitable and ineradicable. In his mind the "Negro question" was linked to the larger problems confronting all workers. Any lasting offensive against race prejudice, Randolph insisted, must commence with the building of strong, progressive unions, white and black. It was this premise that moved Randolph to unionize the Pullman porters and to show all workers thereby that Negroes could undertake militant organization.

Despite the calamitous predictions of critics who saw in the Pullman corporation an invincible foe, Randolph's hard work welded together more and more porters. Even throughout the doldrum years of depression, union recruiting continued, unchecked by the company's "retrenchment" program that decimated porters' ranks. Nor did the porters in their campaign for union recognition receive much-needed assistance from the other railway brotherhoods. When, for example, the Railway Act of 1926 was in the process of amendment in 1934, the leadership of the brotherhoods ignored the porters and willingly agreed that the new provisions of the Act need not apply to Negro sleeping-car employees. Only after Randolph's insistence before the Senate and House Committees was the Act expanded to include porters as well as other railway workers.

The amendments to the Act supplied the Brotherhood with a new tactic which it immediately pressed into service. Randolph called for a vote under the supervision of the National Mediation Board to determine whether the porters desired to be represented for collective bargaining purposes by the Brotherhood or by the company-controlled Pullman Porters and Maids Protective Association. The corporation, of course, protested loudly against such a poll. But in May 1935, the porters carried their point; the vote of 5,931 to 1,422 upheld the Brotherhood's claim to speak for Negroes employed on Pullman sleeping cars.

The vote had great significance. Never before had an all-Negro union succeeded in gaining recognition from a major corporation. Victory also transfused new life into the Brotherhood, which immediately sought, among other demands, a wage increase of 20 percent, a reduction in monthly mileage requirements from 11,000 to 7,000 miles, and a lower work month of 240 hours in place of the existing 440 hour schedule. The Pullman Company gathered its lawyers in opposition and the union's demands went to the National Mediation Board in April 1937, for settlement.

But while Randolph's dream of recognition was fulfilled, he was still confronted with other difficulties. The employers continued to maintain their spy infested company union, except that it now operated under the pretentious title of Pullman Porters and Maids Protective Association. In addition, questions of jurisdiction hampered Brotherhood progress. In seeking to organize Filipinos employed by the Pullman Company, the porters were forced to contend with owner objections that Filipinos were attendants, not porters. The Brotherhood responded that regardless of title the Filipinos performed work identical with that of the Negroes. Again, Randolph's plan to enroll red cap porters, particularly after they had expressed their desire to join the Brotherhood, brought protests from the Brotherhood of Railway Clerks, though the clerk's constitution barred Negroes from membership in the union. Randolph made clear that in those instances where other unions accepted Negroes, the porters advanced no jurisdictional claim, pointing out that the porters had always urged Negro dining-car waiters to join the hotel and restaurant union and the bartenders' league.

Withal, the Brotherhood had come a long way. A decade of struggle taught it the value of democratic conduct of union affairs untrammeled by the tenets of Gompersism. Of necessity, the Brotherhood had adopted a craft union form: discrimination, and the problem of bringing unionization to a limited category of workers, in an industry already organized solely into crafts, precluded industrial unionism. But in convention the Brotherhood supported the C.I.O.; for as Randolph expressed it, "The craft union invariably has a color bar against Negro workers . . ."

The C.I.O. took active steps to organize Negroes. Philip Murray, director of the Steel Workers Organizing Committee, addressed a conference of Negro C.I.O. organizers in February 1937, at which he pledged the full support of the C.I.O. to bring Negro workers into the unions. Yet Randolph and the majority of the Brotherhood's membership were not content with this advance, important as it was. "The next instrumentality which workers must build and employ against economic exploitation," Randolph declared, "is an independent working class political party. It should take the form of a farmer-labor political organization." Such a political alliance, Randolph added, should "embrace all the progressive political movements such as the Farmer-Labor Party of Minnesota, the American Labor Party, the Socialist and Communist Parties, and the various liberal political organizations throughout the country," and could protect the labor movement from fascism and war. Through it, Negroes would gain an equal voice in the unions and the government. Even more, political action would teach the workers the invaluable lesson that by protecting minorities — the most vulnerable groups within the working class — they would at the same time guard the security of all.

Beyond its immediate tasks, Randolph looked upon the Brotherhood of Sleeping-Car Porters as an example to other Negro workers, helping to draw them into the union movement. In addition, if Negroes were organized "the barriers against race and color will be broken down and eventually destroyed. . . . If race prejudice is to be eliminated from the trade union movement, it is going to be eliminated by the workers themselves . . . and not by polite, deliberative interracial conferences." To A. Philip Randolph the goal was to convince all workers that "only solidarity can save the black and white workers of America, and this solidarity must be developed in mixed unions, composed of black and white, Jew and Gentile, native and foreign, Republican and Democrat, Socialist and Communist."

VII. HARRY BRIDGES

Voice of the Rank and File

UNTIL THE SHIPOWNERS encountered Harry Bridges, they thought they knew what to expect from a labor leader. As much. masters of the Gompers tradition as William Green or William Hutcheson, they felt safe in assuming that Bridges would quickly be transformed into an acceptable labor official whose sole concern would be to hold on to his job. They could understand, though they did not approve, his rise to leadership in the 1934 maritime strike. They could also understand, while approving still less, his ability to survive the slanderous attacks on his character and principles, and the willingness of other workers after the strike to elect him president of the San Francisco local of the International Longshoremen's Association. What exasperated the bankers and industrialists was that once Bridges gained authority in the union, success did not temper him as they had predicted. Instead, the defiance of this slender, resolute longshoreman persisted and began to affect unions other than those on the waterfront. The owners grew panicky. Particularly as Bridges insisted, smiling quizzically in a way that infuriated them, "What a union representative should never forget is the power of the men behind him."

Some accounted for Harry Bridges' purposefulness by pointing to his six years' service at sea. Certainly Bridges knew conditions in the merchant marine and on the waterfront where he had spent twelve years as a longshoreman. Sailors, who in turn influenced the longshoremen, had a tradition of militancy. The isolated life at sea, the miserable and humiliating living conditions, the ever-present struggle against the captain's autocratic power, the discussions held with sailors in foreign ports or the talk that went on in the fo'c'sle, the international character of the crews — all seemingly tended to illuminate class relationships. Accordingly, most seamen took for granted that, in the last analysis, the interests of the workers were — had to be — fundamentally opposed to those of the employers.

"Everything is produced by the workers . . ." Harry Bridges expressed it, "and the minute they try to get something by their unions they meet all the opposition that can be mustered by those who now get what they produce."

HARRY BRIDGES' FATHER, Alfred E. Bridges, was a fairly prosperous real estate agent in Melbourne, Australia. While still a young man, Alfred Bridges married Julia Dorgan, whose family of devout Catholics, recently migrated to Australia from Ireland, had for years energetically supported the struggle for Ireland's freedom.

Alfred and Julia Bridges' first son was born on July 28, 1900. He was christened Alfred Renton Bridges. Young Alfred (later renamed "Harry" by American sailors), began school before he was five. He did well, graduated at twelve, and entered St. Brennan's parochial school where he remained until he was sixteen. At thirteen or fourteen, his father started to teach him the real estate business, sending the boy out to collect rents from occupants who had taken houses and flats through the Bridges' office. Many of the families were poor; many were unable to pay. The boy disliked the job; years later he remarked that no person with any sensitivity to suffering could have collected rents in Melbourne and not have had his opinions colored by the task.

At home, the boy heard politics argued continually. His father was conservative; but two uncles took an active interest in the Australian Labor Party. Charles Bridges was elected years later (1936) to the state legislature on the Labor Party ticket. Another uncle who owned a ranch and who later was killed in France during the war, influenced the young boy particularly. On visits to the ranch, Alfred would listen intently to the older man's discussion of labor's needs, impressed by the repeated refrain stressing the value of a powerful Labor Party.

On leaving school, young Bridges clerked for a time in a retail stationery store. He had no real interest in the work, no ambition to enter his father's business. Whenever he had a chance, he rushed to the docks where he could talk to foreign sailors, and watch the boats slip in and out of the harbor. He craved adventure, the chance to know other lands. Finally, he appealed to Captain Suffern, President of the Mercantile Marine Board, to persuade his father to let him go to sea. Captain Suffern spoke to the elder Bridges, told him that if he encouraged his son, the boy would certainly prove a success.

Alfred Bridges would have preferred the boy to remain in Melbourne and enter the real estate business. But, as he related many years later:

"To test the boy's love of the sea I hatched a plot with an old Norwegian skipper who ran a ketch between Tasmania and Melbourne. The boat was very small, although seaworthy and making a stormy crossing in it was guaranteed to test the stoutest heart. During the passage with Alf aboard a storm arose. That was on the homeward trip, and the boat was blown more than 100 miles out of its course. Alf was delighted and refused to leave the deck. The skipper expected him to be washed overboard with every wave.

"After that there was no stopping the boy from going to sea. He was in two shipwrecks, including the wreck of the 'Val Marie' off the Ninety-Mile Beach. Alf went overboard with my mandolin and kept afloat on it until he was picked up."

In 1920, Bridges shipped on the South Sea Island barkentine, "Ysabel." The ship headed out across the Pacific for San Francisco. On the way, Harry and several other men objected to the captain's order that they work on Easter Monday, a regularly recognized holiday for Australian workers. Still angry when the "Ysabel" docked in San Francisco, Harry Bridges left the ship and, after paying the required head tax of eight dollars, entered the United States.

Immediately he looked for a job on an American vessel. For two years he sailed up and down the West Coast, and to the Gulf. In 1921, his ship steamed into New Orleans, where a maritime strike was in progress. The next day Harry Bridges reported for picket duty: by the end of the strike he was in charge of a picket squad. "I was arrested once during that time," he said, describing his introduction to police intimidation, "and held over night but released without a court hearing; no charge was placed against me, my offense being that of a striker on picket duty."

Following the strike, he was employed as quartermaster on a government ship chasing rum runners. When he received an honorable discharge, he decided that he had spent enough time knocking around from port to port. In October 1922, he started to work on the San Francisco waterfront as a longshoreman.

The workers along the Embarcadero, the wide half-moon of boulevard that bounds the expanse of concrete docks, found the young Australian engaging and witty. They joked about his cockney twang and nicknamed him "Limo." Harry Bridges, rangy and thin, with a long, narrow head and black hair brushed in a pompadour, with a thin smile and sharp eyes under heavy lids, settled down to a dockworker's life. At first, he attempted singlehanded to defy the company union that dominated the waterfront. But he found that unless he paid dues to the clique that ran the docks, he would soon be blacklisted and unable to get work on the waterfront. Back in 1919, when longshoremen struck for better conditions and higher wages, the owners had smashed the local of the International Longshoremen's Association in San Francisco. At that time, the union could not secure the coöperation of seamen and teamsters. The I.L.A. had disintegrated as scabs unloaded the ships and teamsters delivered goods to the pier heads. With the I.L.A. destroyed, the shipowners had decided that perhaps a union had its use — if the employers controlled it. Accordingly, they set up the Longshoremen's Association of San Francisco and the Bay Region (known as the Blue Book Union) and instituted a closed shop — for the company union.

The Blue Book ushered in all the abuses of company unionism. Speedup flourished, while breakneck competition between gangs forced longshoremen to load more and more cargo each hour. The strained slings, the absence of safety devices brought an appalling increase in the number of accidents. To meet the growing rebellion among the longshoremen against the terrific pace, the corporations placed spies on the docks to ferret out the more militant workers for dismissal and blacklisting. Disputes were settled perfunctorily, in a manner designed to place the companies at no disadvantage. Favoritism grew, workers were played one against the other to obstruct unity of action, men were required to pay tribute to the foremen and the Blue Book officials in order to obtain work.

Harry Bridges, too, found himself compelled to knuckle under in order to keep his job. "I continued to pay my dues to the Blue Book Union," he testified at the National Labor Board hearings during the 1934 strike. "However, after I was on this job for a while (on the

Luckenbach dock), I entered a complaint with reference to not obtaining full pay for actual time I worked. The company refused to pay me and I complained to the Blue Book delegate, with the final result that I never received my money for the time I worked and I lost my job in the bargain. . . ."

Despairingly, the longshoremen turned to the American Federation of Labor for help. In the succeeding years they witnessed a grim farce, played at their expense, unfold between the local A.F. of L. potentates and the company union officers. The officials of the International Longshoremen's Association tried to persuade the Blue Book to affiliate with the international union. The owners naturally refused. Nevertheless, the company union saw the value of membership in the San Francisco Labor Council and the State Federation of Labor. For if the employers were able to place representatives in those high councils, they would have a voice in determining labor policies. The president and secretary of the Blue Book were close friends of Paul Scharrenberg, secretary of the State Federation, and of John O'Connell, secretary of the San Francisco Labor Council. The deal was made with the approval of Joseph P. Ryan, international president of the I.L.A. The state and city councils welcomed the Blue Book delegates despite the express provision in the A.F. of L. constitution forbidding membership in labor councils to groups not affiliated with the Federation. But illegality did not deter Scharrenberg and O'Connell, any more than such considerations deterred the A.F. of L. executive council ten years later when it decided to suspend unions affiliated with the Committee for Industrial Organization. On the Pacific coast, the Blue Book company union was blessed by the A.F. of L. high priests — and only the longshoremen suffered.

Still, President Ryan felt he should not be completely excluded from participation in the benefits resulting from the West Coast bargain. He wanted his share of the dues collected from the workers by the Blue Book. Once again he demanded that the company union likewise affiliate with the I.L.A. The owners conducted a farcical vote among the Blue Book "membership," and announced that the results opposed affiliation with the international. Infuriated by what he considered traitorous ingratitude, Ryan suddenly remembered the A.F. of L. constitution, resolving that if he could not share the benefits sweated from longshoremen by the Blue Book, neither should

Scharrenberg nor the rest of the California officials. Ryan insisted, on pain of creating a scandal, that the Blue Book be unseated from the Council and the State Federation. There was no alternative. The company union was forced to drop out of the labor councils.

Bickering over the spoils in no way lessened the Blue Book's ability to maintain its throttling grip on the rank and file longshoremen. Ryan lost interest once the company union was thrown out of the two labor bodies, and made no attempt to organize the docks. Bridges and the rest of the workers remained helpless while the company union stifled real organization, prevented any attempt to improve wages or working conditions, allowed the companies to hire and fire, demote and transfer workers whom they deemed undesirable. All the official fulminations of the A.F. of L. did not break the Blue Book's hold, any more than the Federation's pious words blocked the growth of company unions elsewhere in America.

So Harry Bridges, like the other longshoremen, suffered and waited. In the shape-up (the line of men waiting each day in front of the docks for a job in a longshore gang) the workers guardedly discussed conditions among themselves. Sometimes they stood for hours, only to be turned away in the end; sometimes they wasted half a day to obtain an hour's work; sometimes they saw men at the end of the line given preference over those at the head — because previous payments of high tribute to the foremen bought jobs. As the longshoremen hung about in the early morning fog, as they shivered in the rain and wind, or loitered in the fresh sunshine, they talked and Harry Bridges listened to their complaints. He would nod his narrow head, a smile curving his thin lips, "Of course," he would snort. Workers on the waterfront learned to expect those two impatient words from Bridges, the cocksure "of course" that invariably greeted their grumbling and preceded the angry explanation of how they could combat the employers. "Organization . . ." went the refrain, "rank and file control . . . unity of action . . . union democracy . . . solidarity among all Coast ports . . . among all unions. . . ."

Like most longshoremen, Bridges enjoyed a drink and liked to hang around talking in the saloons along the waterfront. He preached the same sermon endlessly, often arrogant in his certainty and impatient of those who had other ideas. But Bridges also had a sly humor that amused other workers, and an integrity that impressed them. He read little, but his ideas were rooted in what he heard and saw about him, and he learned by listening to others, observing them through half closed, heavy lidded eyes. One thing Bridges grasped — and repeated endlessly — that class was aligned against class, that workers and employers were ever opposed, and that their struggle could not be solved by compromise. Bitterly, Bridges attacked the A.F. of L. officials who practiced coöperation with the owners and thereby misled the workers and sacrificed their interests.

Twice Harry Bridges attempted to revive the I.L.A. on the waterfront. In 1924, he and a few other militants organized a local, but it lasted only a few months and collapsed ignominiously when an organizer embezzled the union funds and disappeared. Again in 1926, Bridges and the small group around him tried to interest other workers in the I.L.A., but they turned away, fearful of the blacklist, recalling too vividly the unsuccessful strike of 1919 that had killed the union and subjected them to bitter reprisals from vindictive owners.

But Harry Bridges persisted. Eventually, he believed, desperation would overcome fear, intolerable working conditions would replace apathy with revolt. He continued on the docks: on two occasions he was injured in accidents caused by the terrific speedup. Improper gear failed to secure a load and he was badly bruised when three tons of steel crashed to the dock beside him. In 1929, another load fell and broke his foot. But such mishaps were daily occurrences: speed cut down costs and boomed profits — and there was no difficulty replacing men incapacitated or, as often happened, killed. The Blue Book union prevented repercussions that would have dislocated production on the docks; the employers rode high, secure from bothersome labor troubles, enjoying "industrial peace."

Though some of the foremen and Blue Book delegates objected to Harry Bridges, to his complaints and to the opinions which he so freely expressed, he was more fortunate in securing jobs than the average longshoreman. He had married in 1925 and now had a family to support. An expert workman, an able winch driver, he became a member of a "star gang," which included the most efficient longshoremen on the 'front. The star gangs worked the longest stretches, often twenty-four to thirty-six hours without sleep, but they got the best jobs, and though they were severely abused, the members were willing to put up with danger and pressure in exchange for steady employment.

By 1932, conditions on the docks had become so bad that the small group of militants decided to launch a third attempt to build the I.L.A. But this time they planned first to give the longshoremen a more thorough understanding of just what unionism could do for them. The handful of progressives published a mimeographed, clumsily constructed little bulletin which they called *The Waterfront Worker*. Often the *Worker* was hard to read because the ink blurred on the cheap paper; usually the drawings were crude. But the bulletin circulated rapidly up and down the Embarcadero and longshoremen were impressed by the sound sense that filled the four pages. Some of them recalled that the slogans stressed by the editors echoed the words that Bridges had so often repeated in the saloons across from the docks, or while standing in the shape-up line: "rank and file control," "unity of action," "union democracy." Longshoremen picked up these phrases, mulled over them until they took on a sharp meaning. The waterfront hummed with union talk. The Marine Workers Industrial Union, affiliated with the Trade Union Unity League, lent powerful aid to the agitation for organization. Then in July 1933, the campaign to form a San Francisco local of the International Longshoremen's Association commenced. Within six weeks, the overwhelming majority of longshoremen had deserted the Blue Book and signed with the union. President Joseph P. Ryan from his New York office saw no reason to refuse the dues of several thousand recruits: he issued a charter and forgot the incident.

DELEGATES from every West Coast local arrived in San Francisco for the 1934 district convention of the I.L.A. During the fourteen years that the Blue Book had dominated the Embarcadero, the I.L.A. maintained locals in most of the other Pacific ports, but lacking a strong union in the main shipping center of San Francisco, the I.L.A. in Portland, Tacoma, Seattle, and elsewhere had remained, almost of necessity, inactive. With San Francisco returned to the union domain, maritime workers looked hopefully to the convention to challenge the shipowners. True, they knew that the I.L.A. officialdom was steeped in the Gompers tradition of compromise, and that the president, William J. Lewis (no relation to John L. Lewis), was both suspicious of the progressives and fearful that they would sweep him from office. True, they knew that Joseph P. Ryan, international president, supported Lewis and his clique. But the rank and file trusted the young militants, headed by Harry Bridges, who had successfully revived the union in San Francisco. And though at the convention the old guard urged a "reasonable" attitude, the majority of delegates followed the militants in voting for immediate negotiations with the owners to achieve recognition of the union, higher wages than the prevailing weekly wage of $10.45, a thirty hour week, and most important of all, a coastwide agreement.

The employers jeered at the demands. No steamship company, they argued, would sign. Behind their obstinate refusal to consider a coastwide contract was the determination to prevent unity among longshoremen in different ports. Besides, the shipowners did not take the strike threats seriously. Even if the longshoremen walked off the docks, the shipowners expected to demolish the young San Francisco local as they had in 1919. Once San Francisco was out of the way, the I.L.A. would again be helpless. Nor were the shipowners without allies; they counted on the federal government and the international president of the I.L.A. for help against the longshoremen.

Joseph P. Ryan had studied William Hutcheson's methods and had proved an apt pupil. Like Hutcheson, Ryan had his fingers in more than one pie: as president of the New York Central Trades and Labor Council, as president of the Joseph P. Ryan Association, he had influence wherever the power of Tammany Hall extended. "I'm a machine man," he boasted, "and I head a machine." For twenty years he had dominated the East Coast, and his business agents — "gorillas," the longshoremen called them — "dominated" the docks and succeeded, for the most part, in keeping them free from progressives. Ryan did not differ from most of the top officials of the A.F. of L. in his hate and fear of militants. When, therefore, the western shipowners informed Ryan that the rank and file along the Pacific was controlled by "Reds," and when William J. Lewis confirmed this report, Ryan did not hesitate to coöperate with the employers.

His collaboration wasn't enough. The rank and file countered the owners' refusal to discuss the union's demands by voting to strike on March 23, 1934. The workers pointed to the N.R.A. which promised them the right to organize into unions of their own choosing for purposes of collective bargaining. In desperation, the employers turned from Ryan to the federal government. The Regional Labor Board, in the person of George Creel, offered to mediate: the employers agreed, except that they refused to deal with the union or discuss the I.L.A. demands. As March 23 drew too close for comfort, Creel appealed to President Roosevelt, who requested the longshoremen to wait and in turn appointed his own mediation board. The owners smiled to themselves, knowing that nothing demoralized workers so successfully as postponement and indecision.

Negotiations dragged on. The shipowners flatly declared that they would never recognize the union or consider a coastwide contract. But they did persuade William J. Lewis, eager to prevent the strike, to endorse a meaningless agreement which despite its verbiage did not change conditions on the docks. The longshoremen balked, and on May 9, 1934, walked off the docks. The strike was on.

Immediately, the strikers expanded their demands to include union control of hiring halls in place of the shape-up system, and institution of the closed shop on the waterfront. Calling on all other marine unions for support, and on the teamsters not to haul to and from the docks, the longshoremen stretched picket lines along every waterfront from Vancouver to San Diego. Immediately, the Marine Workers Industrial Union struck in full support of the longshoremen and helped to swell the picket lines.

The pressing problem was to spread the strike. Harry Bridges and other rank and file leaders were determined not to repeat the mistakes of 1919. Though strongly opposed by Michael Casey, for forty years president of the teamsters, the longshoremen induced the teamsters to stay away from the docks for the duration of the strike. Engineers, cooks and stewards, mates, pilots, seamen filtered off the ships. Their officials harangued, threatened, promised them anything if they would only return to work. But in a week, Paul Scharrenberg, head of the Sailors' Union of the Pacific, wired William Green, lamenting that he could no longer restrain the membership, and was forced in self-preservation to declare a sympathy strike. A week later the sailors presented their own demands to the employers. The experience of the Sailors' Union was repeated in the other marine unions whose membership joined the picket lines and presented demands to the shipowners.

Shipping stopped. But the shipowners were still not overly disquieted. They could starve the men out and in the meantime they had their government subsidies. These amounted in many cases to more than the companies expended in annual wages, subsistence, maintenance and repair charges combined! In a report to President Roosevelt, Postmaster General Farley estimated that the subsidy cost the government altogether $70,618,096.06. The salaries of corporation officials, largely paid out of subsidies, reached staggering figures: four stockholders of the Dollar Line received from 1923 to 1932 a total in salaries, profits, and bonuses of $14,690,528. So when the strike stopped shipping, the corporations anticipated no great loss — the government paid the deficit. The corporations sat back and waited.

To put the strike on a firm footing, the militants proposed that no union settle or arbitrate its demands until all other unions had received agreements satisfactory to their memberships. The unions agreed, and further pledged themselves to hold out for a coastwide agreement. To coördinate their activities, they set up a Joint Marine Strike Committee, composed of five delegates from each union elected by and responsible to the rank and file, with Harry Bridges as chairman. For the first time in American labor history, both licensed and unlicensed personnel coöperated on an equal basis, breaking down craft jealousies which had riddled the marine industry. And for the first time in many years, the rank and file fully controlled the conduct of a major strike.

It was not all smooth sailing. The unions coöperated willingly enough, but the employers too were mobilizing. Edward F. McGrady, government "trouble shooter," arrived in the West, and set to work to break the strike. He got nowhere. "I've been able to crack other strikes," he complained, "but I can't crack this strike." At McGrady's suggestion, Angelo Rossi, mayor of San Francisco, summoned Joseph P. Ryan. But Ryan lacked authority: in 1911, when the Pacific Coast district had rejoined the I.L.A. from which it had previously seceded, the international granted the district complete autonomy, and agreed that international officers should have no jurisdiction in Coast affairs unless their assistance was specifically requested. When he arrived in San Francisco in May 1934, Ryan strutted and wheedled, bullied and argued, and finally signed a secret pact with the employers ending the walkout. Hutcheson had used the same trick many times. The newspapers rejoiced at the strike's termination. But when the longshoremen read the terms which failed to provide any improvement in working conditions, and in addition violated the pledge entered into by all striking unions that any settlement must include every union involved, they repudiated Ryan and the agreement. The international president hurriedly left for the East — miserable over the miscarriage of his most zealous strikebreaking.

All hope of ending the walkout by bartering with corrupt union officials melted away. Nor had attempts to "buy" Bridges helped the employers' cause. They turned to force and calumny. With Hearst leading, the press attacked Bridges as a Communist and alien, and demanded his arrest and deportation. The police harassed the picket lines, jailed militants, slugged, beat, terrorized. The workers only drew their lines tighter about the docks. More than ever they looked to Bridges for leadership. The Red scare fell on deaf ears. "I neither affirm nor deny that I am a Communist," Bridges replied to newspaper charges, and pointed out that political beliefs had nothing to do with the issues of the strike.

Yet Bridges did not hesitate to accept aid from the Communist Party. Two years later, John L. Lewis also learned to welcome all support from workers regardless of their political affiliations. To Harry Bridges, it was obvious that the Communist Party would not only coöperate wholeheartedly and effectively with the maritime workers, but could also give invaluable advice on the conduct and development of the strike. In addition, the rank and file of the waterfront unions found that the Communist workers were the most militant, the most self-sacrificing, and the most consistent elements in their ranks. The membership of the various unions adopted the *Western Worker*, official party organ, as the official newspaper of the strikers.

Such direct acceptance of Communist assistance and advice naturally gave rise to the owners' cry that the strike was "Moscow-made," that it was supported by "Red gold," that it was dominated by the Communist Party and aimed at revolution. The answer, in the strikers' minds, was simple. The gold was not forthcoming, and no one from Moscow told them what to do. More important, while the Communist Party gave guidance, every policy had to be voted upon by the membership of the unions, who selected the most logical and most efficient methods of all those proposed and discussed. If the Communists gave the best advice, then, the men asked, why not benefit by it? It was ridiculous to claim that the Communists "dominated" the strike, since the rank and file had the final say in every policy. But the Communist Party did influence their tactics and their understanding of the strike, and the men were frank in admitting the influence. That the aim of the strike was revolutionary seemed to them ludicrous: the aim was to establish the rights of thousands of men to strike, to picket, to control their own organizations, to protect their unions, to raise wages and improve working conditions. The Communist "plot" was revolutionary only in the eyes of the owners whose stranglehold was menaced.

The docks lay idle. Frantically, the employers called on the San Francisco Industrial Association for assistance. Composed of the largest, most ruthless, and most reactionary interests in the West, the Industrial Association counseled violence, and demanded that the police "open the port" forcibly. On July 5, "Bloody Thursday," the police charged the workers' lines, gassed pickets, shot into the ranks of unarmed men. Over one hundred fell wounded, two men lay dead. That same evening, the national guard marched into San Francisco and Governor Merriam — whose campaign chest was immediately enriched by a $30,000 "voluntary" contribution from the shipowners — declared martial law along the Embarcadero.

The two murdered strikers, one of them a Communist, lay in state in the I.L.A. hall one block from the waterfront. For seventy-two hours, a double line of workers shuffled past the biers. On the fourth day following the killings, with troops patrolling the docks, the workers of San Francisco and their sympathizers gathered to bury the dead. Bareheaded, jamming the street for five blocks, they listened to the funeral oration thunder from the amplifiers above the doorway of the union hall. "You have been killed because of your activity in the labor movement. Your death will guide us to our final victory. Your killing has been inspired by the Industrial Association and the Chamber of Commerce. But organized labor will answer that deed many-fold throughout the land." The two coffins were carried to the street, placed reverently on the waiting trucks. As they moved slowly into Market Street, the procession of workers formed — forty thousand tense, silent, bitter men, women, and children.

Chief of Police Quinn had "forbidden" the funeral. But when the ominously quiet tide of marchers flowed into the streets behind the trucks and muffled drums, the police disappeared. All that long July afternoon the cortège tramped through the city, through walls of hushed spectators massed on the sidewalks.

Almost every Bay Region local demanded a general strike in protest against the Industrial Association's killings and against the militia on the waterfront. Labor Council officials, when they could no longer resist the demand for a general strike, decided to head the movement. They organized a Strike Strategy Committee. On July 16, all industry (except for gas and electricity, telephone, water, and the press) ceased. San Francisco was gripped by the first general strike in America in fifteen years, the second in the history of American unionism.

To meet it, reaction mobilized its entire strength. In California, 7,000 national guardsmen, equipped with tanks and field pieces, reinforced by police, special deputies, "citizens' committees," were arrayed against unarmed strikers. Mayor Rossi of San Francisco declared: "Those who seek the dissolution of the Government shall find no comfort in this community." Over the radio, Governor Merriam fumed, "It is the plotting of such alien and vicious schemers — not the legitimate and recognized objects of bona fide American workers — that has intensified, magnified and aggravated our labor problems." William Green pronounced the strike illegal, unauthorized, harmful, "purely local." Matthew Woll and Joseph P. Ryan screamed that West Coast workers were being manipulated from Moscow. General Hugh Johnson of the N.R.A. denounced the workers as "rats." Local A.F. of L. officials at the San Francisco Labor Temple joined the chorus against Harry Bridges and the other militants. The press foresaw starvation, revolution, anarchy, assassination. But the Industrial Association, though it continued to censor all strike news published in the press, and, in conjunction with Hearst, dictated editorial policy to every Bay Region newspaper, did not depend on words alone. On the second day of the general strike, armed vigilantes swept through the city, beating, looting, destroying workers' meeting places. To mop up after them, came the police, who arrested over 300 militants. "We want it clearly understood," Police Chief Quinn announced, "none of these hangouts can be reopened." San Francisco experienced, as *The Nation* commented, "one of the most harrowing records of brutality to be found outside of Hitler's Third Reich."

Not surprisingly, the general strike collapsed. The vigilantes, none of whom was arrested, continued to terrorize the city, and employer-inspired violence broke out in San Pedro, Portland, Seattle, and elsewhere. In San Jose, fifty miles south of San Francisco, a score of workers were kidnapped by vigilantes and driven three hundred miles down the Coast. Yet, despite unprecedented savagery, the marine unions maintained their picket lines even after the general strike had ended. Nevertheless, it was obvious that the three months' battle had reached its climax. The federal government had set up a National Longshoremen's Board; the state sanctioned terror, the use of troops, the railroading of workers to jail. In the face of these conditions, the Joint Strike Committee, with the approval of the rank and file, accepted arbitration. The strength of the waterfront unions, the support they had gained from all labor in the general strike, the public sentiment in their favor — all seemed to assure an award which would recognize the principal demands of the maritime unions.

In San Francisco and other ports, strikers from every marine union lined up on the waterfront. Together they marched across the street to the docks. All unions resumed work simultaneously, their solidarity intact even after the terror. The West Coast maritime strike had ended.

When the arbitration board handed down its award, the longshoremen were granted hiring halls jointly controlled by the shipowners and the union, but with a union despatcher that in practice assured the closed shop. They gained a thirty hour week, higher wages, union recognition, coastwide contracts — substantially every demand they had made in February. The Board had heeded the warning of the general strike and Bridges' solemn words:

"The main issue is the right of labor to organize. This is the significance of the issue in the fight for control of our own hiring halls by the I.L.A. men. It is the only guarantee against discrimination and blacklist, and therefore against the destruction of unionism by the shipowners. The working class will judge the decision rendered by the Board from this point of view."

Though the other marine unions made advances less decisive than those of the longshoremen, the strike had been a triumph for rank and file leadership. The Marine Workers Industrial Union dissolved and its members for the sake of greater unity, entered the A.F. of L. marine unions. Workers in every Coast port had demonstrated their ability to resist violence and provocation, and had forced basic concessions from the employers. They had cemented unity among the maritime unions. They had established the closed shop for the longshoremen. They had exposed the cowardice of the A.F. of L. old guard and had greatly weakened its control of the unions. They had, moreover, raised Harry Bridges and other militants to positions of leadership in the West.

The dismayed shipowners immediately set about recouping their losses. The greatest threat to them, they realized, was the unity of the maritime unions. This unity had been largely the work of Harry Bridges. If they were able to break Bridges, they could more easily demoralize the workers and promote dissension. With that accomplished, it would be only a matter of time before they could again enjoy the good old days of employer dictatorship on the docks.

Attempts to bribe Bridges were futile. Moreover, the longshoremen's young leader failed to crumple before intimidation, even before threats of death, and he proved impossible to railroad to jail. There remained the Red scare, already badly overworked during the strike and among the maritime workers dishearteningly ineffectual. But the shipowners still believed that constant repetition of slanders and innuendoes could wear down the workers' resistance. Consequently, they bombarded the Coast and particularly the waterfront with Red-baiting, hysterical warnings, with "exposés" of Communist "plots," with stories of Red "atrocities," with predictions that shipping in the West would cease. They threatened that the large companies would shift the bulk of their operations to San Pedro, the least organized port on the Coast, which would permanently reduce employment in San Francisco. The longshoremen and maritime workers remained unimpressed by the propaganda, and continued to build their unity.

But the Red scare did have effect — in financial and industrial circles. For to the employers, every militant was a "Communist," and only William Green, Matthew Woll, and William Hutcheson were exempt from this general condemnation — though even the triumvirate was considered "sanely radical." Hugh Gallagher of the Matson Navigation Co., half-seriously, half-jokingly, referred to Bridges as the "Commissar." Not to be outdone, when he arrived for a conference at the head of a delegation of militants, Bridges sent word to Gallagher that "Bridges and the Reds" were ready to negotiate. And the Red scare, from which the employers hoped so much, became a joke on the waterfront and in the Bay Region, and only the Industrial Association and the Chamber of Commerce found it useful as material for circulars to be sent to their membership and to keep fellow industrialists in a dither of excitement over some unseen force that was always on the point of perpetrating some vague, unnamed horror.

"Red Harry," as the employers shudderingly referred to Bridges, was elected to the presidency of the San Francisco I.L.A. local, despite the owners' campaign of villification. "Alien!" shrieked the press, "whose record of violence, destruction, and class hatred is all too fresh in the memories of our people." The American Legion demanded his deportation. The Department of Labor investigated: Bridges had twice taken out first citizenship papers, had twice allowed them to lapse. But at the time of the investigation, he had again obtained his first papers. Moreover, he had entered the United States legally. The Commissioner of Immigration and Naturalization could uncover no lawful ground for deportation. In addition, fear of the repercussions on the waterfront that deporting Bridges would arouse caused many industrialists to counsel caution.

Furthermore, fabulous stories of the private fortune amassed by Bridges, of the $100,000 banked in some secret place, missed fire. The rumors of his huge salary struck the rank and file as amusing, particularly since it was Bridges who insisted, when he became president of the San Francisco local, that all local officials, himself included, should receive the same salary — forty dollars a week, which was what a longshoreman could earn on the docks. Later, in 1936, when Bridges was elected president of the West Coast district of the I.L.A., his salary rose to seventy-five dollars a week, and was paid by the international office. Joseph P. Ryan saw a chance to get even with the West Coast: he cut off the salary as a "disciplinary measure." The Pacific Coast district thereupon paid Bridges from its treasury.

While the employers terrified one another with Red bugaboos, the waterfront unions were not idle. Workers had won substantial gains in the strike; but without rigid enforcement, the concessions would prove meaningless. From the moment work commenced on the docks following the strike, the shipowners had tried every ruse to circumvent the arbitration award: provocation, increasing the weight of the sling loads, blacklists, dismissals of militants on faked charges. The union met these violations with job-action strikes, or as they were nicknamed, "quickees." When the straw boss fired without cause, the gang affected quit work until the union had investigated and made a settlement. When scabs appeared on boats, "quickees" forced them off. When slings were consistently overloaded, the longshoremen laid down their hooks. The "quickees" provided an immediate, powerful means of enforcing conditions without calling a strike of all longshoremen and all other members of the marine unions. And job action impressed upon the shipowners that they could not chisel on the award.

The employers raged and the "quickees" continued as union workers retaliated against employer cheating. The shipowners protested that "quickees" violated agreements. The unions replied that if the shipowners did not abide by the award, then workers were likewise not committed to it. Gradually, the owners realized that they were dealing with a resolute group of rank and file leaders far different from the usual A.F. of L. officials who tolerated any employer abuse and talked "sanctity of contract" — which bound only the workers. The industrialists learned that while they could trust Harry Bridges' word implicitly, they could not violate an agreement without facing countermoves by the unions.

At all times Bridges promoted consolidation. Unity, he contended, which had won the 1934 strike, could be preserved only by assuring future coöperation among maritime workers. In 1935, he urged the formation of the Maritime Federation of the Pacific, with which all marine and waterfront unions would affiliate and which would co-ordinate the activities of all members. Accordingly, seven marine unions voted to set up the Maritime Federation, pledged to carry forward the campaign to organize the unorganized which John L. Lewis had advocated at the 1934 A.F. of L. convention.

The formation of the semi-industrial Maritime Federation impressed non-waterfront workers with the success of union democracy. Harry Bridges explained what this democracy meant to him as a union officer: "I speak for the men," he made clear, "I act and talk as they want me to." His task as he saw it was "to keep as close contact as possible with the rank and file membership, not to let my new position isolate me from the men." The need to reflect the thoughts and desires of the I.L.A. membership was the core of Bridges' trade union philosophy. No phrasemaker, never a spell-binder, he approached the workers with a cold logic, both simple and straightforward. He paced the platform at union mass meetings, punctuating patient explanations with an odd little hop at the end of his sentences. He had no desire to stampede his listeners with dramatics. A quick negotiator, sure of mass support since final authority rested with the membership, Bridges maintained a detached calm even under attack, and a self-assurance that maddened the employers.

If Harry Bridges had been satisfied only to talk democracy and had done no more about it, the A.F. of L. officials would not have been disturbed. But like John L. Lewis, who insisted on more than lip service to his demand for industrial unionism, Bridges carried out the methods he advised. "A lot of fellows," he commented, "want to get up and express themselves. It has been a terrific job to get the floor for them. Our rule is that they shall have their say . . ." Talk, however, was not sufficient. ". . . if they tear down, they must offer a substitute . . . I believe in free expression and explaining every policy."

The rank and file of other unions, influenced by the example of the longshoremen, began to agitate for similar benefits in their own organizations. Their attitude threatened the domination of the old line officials. Paul Scharrenberg (whom seamen dubbed "pie-card conscious" because of his concern for job and salary) had for thirty years been secretary of the California Federation of Labor and head of the Sailors' Union of the Pacific. His resentment against Bridges during the 1934 strike turned to loathing as he realized that West Coast workers were no longer docile, or content to let him arbitrarily run their affairs. Scharrenberg therefore planned to trap and destroy Bridges while there still remained a chance of undermining the rank and file's confidence in the young longshoreman.

Backed by the shipowners with whom he had long been on over-friendly terms, Scharrenberg suddenly called an unauthorized strike of coastwise tanker workers without submitting the call to a referendum vote. His strategy was designed to cause dissension among the waterfront unions and through the demoralization that Scharrenberg hoped would accompany an unsuccessful strike, to create antagonism against the militants who had been elected to union office. Bridges exposed Scharrenberg's intrigue. Forced to retreat, Scharrenberg abandoned all caution. Before an arbitration board, he asserted: "I hope we have a war with Japan because we will be sitting on top of the world then," and "We don't care how much the ship-owner is able to make out of the government as long as we get our share." The sailors promptly expelled Scharrenberg from the union. War mongering touched no responsive chord among the seamen. Instead they agreed with Bridges: "One of the main reasons for war against us is that there is a war in the making. And when there is a war in the making, such things as strong unions which don't believe in war are not wanted by those who make war."

The discredited Paul Scharrenberg trailed his fellow reactionary, Joseph P. Ryan, to the East Coast, where he demanded the "revocation of West Coast charters and the reorganization by the convention" of the Sailors' Union of the Pacific. Expulsion of the West Coast sailors by the International Seamen's Union followed. But unity among the maritime unions remained unimpaired, and if anything, more complete. The A.F. of L. officials on the Coast took Scharrenberg's fate to heart — his repudiation became the dreadful example, the nightmare that haunted them. Henceforward, the reactionaries were wary how they opposed the militants. Many union heads tagged cautiously after their membership, posing as progressives, which only made their subsequent retreats more glaring. Other union officers, formerly conservative but who at the same time were genuinely eager to forward the labor movement, began to acknowledge the fruitfulness of Bridges' tactics. In addition, the composition of the San Francisco Labor Council altered as rank and file delegates replaced tories. From a backward, static gathering lacking both direction and hope, the Council changed into one of the most progressive and dynamic assemblies on the Coast or in the nation. And similar shifts in the composition of central labor bodies occurred in Seattle and elsewhere on the Coast.

With the docks solidly organized, with not a single member of the San Francisco I.L.A. local on relief in the fall of 1935, with unemployment practically abolished on the Pacific waterfronts, the rank and file demanded the spread of unionization to all categories of workers. Early in 1936, the maritime unions' "march inland" commenced in earnest. The slogan of the Maritime Federation, "An Injury to One Is an Injury to All!" was not merely an insistence on solidarity among affiliated unions; it was likewise an acknowledgment that an advance achieved by one sector of the working class could be preserved only if all other sectors were organized.

The longshoremen led the way. Warehouse workers had been placed under the I.L.A. jurisdiction in 1917, yet at the conclusion of the 1934 strike, the Warehousemen's Union had recruited at most 300 members. The I.L.A. set out to bring the warehousemen into the union. By the end of 1936, 4,500 workers had been enrolled, and had obtained a closed-shop agreement, substantial wage increases, a forty hour week, and other major concessions. With the encouragement of the I.L.A., the union organized in San Francisco all wholesale coffee houses, wholesale grocery, hardware, drug, hay, fuel and feed firms, as well as cold storage plants and the general warehouses. Bargemen and workers in sugar refineries received aid from the longshoremen in unionizing their industries. Inspired by the solidarity on the waterfront, bakery wagon drivers in various parts of California unified their locals. The retail clerks, affected by the upsurge of militancy in other unions, invaded department and chain stores. Striking lettuce pickers in Salinas, one hundred miles south of San Francisco, turned to the I.L.A. for financial aid when vigilantes attempted forcibly to break their union. Unemployed organizations received longshoremen's backing in their opposition to curtailment of relief and the lowering of relief standards and wages. In the Northwest, lumber workers set up an alliance similar to the Maritime Federation and pledged to coöperate with the waterfront unions. Industrial workers rallied to the support of the Newspaper Guild in Seattle, with the result that the success of the *Post-Intelligencer* strike caused every major newspaper in the Bay Region to enter into agreements with the newswriters. Even Los Angeles, stronghold of the open shop on the Pacific Coast, was invaded by the unions with increasing success.

Harry Bridges, elected president of the West Coast district of the I.L.A. in the summer of 1936, was also anxious to enlist agricultural workers into powerful unions. "The sources of scabs," he stated, "are the universities and the itinerant agricultural workers. It is difficult to recruit scabs among workers who are unionized. The I.L.A., if only from a selfish standpoint, is concerned with the drive to bring organization to those who work in the fields."

The Industrial Association watched the spread of organization with helpless fury. "The 'march inland'," they wailed, "as it is termed by the maritime unions, is a part of a well laid plan of Harry Bridges and his fellow radicals to extend control over the movement of all merchandise in San Francisco, as well as on the waterfront." What they really dreaded was that Bridges' course would coördinate all unions as they had been coördinated on the waterfront. For did not Bridges admit in 1936:

> "Of course, we favor industrial unionism . . . We are strongly opposed to splitting the labor movement. But as yet possibilities of industrial unionism on the West Coast are hard to predict. The first job here is to organize the unorganized on an industrial basis . . . the real drive, of course, must start in the mass industries — in steel, auto, rubber. On the waterfront here our organization is not dissimilar to the industrial setup."

In addition, Bridges pointed out that refusal to tolerate the split promoted by the A.F. of L. mikados would mobilize the rank and file of the craft organizations in support of the Committee for Industrial Organization. When it became obvious that the executive council had no interest in unity, Harry Bridges took the leadership of the progressives who advocated that the maritime unions join the C.I.O. At the convention of the Maritime Federation of the Pacific in June

1937, the delegates overwhelmingly supported Bridges' position and instructed all member unions to hold immediate referendums on the question.

Neither the progress of the inland march nor the invasion of the central labor bodies by the progressives satisfied Bridges. He urged extension of the battle to still another front. The Gompers tradition, which taught avoidance of independent political action and denied the existence of class relationships, limited the labor movement to temporary advances, usually counteracted in short order. Bridges contended that workers could preserve economic gains won in strikes or negotiations and compel favorable legislation only by exercising their political power. Long before John L. Lewis began to concede the importance of labor's independent action, Harry Bridges advocated labor's political as well as economic organization. Class antagonisms, he knew, could not be eliminated by denying their existence. When labor learned to acknowledge the fundamental opposition between workers and owners, it would then organize realistically to keep and extend democracy, civil rights, free speech. Logically, therefore, labor must enter politics with its own program, fostered by its own political party.

"I am in favor of a Farmer-Labor Party composed of workers, farmers, small tradesmen and professional people," Bridges declared. "The workers must have a Farmer-Labor Party to maintain their economic position, to protect the six hour day, the thirty hour week, maintain a decent wage scale, keep down prices and otherwise insure a standard of living of health and decency." As a step toward this end, Bridges endorsed the San Francisco Labor Party's mayoralty campaign in 1935, and a year later backed the program of the progressive Commonwealth Federation of the Northwest. By 1937, Bridges felt that world events had moved so rapidly that he concluded: "The Farmer-Labor Party is necessary to make democracy work and to prevent the rise of Fascism."

It was clear to Bridges that friction between Negro and white, foreign born and native workers weakened the cause of labor. Discrimination, he told the rank and file, must go. Only by ever widening the base of the labor movement could solidarity, already partially achieved, be reinforced.

After all, he pointed out, the slogan "An Injury to One Is an

Injury to All," implied a unity attainable only after the misconceptions of Gompersism have been repudiated. Workers must learn that no matter where labor suffered defeat, whether in Germany or Italy, whether in Alabama or Colorado, the reversal menaced the labor movement everywhere. Fascism meant the end of unions. Fascism meant war, and war bore most heavily on workers, farmers, and their allies. Thus Harry Bridges, who had seen the employers resort to fascist methods in San Francisco, frankly admitted, "I have tried during the term of my office, to have . . . the I.L.A. adopt such policies as will defend the democracy of the world, and oppose the fascist nations." When a German ship sailed into San Francisco flying the swastika, the longshoremen refused to unload the cargo until the Nazi flag was hauled down. Again, during the Italian invasion of Ethiopia, dock workers refused to load war materials on an Italian freighter. While, according to Bridges, "the union was finally forced by the shipowners, with whom the union had a contract, to load this ship . . . our organization intends, in the future, to prevent all war supplies from being shipped to fascist nations, for war on defenseless or democratic people."

NEW RANK AND FILE LEADERS emerged on the Pacific Coast. In 1935, Bridges backed Harry Lundeberg, formerly close to the Industrial Workers of the World, to head the newly formed Maritime Federation. Lundeberg, a handsome, impetuous seaman, far surpassed Bridges in militant phraseology. To Bridges — still inexperienced and too readily impressed by Lundeberg's vigor — and to the rank and file leadership of the marine unions, it seemed important to utilize Lundeberg's energy. Lundeberg's enthusiasm compensated for a certain lack of stability; Bridges and the other militants assumed that he would outgrow immature, ultra-left posturing once he was involved in day-by-day union tasks. Furthermore, Lundeberg showed a healthy disregard for the A.F. of L. bureaucracy and its opposition to the Maritime Federation.

Bridges seriously misjudged Lundeberg, who proved vain and inordinately jealous of the respect and authority won by Bridges and the militants. Influenced by empty leftist phrases rather than by sound reason, Lundeberg was prone to accept any extremist position as necessarily the correct one. He lacked ability to negotiate with the employers, refusing, even for the sake of preserving important advances, to retreat strategically or to bide his time. He rejected all compromise, even when compromise forwarded the interests of the workers. Like an enraged bull, he charged head down into a stone wall before he had ascertained whether the wall could be scaled or circumvented.

When the corrupt International Seamen's Union expelled the Sailors' Union of the Pacific, Lundeberg, who replaced Paul Scharrenberg as head of the union, only half-heartedly attempted to bring the sailors back into the A.F. of L. Favoring a vague "one big union" plan that echoed his I.W.W. past, Lundeberg went so far as to turn down an offer made by the I.S.U. officialdom in 1936 to reinstate the West Coast sailors — an offer that Harry Bridges had succeeded in obtaining and that granted most of the rank and file's conditions for reinstatement. Lundeberg, the individualist, hostile to the A.F. of L., claimed that the terms were unsatisfactory and that the Sailors' Union was better off outside the A.F. of L. In the middle of 1937, rank and file pressure forced Lundeberg to abandon his isolationist position and to agree to a referendum on whether or not the Sailors' Union should affiliate to the C.I.O.

Lundeberg also antagonized the other maritime unions. In contrast to Bridges who conceived of the "quickee" strikes as a device to consolidate the unions and preserve the 1934 award, Lundeberg resorted to job action without proper consideration and long after the method menaced waterfront unity. Often he ordered individual walkouts of sailors without consulting the rest of the crew, or used the "quickee" to raise basic demands that could be won only through a major strike. Overlooking the ultimate effect of his impetuousness, Lundeberg failed to visualize the goal that Bridges kept constantly in mind: the objective was not merely attainment of local or immediate gains but rather the welding of labor's strength so that it could weather the hurricanes ahead as well as the current squalls.

Naturally the employers utilized Lundeberg to embarrass Bridges. Along with dissident and reactionary minorities on the waterfront who found Lundeberg easy to flatter, the shipowners attempted to play one union against the other and thereby split the unity of the Maritime Federation. Disruptive groups encouraged the head of the sailors on his erratic course which led unwittingly into the hands of the employers. Lundeberg more and more fell under the influence of a group who were the leaders of a small but exceedingly vociferous and unscrupulous band of Trotzkyists. This clique, with Lundeberg's aid, appointed an ex-convict, Barney Mass, as editor of the Maritime Federation's official paper, *The Voice of the Federation*. From this vantage point, Mass attacked Bridges, refused to print the speeches and statements of rank and file officials in the various marine unions, and later, during the 1936 strike, sabotaged the unity of the Federation by slandering the leaders of the strike and excluding all statements of the joint strike committee from *The Voice*. In the end, the rank and file ousted Mass in disgrace. But the Trotzkyists continued their sniping and their intrigues, and Lundeberg made no objection.

Nevertheless, Bridges refused to allow Lundeberg's personal animosity or jealous ambition to precipitate an ill-advised fight. Conciliatory, subtly restraining Lundeberg's assaults on the Maritime Federation's unity, and guiding his rashness whenever possible into healthier and wiser channels, Bridges forced the sailor's head to coöperate with the militant rank and file leadership, and successfully countered destructive tactics by healing wounds and mending the solidarity of the maritime unions.

The experience with Lundeberg also aided Bridges in overcoming his own weaknesses. More and more he abandoned the pretense of being fully informed of all facts in a given situation. He gave greater attention to the training of subordinates. Willing enough to follow advice of associates whom he trusted and whose judgment he respected, Bridges had difficulty delegating authority. Though he was not jealous of others, Bridges still doubted that a task was properly accomplished unless he attended to it himself. The result was needless concern with details, overwork, a constant killing pace that seriously undermined his health.

UNIONIZATION on the West Coast swept forward. Seriously worried, the shipowners began elaborate preparations for a showdown. As they amassed a huge war chest and stocked great quantities of goods in warehouses, the owners intensified the anti-Red, anti-labor propaganda. At what they considered the psychological moment, they launched an intensive offensive against the Maritime Federation.

The 1934 award lapsed in September, 1936. The employers refused to renew contracts unless the maritime unions made sweeping concessions, which in practice would cancel all the gains of the 1934 strike. The unions countered by demanding that further concessions by the employers be incorporated in the new contracts. Clamoring for "arbitration" of the terms granted in 1934, the employers threatened to lock out all unions affiliated with the Maritime Federation. The unions objected that to reopen arbitration proceedings would only enable the shipowners to prune benefits already granted. For a month after the contracts expired, negotiations continued; but it was obvious that the employers had no intention of signing new agreements. In an attempt to split the unions, they suddenly offered to settle with the longshoremen, though they refused to listen to the demands of the other maritime organizations. The longshoremen responded that the offer meant "nothing but another attempt of the shipowners to divide the ranks of the waterfront unions."

On October 30, all unions affiliated with the Maritime Federation issued a strike call. Pacific Coast shipping halted immediately. Unlike 1934 when workers still drifted off the boats two months after the strike had commenced, in 1936 forty thousand men stopped work simultaneously, and paralyzed all sailings for the duration of the strike. In 1934, the unions had fought for recognition, struggling to build their organizations; in 1936, they walked off the ships and docks in unison with consolidation already achieved. They had so built their defenses that the employers dared not use violence against them, dared not enlist scabs and strikebreakers or attempt to mobilize the vigilantes. And the 1936 stoppage was rapidly transformed into a display of militant power by workers who had completely organized an industry and had set up an effective instrument, the Maritime Federation, to guard their unity.

When the strike ended in February 1937, the seven waterfront unions were stronger than ever. Sailors, engineers, firemen, radio telegraphists, masters, mates and pilots, cooks and stewards received contracts which equalized their conditions with those won by the longshoremen two years before. For the most part, the unions gained increases in wages, shorter work days, union-controlled hiring halls. The Maritime Federation had been immeasurably strengthened. The lesson that solidarity meant victory had again been impressively illustrated.

Furthermore, the strike crystallized the revolt against corrupt A.F. of L. officials and oppressive conditions along the East Coast and Gulf. The desire for organization similar to that existing in the West and already beginning on the Gulf caused East Coast sailors to strike in support of the Maritime Federation of the Pacific. Just as the 1934 West Coast strike brought forward rank and file leaders, so the East Coast strike developed Joseph Curran and other militants. The strike won shorter hours and higher wages. Likewise, Joseph P. Ryan's disgraceful collaborationist policy became startlingly clear to East Coast longshoremen when Ryan joined the shipowners in a frenzied attempt to break the seamen's strike. And again the executive council of the A.F. of L., by "outlawing" the East Coast walkout, revealed itself as currying favor with the shipowners.

On the other hand, C.I.O. leaders showed a sympathetic interest, and John L. Lewis later aided the seamen by opposing the black-listing, continual-discharge book that the shipowners' lobby had railroaded through Congress. On every waterfront the demand arose for a National Maritime Federation modeled after the Federation of the Pacific. But first, Harry Bridges told the East Coast seamen, they must achieve unity:

> "And if they can't get unity, if they can't get it because of these so-called labor leaders, these people lined up with the shipowners . . . we will understand on the Pacific Coast and will do our best and still gamble for unity and for a National Maritime Federation."

It was a good gamble. The termination of the East Coast strike did not end the fight between the rank and file and the I.S.U. overlords. Rank and file elections, though opposed by the I.S.U. officialdom, overwhelmingly endorsed the "outlawed" militants. And immediately after the Supreme Court declared the Wagner Labor Relations Act constitutional in April 1937, the International Merchant Marine, largest American shipping corporation, recognized the rank and file group along with the American Radio Telegraphists which had recently affiliated with the C.I.O. In the late spring, the militants formed the National Maritime Union, pledged to join the C.I.O. The new union included the great majority of seamen in eastern and Gulf ports, and preparations were made to determine whether it or the International Seamen's Union should represent the men in collective bargaining. That the referendum would give the C.I.O. union an overwhelming endorsement was an almost foregone conclusion. Once the ballot had been taken, the formation of a National Maritime Federation similar in form to the Federation already existing on the West Coast, affiliated with the C.I.O. and in the hands of progressive, militant leaders, no longer appeared a remote dream.

THE MARITIME UNIONS had traveled far in three years. They had illustrated what the rank and file could accomplish once the false premises of the Gompers heritage were discarded. They had raised to leadership a young longshoreman who never forgot that his rôle was to act as spokesman for the masses of workers who trusted and admired him. Harry Bridges, resolute and flexible, modest and courageous, insisted that the final decision, the final power in the labor movement must rest securely in the rank and file. His duty as a class conscious leader was continually to spur the workers to greater efforts, to urge them not to rest content no matter what benefits they obtained.

No labor leader in present day America won greater confidence and affection from the members of his own union. When in May 1935, Harry Bridges was rushed to the St. Francis Hospital in San Francisco for an emergency operation, hundreds of workers waited late into the night to hear the doctor's report. More flowers than had ever before been received by any patient in St. Francis Hospital arrived for this worker who had revitalized the West Coast labor movement. And from San Quentin, the penitentiary across the Bay, came a short note. "Get well," Tom Mooney wrote, "for the working class needs you."

VIII. GIANT KILLERS

A CHANGE came over the American labor movement in 1936. Only four years before, trade unions, because of the A.F. of L. practices, were almost non-existent in the huge basic industries. But by the middle of 1937 the C.I.O. was advancing in a lightning offensive which had forced terms from many of the corporations forming the backbone of American finance. Everywhere, in unprecedented numbers, workers flocked into the young industrial unions. What had revived the labor movement in such a short time? Why were the new unions able to wrest recognition from employers who had until then forestalled all attempts at organization?

The full answer to these questions lay buried in the substratum of events following 1929. When Franklin D. Roosevelt took office as 32nd president in 1933, the nation was racked by the blackest panic in its history. Bank failures, which had commenced several months before in the rural areas, had so spread to the larger institutions that state after state declared bank holidays. To avoid financial disaster, the first act of the incoming president was to extend the holiday nationally.

Moreover, production had sunk by March 1933 to about half the 1929 peak and to below even the worst level reached in the 1920–22 depression. Especially had heavy industries suffered: the index for steel and iron output had fallen by 85 percent; for lumber by 77 percent; for cement by 65 percent. Decreases had been proportional in other basic industries and only slightly less severe for those industries producing consumption goods. Agriculture was paralyzed. Foreign trade had slumped disastrously.

To rescue the nation's prostrate economy, the administration realized it must move with utmost speed. The terrified ruling class, its morale undermined, clamored for a blood transfusion to revive capitalism which in its eyes seemed just about to expire. Hastily, the administration pulled the National Industrial Recovery Act out of the legislative hat, exhibiting it as the panacea that would put vigor into the anaemic profit system and restore it to some sort of health. The bankers and industrialists applauded with uncritical enthusiasm.

Still, the government needed more than the ruling class' eagerness to be saved if the New Deal were to fulfill its purpose. The all-important task was to sell the idea to the workers who were in anything but a trusting mood. Faith in capitalism had worn a little thin for the seventeen million unemployed, for the wage earners who watched the number of men on factory payrolls dwindle by 44 percent and the size of those payrolls in dollars decline by 65 percent. Nor had their faith been fortified by the halving of working class income while the cost of living fell barely 30 percent. Workers expressed their disgust and desperation through spontaneous strikes; through unemployment demonstrations that grew more militant and more insistent; through hunger marches that converged on state capitals and on Washington with alarming frequency; through farmer revolts that were characterized by an ugly bitterness.

It was obvious that the administration would have to sugarcoat the N.R.A.'s huge grants to industries if it expected to win support among the people. Accordingly, in Section 7-A of the recovery plan, which proposed "to encourage national industrial recovery, to foster fair competition, and to provide for the construction of certain useful public works, and for other purposes," the government admitted that labor had the right to organize into trade unions and to bargain collectively for its own advancement. In addition, codes of fair competition authorized by the Act, vaguely provided for maximum hours, minimum wages, and the elimination of child labor.

The N.R.A. did not look bad on paper. It was one thing, however, to offer such grants and quite another to carry them into practice. Workers learned before long that New Deal gestures had meaning only if labor could compel employers to recognize unions and to bargain with them. On the other hand, most workers had no unions through which to take advantage of the codes. True, the United Mine Workers immediately launched a recruiting campaign that enrolled almost all of the coal miners. Similarly, the needle trades unions did not delay in profiting from the N.R.A. But the craft unions failed to rally — or if they did, were soon enmeshed in stultifying jurisdictional wrangles.

During 1934, strikes erupted throughout the country. On the West Coast, maritime workers won a spectacular victory over the combined opposition of the Federation's hierarchy, the government, and the employers. Close to half a million textile workers walked out of the mills along the eastern seaboard. Teamsters in Minneapolis, meat packers in Iowa, longshoremen on the Gulf, silk-dye workers in Paterson, taxi-drivers in New York City, rubber workers in Akron — all fought against exploitation. In twelve months, 1,856 strikes had involved a million and a half men and women. Federal unions sprouted like mushrooms after a spring rain. But alarmed by the insurgency of the masses, the A.F. of L. executive council thwarted organization in the basic industries by refusing industrial charters to the federal unions and by insisting that members be parceled out to the various craft unions.

While the A.F. of L. discouraged any worker attempt to benefit from the N.R.A., the employers had shown no reluctance to accept federal aid. Profits once more replaced deficits. With the crisis weathered, bankers and industrialists began to regret even the left handed generosity shown to labor by the federal government during the panic. The need had passed for the few regulations set up by the N.R.A. to aid the largest corporations; therefore, they desired to cancel the Act and allow capitalism to revert to the happy pre-depression days of dog eat dog. Above all, they wailed, Section 7-A must go. As always before, the Supreme Court complied by delivering decision after decision invalidating New Deal legislation and wiping the slate clean of embarrassing admissions.

The erasure of statutes from the record presented no difficulties. It proved another matter, however, to convince workers that the partial admission of labor's rights granted in the days of despair could be blotted out the moment the employers succeeded in catching their breath. Section 7-A, for all its weaknesses and despite the Federation's refusal to take advantage of it, had stimulated the rank and file's desire for organization. The reanimation of the profit system had not lessened the need for collective bargaining.

This need impelled the executive council at the 1934 San Francisco convention to sanction a resolution favoring industrial forms in the mass-production industries. Of course, the council had no intention of taking the resolution too seriously. Consequently, by the time the 1935 convention met, with N.R.A. a memory, the chasm between those who advocated immediate action and the unwilling craft leaders had widened to a point where revolt could not be

stopped. Pressure from below led to the formation of the Committee
for Industrial Organization.

The birth of the C.I.O. answered the pressing impatience for
leadership. Immediately organization advanced in the mass-production industries. The working class gained a new solidarity. And
as the first skirmishes took place, Labor's Non-Partisan League
rallied workers politically in preparation for the 1936 presidential
election. If the program of the League remained elementary, it
represented, nevertheless, a definite break with the "pure and simple" past. The main issue of the election was clear enough: the turning
back of incipient Fascism inherent in the Republican-Liberty League
platform. Conscious of the gathering forces of reaction throughout
the world, workers contemplated the desperate fight to preserve
democracy that raged in every country of western and central
Europe. They beheld the defeat of unionism in Italy, Germany, and
Austria; they saw democracy battle for survival in England, France,
and Spain. The struggle abroad was only a development, an intensification of the conflict at home.

American workers translated the example of Europe into a spectacular defeat of the Republican Party. The repulse of reaction at the
polls gave wage earners a sense of their political and economic power.
Renewed confidence expressed itself immediately in sit-down strikes
that brought C.I.O. unions to industries never before organized.

The A.F. of L. old guard, of course, did not welcome the growth of
industrial unionism. Abandoning any pretense of trying to win benefits for the worke 3, the officials scurried to the employers with offers
to bolster certain company unions, to defeat progressives by terror,
scabbing, falsification — in fact, by any means even if opposition
meant the complete annihilation of all unions. The split between the
C.I.O. and the A.F. of L. shifted to open warfare, declared by the
executive council — a war that could result only in the victory or the
wiping out of unionism, only in the defeat or supremacy of Fascism in
this country. Gompersism had finally — inevitably — developed into
a powerful employer weapon against the American labor movement.

THE UNITED RUBBER WORKERS was the first C.I.O. union to
win recognition from large corporations. In no industry — with the
exception of textiles — did more intense speedup and stretchout

systems prevail; no industry levied a greater toll on the health and endurance of factory workers. At forty, the unrelenting pressure had so burned out the average rubber worker that he could no longer obtain a job in the mills. In addition, rationalization of manufacturing processes had raised the average output per man from an index point of 499.1 in 1921 to 1,015.5 in 1931. From 1928 to 1931, the six leading rubber factories had reduced the man power required by 41 percent: almost three-quarters of the industry's unemployed in 1931 had been thrown out of jobs by speedup and stretchout devices, and only 29 percent were jobless because of lowered production. While in 1920 the Akron plants hired 75,000 workers, in 1936 payrolls had been reduced to 40,000 men. Yet the number of tires produced had more than doubled.

To be sure, workers in the rubber mills had made repeated efforts to organize. In 1902, some of them joined the International Association of Allied Metal and Rubber Workers, affiliated with the A.F. of L. Of necessity, the union was a secret body; it progressed until a company agent invaded the hotel room of the union secretary and stole the membership list. The wholesale discharge of militants that followed killed the Association. Shortly afterward, the A.F. of L. granted a charter to the Amalgamated Rubber Workers of America, organized in Washington, D. C., which went out of existence after a brief strike had been broken by imported scabs.

In 1904, Akron companies instituted a highly efficient spy system to keep tab on militants and to inform the employers of any move to organize the plants. The spies earned their salaries of $85 a month many times over; militants were quickly weeded out, no union was able to exist, and one private detective a few years later even succeeded in being elected secretary of the Akron Central Labor Council. Terrorism imposed an "industrial peace" that won for Akron, center of the rubber industry, the dubious honor of being an open shop town unsurpassed in America. For a brief moment in 1912, a spontaneous strike brought I.W.W. organizers to Akron, but employers had only to call on State Senator Green for aid and the future A.F. of L. president won their everlasting respect by Red-baiting the strike to its doom. Once more peace gripped Akron, a peace bolstered in 1919 by the introduction of company unions, a peace of depressed wages averaging even in the boom year of 1929 only $1,390 a year, and in 1933, $1,076 a year.

The rubber workers made an attempt to unionize the mills in 1926. But the venture got nowhere and soon collapsed. Only when the N.R.A. was passed did the drive for unionism take on new purpose. In a few months the federal unions in Akron grew from 2,000 to 30,000 members, amazing William Green but failing to alter his determination to distribute the membership among seven craft organizations. Green sent Coleman C. Claherty of the sheet metal workers to Akron with instructions to make sure that rubber workers abided by his orders. A few militants balked and called a rump convention in January 1934, in the hope of forming an independent and industrial international. Green lost no time expelling the leaders of the revolt; Claherty mopped up later in a series of speeches to the discontented rank and file, promising a convention sanctioned by the A.F. of L. sometime in the dim future.

Yet the rapid rise of union consciousness among the men, which the executive council could not completely prevent, worried the rubber owners. The mounting enthusiasm with which workers advocated a general tire strike boded no good for profits which had increased 140 percent during Roosevelt's first year in office. The employers decided to strengthen the company unions and to import additional spies. Their concern, however, was premature, since Federation officials still retained control of the federal unions and quickly ruled out all thought of a strike in favor of a proposed industry-wide agreement which, the officials promised, would bless the rubber workers with minimum wages, pay increases, a shorter work week, employment insurance, and seniority rights. Claherty called a national convention of rubber unions to approve the agreement, and appointed delegates from different related crafts in such a way that the rubber workers were in the minority. To make sure that nothing went wrong, he also designated seven executive committeemen of which only one was a rubber worker, and had himself named president over all the federal and craft locals.

Claherty's elaborate precautions did not convince the rubber barons that they should sign the agreement. Rebuffed, the A.F. of L. admitted defeat, but was unable to smother the anger of the rank and file. In the General Tire and Rubber Company, for example, 1,100 factory hands walked out in a spontaneous strike. The stoppage, the first major strike in the industry since 1912, lasted a month and mobilized powerful picket lines. Unfortunately, the inexperienced rank and file, with a splendid chance to win concessions, entrusted negotiations to Federation officials who immediately capitulated. Other strikes occurred, but the results were disheartening. By the end of 1934, great numbers of rubber workers who had joined the federal locals a year or so before, tore up their membership cards and deserted the ineffective unions in disgust.

The Federation hoped to recoup losses by reopening negotiations with the companies. Once again employers refused to bargain and laughed at threats of strike. Just to be on the safe side, the big three — Firestone, Goodyear and Goodrich — retained Pearl Bergoff, professional strikebreaker. After some thought, Bergoff in conjunction with his lieutenant, George Williams, hit upon a cheap and efficient scheme that he was confident would end any strike. With a stake of $50,000 paid by the companies, Bergoff set up a vigilante organization known as the Citizens Law and Order Association, pledged "to uphold constitutional rights and liberties of all citizens," and instructed in the latest methods of violence. The American Legion, the Chamber of Commerce, and other big business clubs and associations coöperated. The advantage that the Law and Order plan offered over the usual importation of strikebreakers was the appearance it gave of popular resistance to the strikers — and, of course, the fact that the services of townspeople cost the company nothing.

Bergoff and fifty of his best salesmen, each receiving $25 a day, came to Akron to build the army of vigilante patriots. Bergoff also interested the sheriff in the idea, persuading him to deputize 500 men and to obtain National Guard officers to drill them. At the last moment, the strike did not materialize and the plan fell through. Bergoff got drunk to ease the heartbreak. But barbed wire fences, sandbag fortifications, and flood lights remained to protect plant property, and thousands of army cots were stored for the use of a future battalion of strikebreakers.

The strike had gone the way of all strikes threatened by the executive council — to a "victorious" retreat, which took the form of a no-strike agreement between the A.F. of L. and the companies. The agreement was to remain in force until such time as the Supreme Court settled all questions relating to the constitutionality of the National Labor Relations Boards. Union membership again dropped off — 3,000 members in Akron, of which only a handful paid dues. The few progressives who stuck to the organization kept urging action and particularly the granting of an international charter to the rubber workers. Finally, in September 1935, the executive council bestowed the charter, but one that was not industrial in form. William Green delivered the charter in person and in return demanded that his man Claherty be elected president. The delegates rejected Green's candidate and elected Sherman H. Dalrymple instead.

The new president, a World War veteran, had entered the rubber mills when he was fourteen. Like most Akron workers, he had been born in the West Virginia mountains. He became a highly skilled and highly paid worker, curing tires in the hot steam pits. The companies hired only men with enormous endurance for this task. Dalrymple was over six feet two, broad and powerful. During the World War, he left the plants to enlist in the marines; when he returned from France, Firestone refused to reëmploy him because, as the management explained, the promise to take back veterans did not apply to volunteers but only to drafted men! Dalrymple finally found a job. In 1926, when rubber workers unsuccessfully attempted to form a union, Dalrymple was among the progressives. And in 1933, he was one of the first to join a federal union, and that same year became president of the Goodrich local.

When he was elected international president, Dalrymple still lacked experience and was inclined to lag behind the more militant group within the union. But he had sufficient foresight to join the majority at the convention in vetoing Claherty's resolution that called for the expulsion of "members of a Communist Party or I.W.W." Once the convention ended, Dalrymple found no treasury, few members, and hardly any interest in the union. He did not oppose the attempts of militants to recruit; but neither did he know how to press the drive himself. The United Rubber Workers made little progress.

Yet rebellion against the speedup and threatened lengthening of the work week flared throughout the industry. Workers objected to the pacemakers sent into plants by the employers to establish a new standard of output. In January 1936, desperate Firestone workers interfered with a pace setter and delayed him. A foreman intervened, a fight resulted, and a union man was discharged. The other men demanded his reinstatement. When the company did not take the man back into the plant, Firestone workers suddenly halted the machines and waited for the company to capitulate. It was the first sit-down in the industry. In three days, this method had won the reinstatement of the union worker and payment of wages for time lost during the strike.

The new tactic, stumbled on almost inadvertently, electrified all other rubber workers in Akron. They asked themselves why they had not thought of such a sensible and effective weapon before. Not only had the stoppage been successful but it had recruited from 400 to 500 new members into the union. Sit-down strikes broke out in all the plants. After each, the union grew.

Meanwhile, in October 1935, Goodyear had announced that it would shortly abandon N.R.A. standards and lengthen the six hour day to eight. A government fact finding committee, unable to ignore this violation, rebuked Goodyear. The elaborate, two chamber company union, provoked by the new driving pace, voted in December against the additional two hours. The board of directors vetoed the resolution. The company union again refused to abide by the veto; finally, President Litchfield of Goodyear had to censure the rebellious group. As a result, the company union, revealed in all its impotence, lost whatever influence it had exercised until that time over the workers.

The rank and file as a whole, however, relied neither on rebukes nor on protests against the increase in the working day. Instead it conducted three sit-downs in various departments. Goodyear yielded. But the sit-downs won only temporary postponement of the lengthened day. In February 1936, the numerous small protests precipitated a spontaneous walkout of Goodyear workers.

Within three days mass picket lines had shut down all Goodyear mills in Akron. At first, Sherman Dalrymple refused to authorize the strike — which included a majority of non-union men — confused by its unexpected size and momentum. But almost immediately he recognized that it was imperative to throw all U.R.W. resources behind the struggle. The C.I.O., which, when it was first formed, the United Rubber Workers had joined in order to obtain an industrial charter, sent monetary aid and organizers. On their side, the employers petitioned for and received an anti-picketing injunction, plus the

coöperation of Edward F. McGrady who flew to Akron full of advice
on industrial peace, and eager to find a weak spot in the strikers'
armor. The injunction proved a dud when the sheriff did not dare
attack the mass picket lines. McGrady's smoothest words failed to
impress the rank and file. In the end, the strikers, heartened by
support from the C.I.O. and the Akron labor council, won a settlement granting workers the six hour day, seniority rights, and a curb
on speedup.

It was the first great victory of Akron rubber workers, swelling the
membership of the Goodyear local from 400 to 4,500. Workers returned to the mills with the slogan "Take the picket line back to the
factories." And the U.R.W., revived by the militants, continued to
advance, conducting in the period between the Goodyear settlement
and January 1937, 180 sit-downs important enough to halt production. Each sit-down built the union, until by March 1937, it had
enlisted approximately 40,000 men and women, of which 37,000
worked in Akron.

By March 1937, the union was strong enough to resist speedup
even more directly. A sit-down in the Firestone plant was transformed into a walkout that lasted until the end of April. The U.R.W.
emerged from the strike having won from a major rubber company
the concession that the union must be consulted before the pace
required of the workers was changed. After almost forty years,
industrial organization had gained rubber employees real protection
against the rapacious owners. The United Rubber Workers had
proved that open shop could be beaten, that company unions could
be eliminated, that speedup could be checked, that terror and
intimidation could be overcome.

THE SUCCESS of the rubber workers influenced the rank and file
in the automotive industry. They faced problems almost identical to
those which plagued the U.R.W. Prior to 1933, attempts to organize
the auto industry came to nothing for much the same reasons that
unions had failed in Akron.

At the turn of the century, the automobile industry was a new-
comer to capitalist enterprise. The infant factories employed about
12,000 workers in 1904; twenty-two years later, this number had
increased by about 4,000 percent. The output of automobiles in the

booming late twenties averaged 4,500,000 a year, with a capacity of over 7,000,000 cars. More than five million persons, almost an eighth of the gainfully employed, were dependent for their livelihood either directly or indirectly on the auto industry. Nowhere was the trend toward monopoly and centralization more apparent. Three corporations overshadowed all other competitors: General Motors sold 43.5 percent of all cars marketed in 1934, Ford Motors sold 28 percent, and Chrysler 22 percent.

The first automobile union appeared directly after the World War, an industrial organization independent of the A.F. of L., known as the United Automobile, Aircraft and Vehicle Workers. It disintegrated as a result of a strike defeat, which had been materially aided by the A.F. of L.'s usual tactic of attempting to divide workers into a variety of craft unions. Though the industry remained without organization, the Federation ignored the automobile workers completely until 1926 when delegates to the A.F. of L. Detroit convention urged a campaign to unionize the industry.

The leaders of the craft unions would not listen to proposals that for the duration of the organizing campaign in auto, all unions should waive jurisdictional claims. With this handicap, and as if to make doubly sure that the auto workers would remain outside the labor movement, the A.F. of L. started its drive by knocking at the doors of the Ford Motor Company and the General Motors Corporation and begging permission to form unions. The corporations refused: William Green sadly — and not too harshly — denounced the auto overlords and the campaign died before it had begun.

Here again the N.R.A. spurred automobile workers to demand organization. Wages of the most highly skilled had sunk to less than half the amount received in 1929: tool and design engineers, for example, who had been paid $2,717 a year in 1929, made approximately $1,300 in 1933. Per capita earnings of all auto workers averaged only $25 a week, with 45 percent of the men receiving less than $1,000 a year. As a result 60,000 auto workers entered federal unions between summer 1933 and March 1934. Moreover, independent unions appeared, such as the Mechanics Educational Society which enlisted skilled tool and die men, and after building its membership to 25,000 in six months expanded into an industrial union.

The N.R.A. required that even automobile corporations must sign a code. The owners decided to write their own ticket — neither the Federation nor the government objected to the companies' refusal to consult the workers. The code formulated allowed the manufacturers to hire and fire according to "merit" — in other words, employers had a free hand in sifting militants and thus evaded the clause in Section 7-A that prohibited discrimination. Furthermore, the code was so worded that restrictions on work time applied only to an average of hours worked by a man over several weeks: thus, five 48-hour weeks plus a sixth week layoff counted as six 40-hour weeks. Minimum wages were fixed at forty to forty-three cents an hour.

The rank and file threatened to strike against a code that nullified everything they had hoped to gain from Section 7-A. Trouble shooter Edward F. McGrady and conciliator Professor Leo Wolman devised the Automobile Labor Board as a solution to all friction — and the A.F. of L. officials obligingly canceled the strike until such time as the new Board handed down decisions. Presumably insuring workers against discrimination and guaranteeing collective bargaining, the Board permitted company unions proportional representation. Participation of company unions on the Board prevented workers from presenting a solid front in collective bargaining. This master stroke of compromise so outraged the rank and file that the majority bolted the federal unions. For nine long months, the Automobile Board heard complaints that the manufacturers violated the code, and yet it did nothing about them.

Early in 1935, after postponement was no longer possible, the Board held elections. Ninety percent of the 40,000 eligible participated, although by this time the A.F. of L. had repudiated the Board and advised boycott of the polls. The vote, overwhelmingly in favor of unaffiliated representatives, was proof of the workers' rejection of company unions and also of their disillusion with A.F. of L. policies. At the same time, it expressed the desire for a real collective bargaining agency.

Even the Auto Labor Board could not restrain rank and file restiveness forever. During the second week in April 1934, a federal local in the Toledo Electric Auto-Lite factory struck. The walkout rapidly turned into one of the most bitterly fought battles of the New Deal. Defying injunctions, mobilizing the unemployed, resisting brutal violence on the part of employers and the city government, the workers ended the strike with a partial victory. Again in 1935, what commenced as a local walkout soon threatened to stop all General Motors production. The Toledo strike turned out to be a bottleneck in the process of manufacture. Workers learned that by paralyzing one strategic link in the chain of production, they could cripple a corporation.

The primary problem confronting the 1935 Toledo strike was to keep Francis J. Dillon, Green-appointed head of the federal unions, from taking leadership of the auto local. Fears that Dillon would accept a weak compromise were not groundless. It took McGrady no time to persuade Dillon to sign an agreement — on McGrady's terms. Dillon arrived in Toledo after the strike had been in progress four days. He managed to prevent sympathy walkouts in Flint; but his agreement with McGrady, settling the strike, was speedily rejected by the men. Dillon knew the value of persistence; he again negotiated a settlement which granted practically no gains. Rank and file leaders failed to hold out with sufficient strength and Dillon persuaded the union to accept his contract.

Throughout this period, agitation for industrial unionism became firmer. The federal unions that made up the United Automobile Workers demanded industrial charters which Green and Dillon granted at the August 1935 convention. Green also pleaded that Dillon be elected president. The rank and file rejected the recommendation. Undeterred, Green swept the vote aside and appointed Dillon over the objections of the majority. For a year, the U.A.W. remained more or less inactive, until at the second convention in 1936, the members again repudiated Dillon and elected Homer Martin as president of the international. This time Green was unable to invalidate the election. Almost immediately the U.A.W. joined the C.I.O.

Homer Martin and the other newly elected officers immediately set about building the U.A.W. By the end of the year, auto workers had sufficient strength to strike the General Motors plants. With new forms of industrial organization went new forms of struggle. Adopting the sit-down tactic, the auto workers remained inside the General Motors factories at Flint and elsewhere, and succeeded in enlisting public support. The strikers defied injunctions, resisted gas attacks, withstood violence. For almost two months they stuck to their posts, reiterating their demand that before they vacated the factories the company must grant union recognition and collective bargaining agreements. The C.I.O. threw its full resources behind the U.A.W. Moreover, the strikers challenged Michigan's liberal Governor Murphy. They insisted that the Governor who had been elected by labor should compel General Motors to accede to legal demands incorporated in the Wagner Labor Relations Act.

Outside the factories, pickets massed in support of the sit-downers. Women joined the pickets and helped feed their husbands, fathers, brothers, and sweethearts. Well planned publicity informed the public by radio and newspaper of the strikers' struggle and the reasons for it. Neither the hastily organized vigilantes (labeled "loyal workers" and "citizens' committees" by the corporations), nor the frenzied opposition of the A.F. of L. executive council frightened the strikers or affected public sympathy. The combination of militant stay-in and walkout methods supplemented by elementary political pressure conquered General Motors.

The U.A.W., successful in its first major strike, pushed ahead to organize the rest of the industry. Studebaker, Reo, Hudson, Nash, signed in rapid succession. Chrysler resisted, and sit-downs closed the plants until such time as the union felt strong enough to convert the sit-down into a walkout. Chrysler, too, finally yielded. There remained but one formidable anti-labor stronghold in the industry, the Ford Motor Company. The union had grown by June 1937 to 350,000 members and had raised wages in industry by $250,000,000.

At the head of the U.A.W. stood a militant and progressive leadership that contrasted with the business-minded A.F. of L. officials. By and large, the U.A.W. officers were young, products of the rank and file. Here and there, several of them carried over illusions derived from the Federation. At times, one or two were misled into Red-baiting, but on the whole, the leaders reflected the progressive rank and file, and all were sensitive — some to a greater degree than others — to the desires of the membership.

The president of the United Auto Workers, Homer S. Martin, was born August 16, 1902, the son of a Middle Western school teacher. He was raised in the Illinois coal mining district, and during his childhood saw many a miners' picket line harassed by the local constabulary. By 1928, Martin graduated from the William Jewell College at Liberty, Missouri, where he had been national champion in the hop, skip and jump; by 1932, the young athlete was appointed pastor of the Baptist Church at Leeds, Missouri, a suburb of Kansas City. The life of the auto workers who formed most of his congregation became the subject of his sermons. "The man who pays workers less than a living wage," Martin declared, "and takes advantage of depression to drive down living standards and then comes to church on Sunday is no Christian but a carping hypocrite." The auto workers applauded Martin, but not the deacons of the church, and Martin was out of a job. For a while he worked in the Chevrolet plant. But his attempts to organize pleased the company no more than his sermons had pleased the deacons — and once again Homer Martin was unemployed.

Amiable, with a pleasant voice, bespectacled Martin developed into a sedulous organizer. He became president of a federal auto local, and later vice president under Francis Dillon of the new international. When the workers rebelled against the autocratic A.F. of L. leadership, they chose crisp-spoken Martin as head of the U.A.W., the youngest president until then of an international.

Wyndham Mortimer, first vice president, had a comprehensive grasp of the auto workers' plight. Hardly in his teens, he began to work in the mine pits, and by sixteen held a union card in the United Mine Workers. "My first memory," Mortimer once remarked, "is walking behind the parades of the striking miners in the little coal town where I was born." In childhood, Mortimer learned the first lessons of militant unionism, and was schooled to expect the usual discrimination suffered by an alert rank and filer. Along with his two brothers, Mortimer was dismissed from the mines for incessant talk of the benefits that unions could bring to workers. For the same reason, in 1910, he lost his job with a steel company in Lorain, Ohio. It was no accident that twenty-two years later, when workers in the White Motor Company began to show interest in a union, Wyndham Mortimer spurred them on. Elected president of the shop local, he organized the 2,200 employees who won a working agreement. In the 1936 U.A.W. elections, Mortimer was named vice president. His painstaking and careful preparations paved the way for the victory at Flint over General Motors.

A crop of auto leaders had pushed up from the ranks, and among them was George F. Addes. Born in 1907 in Wisconsin, he was the son of a railroad fireman and union member. After high school, Addes went to work in the Toledo Overland Plant as a metal polisher. In a short time he became a skilled metal finisher. By 1932, he had persuaded other workers to form a federal union and was soon elected financial secretary and shop committeeman. Remembering his leading rôle in the Auto-Lite and Chevrolet strikes, the membership of the U.A.W. in 1935 elected Addes secretary-treasurer.

The remaining vice presidents, Walter N. Wells and Edward Hall, had similar histories. "I absorbed trade unionism," Wells said, "with my earliest food because my father was an organizer for the Drop Forgers and Die Sinkers, and I heard labor principles from my birth." Hall, a large man, over 250 pounds, had a simple, forceful manner and a genial affability that workers liked. He served in France during the World War and was gassed in the Chateau Thierry offensive. In 1922, he obtained employment in the Kansas City railroad shops, but lost his job for activities in the railway shopmen's strike of that year. He traveled to Moline, Illinois, entered an auto-body plant, and by organizing the workers won several wage increases for the welders. In 1933, he formed a federal local of the A.F. of L. in a Milwaukee auto factory; by 1934, he quit his job to do organizational work in manufacturing and part plants throughout Wisconsin.

Aside from the international officials, heads of large locals also exerted powerful influence. There was Robert Travis, Flint organizer, who had worked in the automobile plants for thirteen years. "During this period," Travis explained, "I built up a terrific antagonism year after year to the general conditions of life. While working in the Toledo Overland factory," Travis continued, "I saw the real necessity of organization. We put in ten, twelve, even fourteen hours a night — all at high speed. When we finally decided on organization, we got six people to our first meeting. We were all green, but we decided to stick. . . . Finally attendance went to forty-two. From then on up the shop was organized." The union struck and won. Travis headed the publicity committee in the 1935 Toledo Chevrolet strike. As president of the local, he worked in the shop from six in the morning to two in the afternoon, "then to the office to handle steady streams of the 900 who were laid off" — blacklisted by the company. Travis felt a personal responsibility for these men, helped to pay their light bills, and to buy shoes and milk for their children out of his own salary. But he knew that those who had been blacklisted in Toledo could only be helped in any real sense by unionization of the entire industry. He traveled to Flint, assisted Wyndham Mortimer in the organizational work preparatory to tackling General Motors.

There was Richard T. Frankensteen, organizational director of the U.A.W. in Detroit, ex-football player, writer of musical comedies, law student and honor graduate of the University of Dayton. After working his way through college, he entered the Dodge factory, enlisted in the company union but within two weeks had dropped out in disgust. In its place, Frankensteen helped to organize an independent union, the Automotive Industrial Workers Association. Once the Chrysler strike had ended, he joined Walter Reuther in building the U.A.W. among Ford workers, with the result that both were mercilessly beaten by Ford's "service department" thugs. As a result the National Labor Relations Board charged the Ford Motor Company with responsibility for "malicious and brutal assaults" and with "coercion".

The three Reuther brothers, whose father had been a steel worker and an international organizer for the brewery workers union, had always heard socialism talked at home. Like their father the boys joined the Socialist Party. Walter, the oldest, went to work at sixteen as an apprentice in the tool and die trade. Three years later, in 1926, Walter traveled to Detroit, got a job on the night shift in the Briggs Body plant. As a skilled workman, he earned good pay, as high as $1.40 an hour. But because he campaigned for Norman Thomas in the 1932 presidential election, the Ford Motor Company laid him off. When Walter was discharged, he and his brother Victor decided to tour the world to study working conditions and the progress of the labor movement in other countries. They worked here and there at odd jobs, making their way through Germany, France, Italy, Austria, England, and finally to the Soviet Union where they were employed in the auto factories at Gorky. Walter became a brigade leader in charge of fourteen young Russian workers to whom he taught tool and die making. After a year, with sufficient money saved to resume their travels, they pushed on — through Central Asia,

Manchuria, China, Japan. On returning to America, Walter hurried to Detroit and again entered the auto plants. Discharged in 1936 for union activity, he became chairman of the Detroit organizing committee, and president of the West Side local of 20,000 members.

His brother Victor led a Detroit strike against the Kelsey-Hayes Wheel Company. It was Victor who talked over the loud speaker despite tear gas and police riot guns through the long night of police attacks against the Flint sit-down strikers. His younger brother Roy, after serving as workers' educational director of the Works Progress Administration in Flint, also became active in union work, organizing the successful bus drivers' strike, and later becoming Robert Travis' assistant.

Young, educated, progressive, the leaders of the United Auto Workers were as different from the corrupt A.F. of L. executive councilmen as the principles on which the C.I.O. rested were from the antique philosophy of the Federation. Gompersism rejected progressives, excluded them from leadership in the immobile craft unions, discouraged militancy; the C.I.O. accepted the younger men. By supporting the rank and file, by allowing the membership to control its own industry, by giving workers forms of organization which could resist the centralized management of modern mass-production industries, the C.I.O. leaders disproved the A.F. of L. premise that the huge rubber, steel, and auto corporations could invariably defeat unionization.

INDUSTRIAL UNIONISM gave workers a new form of organization and a new and powerful tactic — the sit-down strike which evolved logically from the centralization and trustification of American industry. Craft unionism had led only to defeat; industrial unionism promised solidarity, singleness of purpose, coördination of the offensive against the employers. As the C.I.O. initiated the campaign to organize the basic industries, the sit-down strategy grew out of the urgent need to preserve solidarity, to stop production in the huge plants, and to keep them shut until the companies agreed to bargain collectively. Sit-downs stole the march on the employers by preventing strikebreakers from replacing strikers, by hindering the usual police terrorization of picket lines. Nor was it an easy matter to eject workers once they had decided to remain within the factory.

The sit-down was not an entirely new weapon. Instances of stay-in strikes had occurred years before. Steel workers seized the Homestead plants in 1892; metal workers occupied mines in Telluride, Colorado, and engaged troops in pitched battle; the I.W.W. staged a good many stay-in and slow-down strikes. In 1906, a sit-down occurred at the Schenectady plant of the General Electric Company. Women garment workers in 1910 ceased operations without leaving the shops. Job-action strikes had occurred countless times in industry — the "quickees" of the maritime workers were similar in intent, as were the "skippies" of the auto workers who when the speedup became too intense would just neglect to work on one out of five cars that passed on the line. But not until 1936 when rubber workers began to sit down was this strategy used with widespread effectiveness in this country.

After the Firestone employees won a decisive victory in the beginning of 1936 by sitting down, rubber workers adopted the strategy as an important part of their strike equipment. Throughout the world the new technique was immediately popularized. And above all, the dramatic sit-down strikes of over a million French workers that followed the inauguration of the People's Front government in 1936 showed the full effectiveness of this new strike weapon.

A short sit-down had occurred in the auto industry as early as 1934. Yet auto workers did not remain in a factory overnight until November 1936. One month later, workers in the Flint General Motors plants inaugurated a sit-down strike that developed on a scale hitherto unknown in America. Thousands of well organized, peaceful, militant men stayed in the factories, while outside the plants huge picket lines guarded and encouraged those inside. The sit-down strike had altered from a spontaneous stoppage into a carefully planned offensive that necessitated highly efficient communication systems; coördination of the strategy of those inside and out of the plants; means of handling the food supply of the occupants, their sleeping arrangements, entertainment, discipline, sanitation, and defense against eviction.

Of course, the sit-down did not invalidate the older forms of strike action. In fact, to be effective, the sit-down had to be supported by large picket lines, and by the mobilization of workers in other industries to support those who remained within the factories. Moreover, in the event of eviction, the strike must be so organized that it could continue. Though the sit-down strikes were in no way revolutionary, since workers did not attempt or wish to seize the plants for purpose of operating the machines for themselves, they took on, nevertheless, a political character. By asserting that workers had rights to their jobs, the sit-downs gave workers' militancy a new meaning and clarified class relationships.

Not surprisingly, employers howled that the sit-downs robbed them of the use of their property. The courts obliged with a series of injunctions — which the General Motors strikers resisted so powerfully that the owners did not dare enforce the eviction order. Legislation declaring the sit-down illegal appeared in Congress — and was passed in several states. Workers, for their part, pointed out that sit-downers "seized" no property nor did they attempt to rob owners of the right to use their property except for the duration of the dispute. In strikes where effective picket lines were formed, production also ceased: the sit-down merely attained the same end more easily and efficiently. So soon as the employer bargained collectively and fairly with the union, the strikers willingly relinquished possession of the occupied factory. Workers, through their new tactic, matched rights enjoyed by the owners of property with the only property right they possessed — their vested interest in their jobs.

Lawyers debated the "legality" of the sit-down at great length, particularly the lawyers retained by the corporations. "Unconstitutional," "revolutionary," "subversive," "destructive of law and order" became familiar epithets. In essence, the argument was the age old conflict between workers and employers. The right to strike, the right to form unions, the right to picket had been greeted in the past by similar objections. The legality of the sit-down would in the last analysis be determined by the refusal of workers to relinquish a valuable form of struggle against oppression. Social change did not mark time until legislatures or courts controlled by the industrialists and bankers gave their sanction; new forms developed and gradually compelled the courts and politicians to acknowledge their existence. Until that time, workers would continue to sit-down despite employers and courts, legislatures and government officials, William

Green and the A.F. of L. executive council — despite all the reactionary groups that had always fought strikers. The verbiage of attorneys hired by corporations failed to refute the simple statement by Wyndham Mortimer, vice president of the U.A.W.:

> "The ethical issue in the sit-down strike concerns itself with the right of an employee to his job. According to the average standard of wages in industry today, practically every working family is only a few days removed from starvation. We must therefore ask ourselves whether the right of hiring and firing at a time when jobs are at a premium, can possibly be construed to be surrounded by such absolutistic and unassailable property prerogatives that it can literally place within the hands of an employer the power of life and death over the men who work for him.

> "No social conscience will grant any man such a right. By the same token, the worker has certain rights in his job. If he feels that collective bargaining through a national labor union is necessary for the preservation of those rights, he is definitely entitled to pursue such orderly methods as may force the employer to meet with his representatives in collective bargaining."

THE APPEAL by giant corporations to "law and order" which they pretended had been shattered by the sit-down technique, did not prevent industrialists from expending fortunes on spies, gangsters, and thugs in their efforts to intimidate employees into docilely submitting to the frightful conditions that prevailed in American industry. In 1936, labor spies and anti-union agents cost industry at least $80,000,000. Stoolpigeons and undercover operatives overran the plants; their function was to spread dissension in unions, spy on organizers and report workers' meetings, draw up blacklists and sway the policy of the rank and file so that attempts to improve conditions would meet with defeat. Spies were instructed to steal union files, to report conversations among the men, to attend meetings and get themselves elected to office, to offer bribes, to blackmail, advocate violence, force strikes prematurely, even to call on the wives of union workers and build up antagonism between them and their husbands.

Spying became a major industry. Seventy-five percent of the operatives involved in industrial undercover espionage worked in various labor organizations. Agencies employed Y.M.C.A. directors, educators, clergymen to spread anti-union propaganda, and bribed or tricked workers to inform on other workers, and kept the committed worker, once "hooked," on agency payrolls through blackmail.

During the Molly Maguire days, James McParland who drifted into the mine area was elected an official of the order, and later turned out to be a Pinkerton stoolpigeon. His testimony was sufficient to hang ten workers and sentence fourteen others to life imprisonment. Twenty years later, in 1892, 300 Pinkerton agents traveled by barges down the river to Homestead and opened fire on steel strikers. Thereafter, espionage systems expanded. The agents themselves were frequently ex-convicts. E. J. McDade, professional strikebreaker, testified that twenty percent of the operatives supplied by the Railway Audit and the Bergoff agencies had criminal records. For example, Sam "Chowderhead" Cohen, commissioned to break the 1936 elevator strike in New York City, had been arrested fourteen times, and convicted on five occasions on charges ranging from grand larceny to receiving stolen goods.

Pearl Bergoff started his lucrative strikebreaking and spy business in 1907. He did well but only came into his own during the decade after 1914 when he drew a salary of $100,000 plus bonuses and dividends aggregating $200,000 to $400,000 a year. By 1925, his personal fortune amounted to $4,000,000.

Employers were only too glad to pay handsomely for strikebreakers and spies. The Philadelphia Rapid Transit Company spent $836,856 to break a two months' strike in 1910. It cost the Interborough Rapid Transit $2,025,481 to smash the New York strike in 1916. The New York Railway Company paid $1,019,761 to stop the same strike. And all the big corporations considered the huge sums expended on various spy agencies as necessary overhead. Bell Telephone, American Woolen Company, American Sugar Refining, and Illinois Steel retained the Sherman Service even though a Sherman district agent had been indicted in Chicago, when inadvertently his instructions to operatives came to light and revealed that the "service" had ordered its agents to "stir up as much bad feeling as you possibly can between the Italians and the Serbians," in the steel strike of 1919. The Active Industrial Service ("Specialists in Labor Difficulties Adjustments") served such firms as the Clyde-Mallory Lines and the Erie Railroad. White Motors employed a Thiel subsidiary known as "The American Plan." Rubber companies in Akron engaged Bergoff. Chrysler hired the Corporations Auxiliary Co. General Motors, Texas Oil, Alka-Seltzer, Western Union, Kelvinator refrigerator, and the Chase National Bank, among others, employed the Railway Audit and Inspection Co.

The United States Steel Corporation and the Ford Motor Company perfected their own spy systems. So thorough was steel espionage that corporation files recorded the contribution by a Minnesota miner of twenty-five cents to a Socialist paper, the names of those who held union cards, and the political tendencies of workers in its many plants. Ford's service system, organized by Harry Bennett, coolly shot down five Detroit hunger marchers in 1932 when these workers came to the Ford plant to ask for jobs. In 1937, the Bennett army brutally beat U.A.W. organizers who dared distribute leaflets outside the Ford enclosure. Carefully nursed by reactionaries in the Middle West, the murderous Black Legion was also definitely linked to Harry Bennett. The Black Legion murdered George Marchuk in 1933, because the order disapproved of his union activities; murdered John Bielak of the Hudson Motor Company for the same reason; Red-baited, bombed, terrorized. As voluntary adjuncts to anti-labor organizations, the Daughters of the American Revolution and the National Civic Federation (to which Matthew Woll devoted a great deal of energy as Acting President until the A.F. of L. convention of 1935 made him withdraw) contributed Red-baiting propaganda to aid the corporations.

The case of Richard Frankensteen's friendship of over a year with John Andrews illustrated the ability of spies to worm their way into union offices and to become friends of union officials. John Andrews and his wife were constant companions of the Frankensteens. In 1935, the two families spent the summer together: Andrews' "rich uncle" arrived and paid for the Frankensteens' recreation. For the information that Andrews managed to glean from the young union leader, Chrysler paid nine dollars a day to the Corporations Auxiliary, of which Andrews received forty dollars a month. But Andrews was only one of a number of operatives; Chrysler spent $72,611.89 for agents in 1935. Even this sum was small compared to the $839,-764 expended by General Motors from January 1934 to July 1936.

Wherever big business spread, as the alert La Follette Senate

Committee on Education and Labor revealed, wherever unions threatened the absolutism of management, undercover men filtered into the shops, plants and factories, into union meetings. But the corporations did not rely on spies alone. Certain agencies, catering particularly to hotels, fingerprinted employees, forcing applicants for jobs to sign a contract reading: "I hereby waive all rights and consent that I be photographed and fingerprinted for the purpose of indentification and classification and that such a report shall be a permanent record for the American Confidential Bureau, Inc." If an employee joined a union or participated in a strike, full information about him was circulated by the Bureau to all companies buying the service. Other agencies made a specialty of providing armed guards. In the year 1934–35, Federal Laboratories, Inc., subsidiary of Railway Audit, made a profit of over one million dollars from the sale of ammunition, tear gas, rifles and machine guns.

For the most part, state governments ignored the extra-legal and violent activities of the large corporations; nor did the federal government act with the necessary resolution to stamp out spying and terrorism. True, Congress enacted a law prohibiting the transportation of strikebreakers across state lines. But more drastic legislation was imperative, legislation that would outlaw armed guards and private police, along with espionage departments, blacklists, fingerprinting of workers, and all other anti-union devices.

INDUSTRIALISTS refused to rely solely on spies and strikebreakers. In the post-war years, employers began to contrive schemes that ostensibly granted "organization" to employees, but which at the same time prevented strikes and "outside agitators." Wherever the threat of unionization endangered the management's power to hire and fire, to raise and lower wages at their own discretion, owners introduced company unions.

Immediately after the war such unions appeared in the metal trades, in the public utilities, and on the railroads. As a driving force behind such plans, which varied from industry to industry, lurked the Industrial Relations Counselors, controlled and supported by John D. Rockefeller, Jr. The purpose of the Counselors was to offer expert advice to companies which decided to set up some plan of "employee representation," or some other type of personnel activity.

By 1927, 1,400,000 workers had been sucked into company-dominated "unions"; one quarter of them were railroad workers. A year later, membership had risen to 1,600,000. But it was not until 1934, when the N.R.A. went into effect, that the company unions spurted vigorously ahead. Steel, auto, and other corporations saw the threat of Section 7-A and attempted to forestall unionization by bestowing company unions on the men, which in that year had at least 2,500,000 members.

Such organization was particularly useful in the mass-production industries. If the employees were not over-eager to join the company unions, employers had no trouble coercing men into them. With membership usually automatic, the company plans were not bona fide unions; members did not pay dues or hold regular meetings, have written contracts with the employers or maintain contacts with other worker organizations, retain the right to arbitration of grievances or consult with and receive the advice of outside experts. Company unions masked themselves with elaborate structural disguises, but they varied little so far as the lack of bargaining power went. In the majority of cases, they lacked treasuries; their officers and representatives were employed by the company; meetings were held at rare intervals; changes in the unions' constitutions rested almost invariably with the management. Though for the most part industrial in form, the company groups were limited to one plant, even to one department.

Both the Norris-LaGuardia Act, which outlawed the yellow-dog contract and made federal injunctions more difficult to obtain, and later the N.R.A. accelerated the corporations' desire to build controlled organizations. Often company unions took ingenious forms, some set up with two legislative bodies similar to the national Congress. Through the company unions, workers were able to correct minor abuses, such as improving sanitation, having a door closed or a window fixed. When workers desired better wages, shorter hours, improved working conditions, the right to bargain collectively, the right to outside arbitration, the company unions failed to function. No company union ever struck.

During the twenties, company unions made great progress in the railroad industry. Through these organizations, the companies negotiated wage cuts from 10 to 15 percent, and eliminated time and one-half for overtime. To some* extent, the Railway Labor Act of 1926 as amended in 1934 helped to eliminate company unions; on 77 railroads the brotherhoods replaced 550 false-front organizations. But this gain was made at the cost of a good many of labor's primary rights, in particular the ability of railroad unions to call strikes without endless delays and negotiations which in the majority of cases made walkouts unfeasible or impossible.

At annual A.F. of L. conventions, the executive council had long made it a habit to adopt resolutions attacking company unions, but it failed to take steps against them. The real attitude of Gompersites to company unions was revealed by Matthew Woll who feared that employer controlled organizations were "irresponsible," and therefore could easily be captured in the future by progressive workers who would use them as a basis for revolt against the A.F. of L.'s inaction. More concerned with the "Red" menace than with owners' ruses to defraud the workers, the Federation failed to penetrate the company unions and win them over.

For their part, workers corralled into company unions immediately after the N.R.A. soon began to chafe against them. In steel, discontent crystallized when members of the company unions called conventions of all employee-representation groups where delegates compared notes, and decided to present the management with demands for genuine collective bargaining. Simultaneously, the C.I.O.'s steel organizing committee started its whirlwind campaign. At once members of the company unions looked to the C.I.O. for guidance. Within a few months, with the aid of the Wagner Labor Relations Act which hindered company unions, these organizations had collapsed in the steel industry and the membership had entered the C.I.O. en masse. The United States Steel Corporation ceased to support its former employee-representation scheme. The automobile and rubber corporations transformed wrecked puppet groups into a new type of "independent" union composed of so-called "loyal workers" — actually nests of vigilantes and spies.

Company unions still clung tenaciously to those industries not yet invaded by the C.I.O. The A.F. of L. executive council, frantic at the desertion of hundreds of unions to the C.I.O., attempted to postpone its own death by taking over the company unions. It sent John P. Frey to Pittsburgh to assist the "independent" unions

dominated by the Carnegie-Illinois Steel Corporation — which rejected Frey's offer because the A.F. of L. still insisted on preserving craft forms. The Brooklyn Edison Company hurriedly signed a contract with the A.F. of L. to forestall C.I.O. organization. The contract, in reality a conspiracy between the executive council and the employers to invalidate the provisions of the Wagner Act, tacitly insured the company against strikes. The company's executive vice president made clear that the A.F. of L. contract assured freedom "from the possibility of any interruption in service due to labor disturbance. . . ." In other words, the alliance with the Federation protected the management against strikes as fully as the company union had done. By rubber stamping spurious groups, the council fooled a few of the workers into thinking that they had enrolled in authentic labor organizations. But the energy of the executive council was devoted solely to preventing the success of the C.I.O.

WORKERS in the needle trades had kept the industry comparatively free from labor spies and company unions. Concentrated for the most part in the large cities, the industry included a majority of foreign born workers who still remembered socialist ideas learned in the old countries, and who did not readily accept false theories of class collaboration. Throughout the early history of the garment unions, its workers showed an understanding of class relationships and a dogged militancy; only in the middle and late twenties did the disease of Gompersism begin to enervate the unions' leadership, weakening it and exposing it to factional struggles that resulted in splits and losses of membership.

The International Ladies Garment Workers Union was formed in 1900 with approximately 2,000 members. With a progressive program, the union grew steadily, until in 1920 membership exceeded 105,000, placing the I.L.G.W. among the first ten largest unions in the A.F. of L. It embraced workers producing women's wearing apparel — coats, dresses, raincoats, cloaks — as well as designers, embroidery and accessory workers. The union was organized semi-industrially as an amalgamation of craft locals.

During the twenties, the union faced decentralization of the industry, together with the simplification of styles and work methods which allowed manufacturers to employ at low wages unskilled women workers in rural areas and small communities. The chaotic setup of the industry, with its host of manufacturers, with its jobbers and contractors who often employed a handful of workers for a brief season, added to the difficulties of consolidating the union and maintaining protective standards. Moreover, in the twenties, reactionaries and some outright racketeers managed to infiltrate its ranks. There resulted factional fights and opposition to the officials' policy of collaboration. Revolt of the rank and file led to mass expulsions of militants, the sabotaging of strikes by the bureaucracy, and fierce Red-baiting. Local scabbed on local; the more progressive workers left the I.L.G.W. and joined the Needle Trades Workers Industrial Union affiliated with the Trade Union Unity League. By 1932, the membership had dropped to 40,000.

Throughout the factional struggle, David Dubinsky, the present president of the union, sided with the old guard. As a director of the employers' organization for the garment industry remarked some time later, "Mr. Dubinsky has been a most vigorous and effective opponent of the Communist or Left Wing element in our industry — Mr. Dubinsky's local was the 'last outpost' in the resistance to the Communist invasion of the industry." Yet years before, David Dubinsky had been persecuted as a revolutionary. Born in Brest-Litovsk, Poland, in 1892, he had been arrested for political activity at the age of fifteen, and only a year later, in 1908, was sentenced to eighteen months in prison for the crime of participating in a bakers' strike. Exiled to Siberia, the young Social-Democrat served five months and then managed to escape. He came to the United States in 1911 and immediately joined the I.L.G.W. But Dubinsky's revolutionary zeal faded, particularly after his election as president of his local in 1921. In its place, Dubinsky adopted many of the tenets of Gompersisms. As the I.L.G.W. disintegrated, as employers grew bolder and began to lower wages and repudiate contracts, Dubinsky and the other officers feared to resist, lest the union be smashed completely. Their caution only aided the owners further to weaken the union. In contrast to the officials' nervous reluctance to resist the campaign against the I.L.G.W., the Needle Trades Workers Industrial Union conducted strikes throughout the depression and won $1 to $3 weekly wages increases for 8,000 workers in the industry.

David Dubinsky was elected president of the union in 1932. A year later, when the N.R.A. was passed, the I.L.G.W. energetically recruited members, and after the independent Needle Trades Workers Industrial Union disbanded for the sake of greater unity in the industry, membership of the international rose to 210,000. The union won important concessions, strengthened, too, by the spread of industrial unionism. David Dubinsky, conscious of the influence of progressives in the rank and file, began to show greater willingness to coöperate with the militants. He supported the C.I.O. from its inception, though at first hesitantly. He also joined Sidney Hillman, again with some hesitation, in forming the American Labor Party in New York, which though it supported Franklin D. Roosevelt in the 1936 presidential election, made it clear that it did not accept the Democratic platform. Rather, it stood for independent political action by labor and its allies.

As it became clear that the A.F. of L. executive council would prefer to kill the labor movement than grant even the smallest concession to the C.I.O., Dubinsky's support of the C.I.O. grew increasingly aggressive. His union, one of the most progressive in America, voted large financial grants to the organizing campaign in auto, steel, and textile. Instituting liberal educational, cultural, and social projects, the I.L.G.W. membership also revealed a clear understanding of the danger to the working class from Fascism. The union contributed generously to the defense of the People's Government in Spain. Sensitive to pressure, Dubinsky realized he must keep in line with the wishes of the rank and file, and that he must take his place in the progressive union movement.

Not unlike Dubinsky in background and approach, though a stronger personality, Sidney Hillman had been president of the Amalgamated Clothing Workers since its formation in 1914. Born in Zagare, Lithuania, he entered while still a child the rabbinical school in Kovno, Russia. At fifteen, the boy had definitely decided that his sympathies would never permit him to become a rabbi; he left school to work in the revolutionary movement. During the 1905–1906 revolution, he was among the workers who seized Zagare in the name of the people, and was a member of the proletarian committee that governed the town. When the Czarist police entered Zagare, Sidney Hillman was forced to flee. Three times in 1906 he was arrested because of his political beliefs, and on the last occasion served six months in the Dvinsk jail. In 1907, he left Russia, making his way to England where he remained for a brief time before he took a boat to America. He settled in Chicago, became a clerk for Sears, Roebuck Company, and then a cutter for Hart, Schaffner and Marx, the leading men's clothing manufacturers.

The first great strike of men's clothing workers occurred in 1910 as a result of a walkout by sixteen girls in protest against a wage cut in a Chicago pants shop. The workers sought aid from the only trade union then existing in the industry, the United Garment Workers. Their appeal was received with indifference. Nevertheless, the strike spread, and pressure on the union grew until the U.G.W. was forced to grant the strikers a limited and grudging assistance. The strike compelled Hart, Schaffner and Marx to sign an agreement which set up an arbitration committee of three composed of one arbitrator selected by the workers and one by the employers, with the third chosen by the two already appointed.

To Hillman, the arbitration committee was a vital victory. In 1914, the union sent Hillman to New York to aid cloakmakers who were out on strike. Immediately afterward, Hillman attended the convention of the United Garment Workers at Nashville, Tennessee. The U.G.W. leadership, fearing the younger and more progressive delegates, decided to play safe by disfranchising a great bloc of militants who they expected would oppose them. The ousted delegates called a rump convention and there laid the base for a new union, the Amalgamated Clothing Workers of America with Sidney Hillman as president. The Amalgamated soon succeeded in recruiting a larger membership than the U.G.W., but opposition from the parent union prevented it from affiliating with the A.F. of L.

Scarcely less than a year old, the Amalgamated called a strike of 25,000 men's clothing workers in Chicago. The strike was unsuccessful, but it helped inaugurate a campaign of organization and education resulting in the successful strike of 1919 which finally consolidated the A.C.W. as a national union. The Amalgamated had won major gains for its membership; not only did it establish a forty-four hour week, but it also raised wages throughout the industry. When the union was formed in 1914, only 15 percent of the workers in the industry were earning $20 a week or over; in 1920, at least 85 percent earned $20 or over, and some received as high as $55 a week.

The Amalgamated, vigorous, militant, class conscious, an advocate of industrial unionism, donated $100,000 to the 1919 steel strike. Some years later, the A.C.W. subscribed $167,000 for foodstuffs, clothing, and machinery to be distributed by the Russian Red Cross. It advocated recognition of the Soviet Union, endorsed Eugene Debs for president, and favored labor's independent political action. It launched an ambitious educational program, developed a plan to give workers in the industry unemployment insurance, built coöperative apartment houses, set up sick benefits for the membership. Its progressive policies enabled it to organize over three-quarters of the men's clothing workers.

Sidney Hillman, in this period, had more and more tended to become what he considered a "sane" progressive. So long as the membership of the Amalgamated remained militant, Hillman was ready enough to allude to his revolutionary past, to his desire to see capitalism displaced eventually by some sort of socialist order. But as a false feeling of security and perpetual prosperity began to influence a certain portion of the A.C.W. membership, Hillman also showed signs of shifting his position. Socialism was saved for evening discussions, for quiet philosophical debates that did not affect union policies. Hillman became convinced that the Amalgamated should assist big business by helping to reorganize the clothing industry scientifically in a manner that would guarantee high profits. "Labor must act as a unit in each given industry," he proclaimed, "and, in the process, learn to look upon industry as a matter of vital concern . . . Labor must become industry conscious."

In his attempt to aid the employers Hillman gave his approval to speeding up the workers, condoning the profits of the manufacturers though wages failed to keep pace. Rank and file opposition grew. The quiet, square-chinned president of the Amalgamated made speeches couched in steadily sharper terms directed against the left-wing groups within the union. The Amalgamated began to lose members, and Hillman's denunciations, punctuated by quick, sharp gestures, took on a new bitterness. Employers who had slandered the A.C.W. commenced to praise Hillman: "He has never made demands on an industry that it could not meet economically, and he has been known to make concessions where the realities of the situation proved irresistible." Yet the more Hillman charmed the employers, the more members the Amalgamated lost. In the end, a large portion of the Amalgamated seceded from the union and joined the progressive Needle Trades Workers Industrial Union.

Hillman was also intrigued by what he considered the business opportunities open to the A.C.W. Like the railroad brotherhoods, the Amalgamated set up banks in Chicago and New York City, "to advance the class struggle." The banks lent money to employers out of their combined resources of twenty million dollars. But banking necessitated adoption of big business methods: when it came to cutting wages of employees, Hillman, like any other bank president, reduced pay 10 percent — and neglected to notify the workers in advance. He began to sympathize with the employers' need for cheaper labor: in the depression he abandoned struggle as a means to protect wage levels and instead accepted drastic pay cuts which he hailed as victories, since, he pointed out, each reduction could have been far more stringent. Sidney Hillman was transformed into a labor leader indistinguishable, in many respects, from the A.F. of L. executive councilmen.

As was the case with the I.L.G.W., the enactment of the N.R.A. awakened the smoldering militancy of the Amalgamated's rank and file. The union's large membership had dwindled considerably and was too poor to call a convention in 1933. To Hillman, the N.R.A. which he had been active in framing, represented "the realization of a dream." The Amalgamated recruited vigorously, raised membership in a year's time to 125,000. A strike involving 50,000 workers won new agreements and better conditions throughout the industry.

Hillman had returned to his old idea that without strong organization in the basic and mass-production industries, the labor movement was doomed and the Amalgamated along with it. Some of Hillman's former progressive tendencies reappeared. The Amalgamated, which had been admitted to the A.F. of L. in 1933, eagerly supported the industrial bloc within the Federation. When all attempts to influence the stubborn reactionaries of the executive council failed, Hillman joined John L. Lewis and others in setting up the C.I.O. His support, in contrast to Dubinsky's, was firm and wholehearted from the first. Active in forming the American Labor Party, he

backed it vigorously. With renewed confidence in the Amalgamated's strength, he pressed the employers for a revised contract and
negotiated a thirty million dollar wage increase for the workers in the
industry.

Hillman still refused, however, to press strenuously for a national
Labor Party. He continued to place undue confidence in Roosevelt.
But his advocacy of industrial unionism was both understanding
and progressive. To him was entrusted the campaign to organize
textile workers, probably the most formidable task yet undertaken
by the C.I.O. He was fortunate in having the aid and seasoned
advice of Francis J. Gorman, president of the United Textile Workers. Slowly, carefully, Hillman planned the strategy of the campaign:
it would require determination, patience, and great financial
resources. If Sidney Hillman succeeded in organizing the textile
mills, he realized that he would be delivering a telling, far-reaching
blow against one of the principal mainstays of the open shop.

FAR WORSE CONDITIONS prevailed in textile mills than existed
in any other major American industry. Speedup and stretchout
systems, starvation wages and child labor were taken for granted in
the New England and Middle Atlantic mills; in the South, where the
standard of living for all workers was invariably lower, the lot of textile employees was an ugly exaggeration of every abuse inherent to
predatory capitalism. Particularly was the use of child labor widespread in the industry. In the first years of 1900, over 69,000 children
were employed in the mills along the Atlantic seaboard. Following
the war, overproduction caused the textile companies to intensify the
scramble for profits, with the result that the employment of cheap
child labor increased. Practically every worker in the industry
started in the mills as a child and spent the rest of his life in what
amounted to slavery. Few managed ever to raise their earnings above
$17 a week.

A host of ills afflicted the textile industry: an anarchical system of
distribution; the expansion of the wool industry which increased
equipment by over 30 percent during the War; the construction
of new cotton mills in the South; the invasion of the rayon industry
which cut into the profits of other textile manufacturers; technological advances that reduced the demand for skilled workers and

increased the volume of production per mill hand. All these factors contributed to the establishment of a wage level lower than that paid by any other manufacturing industry, with the possible exception of wages in tobacco plants.

At the turn of the century, cotton manufacturers began to move South to save money on the transportation of raw goods to the mills. Moreover, costs were lower because the southern states did not tax manufacturers so heavily as did the northern states, because power was cheaper and because, most important of all, fewer labor laws impeded owners. Though the union movement was weak in the North, it was almost non-existent in the South. Wages were consequently lower, hours longer. In turn, the new competition of the southern mills helped to reduce wages and lengthen hours in the North.

In 1927, while most industries were at the peak of post-war prosperity, profits in textiles narrowed and the average earnings of workers in the cotton mills fell to 37 percent below the average maintained by all manufacturing companies. In addition, textile mills were crowded, causing industrial accidents to mount. Tuberculosis and pellagra, diseases of poverty, were common among the workers. In an industry that employed approximately one-eighth of all workers engaged in manufacturing, with women constituting about half of the total working forces in the cotton mills, wages of women mill hands dropped in 1928 to $11.88 a week in Alabama; $12.32 in South Carolina; $14.62 in North Carolina. In these states men earned $14.58, $15.46, and $17.41 respectively. The average work week fluctuated between 55 and 64 hours. During the depression, wages fell again; speedup and stretchout further undermined health.

The average woman worker rose at four or five in the morning, prepared breakfast, and then hurried to the mill. In the half or three-quarter hour lunch period, she rushed home to prepare a hasty meal and once again returned to the mill. After a day averaging ten to twelve hours of intense work in the plant, she had supper to cook, housework to finish, children to care for. She continued in the factory until two or three weeks before childbirth, and five or six weeks after the child was born was back in the mills. A Passaic woman described her life: "All time work, night, day — no wonder me skeeny." From girlhood to premature old age, mill town women spent their lives in the plants, a nightmare existence of slavery, sickness, and despair.

Women, who were employed for less wages, competed against the male workers, depressing wages to a starvation level. Mill owners in the South played the unorganized Negroes against the unorganized whites, fostering race hatred. Since Negroes invariably received even less pay than the whites, the employers used them to slash the white's low scale of pay. Meager wages made the struggle to eat a daily haunting worry, and mill workers were forced to send their children into the factories, with the result that the employers had still another weapon to pare wages. The owners encouraged child labor by demanding that textile workers supply their quota of children to the mills on pain of discharge and eviction from company-owned shacks. In Gastonia, a mill worker complained: "We can't get a house from the mill. We've only been married a few years and haven't any children old enough to work in the mill. The Manville Jenckes people insisted that there must be at least three workers in the family before they will rent a house."

But there was nothing docile about the textile workers. Fierce struggles marked the history of the industry. Strikes were suppressed with furious violence and in bloody battles between workers and strikebreakers, vigilantes, state troops, and police. The A.F. of L. offered the textile workers little assistance, even when strikers were members of A.F. of L. unions. The executive council feared organizing among the semi-skilled and unskilled mill workers, feared the militancy such strikes aroused, and the long, hard, bitter struggle necessary to unionize the plants. In 1929–30, when the United Textile Workers, then affiliated with the A.F. of L., was authorized to press an organizational campaign throughout the South, the A.F. of L. top leadership explained that the purpose of the drive was to bring efficiency to the industry (which had already perfected speedup and stretchout to a degree unsurpassed in any other industry), to reduce production costs, to eliminate waste, to introduce business methods. "No chaos and violence," promised the union heads; the campaign must be, in William Green's words, a "mission of peace and hopefulness." As Thomas F. McMahon, then president of the United Textile Workers, explained,

"We aren't talking higher wages. We aren't talking shorter hours, we can't express our objective in those terms. We want to sit down with the mill owners, we want to take up their problems as our problems, we want the mill owners, ourselves, and the general public to sit down and diagnose the industry's ills and seek mutually a means to heal them."

The campaign was a huge success. A.F. of L. officials made speeches and William Green attended countless banquets tendered by Chambers of Commerce and business men's clubs. The only thing the junketeers neglected was to organize the workers. But then this oversight was rectified by the large owners who busily recruited mill hands into company unions which did their bit to aid textile workers by giving "collective" approval to further wage cuts, further intensification of production.

There was, however, nothing new in the failure of organizational attempts among textile workers. As early as 1834, 2,000 girls walked out of the mills at Lowell, Massachusetts, in protest against lowered wages. "As our fathers resisted unto blood the lordly avarice of the British ministry," they stated in a proclamation, "so we, their daughters, never will wear the yoke which has been prepared for us." In 1858, skilled textile workers formed the National Cotton Mule Spinners Association; twenty years later, the International Labor Union, enlisting 8,000 unskilled workers, came into existence. But these early unions were sporadic affairs which fell apart after a few years. The Knights of Labor set up a union that carried on a number of strikes in the cotton mills. With the decline of the Knights in 1891, the International Union of Textile Workers (A.F. of L.) organized some mills in New England. In 1901, this union merged with the United Textile Workers of America, also affiliated with the A.F. of L. The new union included most of the textile unions in the industry, though cotton workers predominated. It had as its purpose the "mutual protection against the grasping combination of organized capital." But this clause was eliminated two years later in favor of a union label to be offered to "friendly employers."

Workers were dissatisfied with the U.T.W. Searching for leadership, they accepted I.W.W. aid in the bitter strikes of Lawrence, Mass. (1912), and Paterson, New Jersey (1913). But with the War, which gave impetus to organization, the U.T.W. overcame some of the dissatisfaction and was able to enlist thousands of members. In 1919, the union again faced revolt when workers from Lawrence, Paterson, Passaic and other textile centers formed the Amalgamated Textile Workers of America which grew to 40,000 in a year. It began as a protest against the failure of the U.T.W. to support locals during strikes after giving promises of benefits, and, in addition, against the arbitrary dictation of the national office, the undemocratic methods of handling grievances, the failure of leaders to listen to the desires of the rank and file, and the reactionary policies and timidity of union officials. The Amalgamated Textile Workers won several strikes, but after losing an important New England offensive in 1922, went out of existence in 1924 and left the field open once more to the U.T.W. Not for long, however. The leadership of the union had learned nothing from the Amalgamated's criticisms. In protest against the failure of the U.T.W. to organize and win benefits, the National Textile Workers Union was formed late in the twenties.

Strikes occurred throughout the post-war decade. At Paterson, New Jersey, an independent union, the Associated Silk Workers, conducted a strike in 1924. The Communists headed long struggles against extreme exploitation in Passaic, New Jersey (1926), and in Gastonia, North Carolina (1929). The Passaic strike against a ten percent wage cut, headed, among other leaders, by Ella Reeve Bloor, William F. Dunne, Lena Chernenko, and Alfred Wagenknecht, forced a few mills to capitulate, but was defeated by terror and Red-baiting. In Gastonia, the terror was augmented, workers were sent to jail for as much as twenty years, and the government took no steps against vigilantism and owner-sheriff violence. Clarence Miller, Amy Schechter, Sophie Melvin, and Clarina Michelson aided greatly in mobilizing the textile workers. The strike, despite its defeat through intimidation, succeeded in exposing the misery of the southern mill workers.

The United Textile Workers was also involved in strikes in Marion, North Carolina, and Elizabethton, Tennessee, both in 1929. But though walkouts occurred repeatedly in the mills, the conditions of textile workers failed to improve. The A.F. of L. leadership spent its time Red-baiting, and denouncing the Communists who were the only group realistically attempting to organize the mills and win the workers some alleviation from oppression. The result of A.F. of L.

blundering was a steady decline in U.T.W. membership, which dwindled from 105,000 members in 1920 to 27,500 in 1932.

The organizational drive that took place in the textile industry following the N.R.A., enlisted approximately 300,000 workers. Minimum wages provided in the textile code called for the low rates of $12 a week for southern workers, $13 for northern, with hours reduced to forty-eight. The code recommended, moreover, collective bargaining and the elimination of child labor. But the employers recognized no code restrictions. Wages and hours failed to conform, children continued to work in the mills. The National Labor Relations Boards for the industry ignored the stream of worker complaints. Yet other provisions of the N.R.A. textile code proved exceptionally satisfactory to the companies; in six months they had wiped out the previous years' deficit of $14,000,000 and had replaced it with a profit of $13,000,000.

Discontent among textile workers grew. The U.T.W., no longer able to prevent a strike, finally called a national walkout in the autumn of 1934. Demanding a thirty-hour week, a minimum weekly wage of $13 for the unskilled, $30 for the highly skilled, elimination of the stretchout, recognition of the union and reinstatement of all strikers, the 300,000 U.T.W. strikers were joined by 175,000 other mill hands still unorganized. At the head of the general strike committee was Francis J. Gorman, vice president of the U.T.W.

Young, stocky, energetic, Francis Gorman had come to America in 1903 from Bradford in Yorkshire County, England. His father had owned a small pub where Bradford mill workers wrangled over their ale about their union and imperial politics. Almost immediately after arriving in this country, the thirteen year old boy entered the textile mills in Providence, Rhode Island, where he worked for $4 a week.

Gorman was named union organizer in 1922. Six years later he was elected vice-president of the U.T.W. His first big task was to organize the 1929 strike in Marion, North Carolina, during which six workers were killed. "We buried them out in the open," Gorman remarked, "under the sky. I'll never forget that."

When Gorman in 1934 took charge of one of the biggest strikes yet conducted by American workers, he faced an immense problem of organization. In the South, Gorman knew that Negroes would be played against whites and that the National Guard, vigilantes, and "loyal workers" would be mobilized in full force. In the North, he realized, the problems would be almost as difficult. Besides, the strike would cover an area of thousands of miles, a walkout of half-starved workers of all races, foreign and native born, for the most part new to the union movement. The union treasury was almost empty.

Gorman's organizational skill, his flare for publicity, his tireless energy kept the militancy of the strikers steadily rising. He perfected a new tactic, the flying picket squadron: after closing one factory, workers would jump into old cars and invade the next mill town before the police could organize to prevent picketing. Despite concentration camps into which, as in Georgia, strikers were herded, despite attempts in all localities to scare workers back to their jobs, the strike closed the large mills and many of the smaller ones.

But Francis J. Gorman, for all his talents, still clung to A.F. of L. traditions. He rebuffed coöperation from left-wing organizations, and even aided the Red-scare raised automatically by the employers as soon as the workers formed their picket lines. Though many of the left-wing groups continued to support the strike, the owners took Gorman's words to use against the strikers.

Just as the strike had reached its height, just as the companies seemed to be weakening, Gorman ordered the workers to return to the mills. The Winant Committee, set up by President Roosevelt to recommend some basis of arbitration, had issued its report which suggested a more thorough investigation of the textile industry. Until then, the report urged the strikers to go back to work under conditions prevailing before the strike. The committee did not even endorse complete recognition of the union, though it indicated that labor complaints could be taken to the Textile Labor Relations Board. But the authorities had been hearing complaints against the stretchout for months before the strike and had dismissed 900 of the 900 complaints presented to it.

Gorman trusted that the investigation suggested by the Winant Board would rectify many of the abuses in the industry. He relied on President Roosevelt's reassuring words, pronounced the strike at an end, and sat back confidently to await the reforms that the liberal New Deal would introduce. He waited in vain. Nothing had changed — except that hundreds of militants had been added to the blacklists. The stretchout and speedup continued, children still worked in the mills, wages remained at $6 to $10 a week. Gorman's faith in the N.R.A. went unrewarded. And naturally the membership of the U.T.W. fell off sharply.

It was a revealing lesson for Gorman. He had been fooled once but he did not intend to be fooled again. Beyond all argument, he now knew that an isolated union could not expect to conquer a powerful industrial group such as the textile owners without full support from other unions. The A.F. of L. executive council had failed to provide this all-important aid. The conclusion was clear — workers could no longer allow antiquated Gompersism to rob them of their strength. Gorman was drawn irresistibly into the bloc that demanded industrial unionism and that later formed the C.I.O.

Even then, the lesson was not complete. Reliance on the government, Gorman saw, had tricked him into relinquishing a powerful strike. Once again, old precepts that the A.F. of L. refused to challenge, had been proven false. And as Gorman considered the problem of the relationship between the labor movement and government, complicated still more by the danger that Fascism held for the working class, he began to grope toward independent political action as a solution. In a year, his troubled questioning had ended and in its place was Gorman's conviction that a Farmer-Labor Party was as essential to the health of the workers as industrial unionism. "We have two courses," Gorman declared. "First, the building and strengthening of our trade union movement until the millions of workers in mass-production industries are organized; and second, building and strengthening our Labor Party until we have a solid People's Front against the power of industry and wealth which keep us in subjugation at the pc ʰt of a bayonet and make us starve without a word of protest."

The membership of the U.T.W. elected Gorman president in 1936 to replace Thomas McMahon who retired to a political job in Rhode Island. By June 1937, the C.I.O. Textile Workers Organizing Committee had started its arduous campaign. But in the few months since its inception, the committee had won contracts that covered 160,000 textile workers and had brought 150,000 into the union. There remained nearly 1,000,000 workers in the industry to be enlisted, but with the C.I.O. behind the textile drive Gorman had confidence in the future. He looked forward to the victory that had been withheld in 1934, and to the impetus it would give toward "a militant, courageous and statesmanlike Labor Party movement, based on the organized workers of America and pledged to a program protecting the rights of the people."

THE LEADERS of the C.I.O. bade goodbye to Gompersism. The executive council still trudged the familiar, meandering path that always circled back to its starting point. But those who followed the council grew steadily fewer in numbers. For the C.I.O. had chosen a clearly marked highway to travel, a highway that had a destination where all workers, whether of hand or brain, would finally be organized.

The progress of the C.I.O. challenged the executive council as it challenged all tyranny that impoverished American life. Desperate in its hate, the repudiated old guard watched the C.I.O.'s advance which presaged its doom. It was a doom deferred only by the industrialists who were willing to keep the council alive so long as it had value in the fight against the C.I.O.

In the words of John L. Lewis, "The C.I.O. has caught the imagination of the American workingman. It offers him hope for the future and he is lending that Committee and the organizations enrolled in it, his strength, his fealty, his service and his influence." Carefully, but with onrushing momentum, the C.I.O. had achieved in two years its immediate tasks. For American workers, that was sufficient proof of the C.I.O.'s integrity and direction.

What lay ahead was clear. With a sure, firm foundation, the C.I.O. promised protection to groups never fully mobilized into labor's organized ranks — to women and youth, to Negroes and other racial minorities, to white-collar and professional employees, and to agricultural workers. In addition, through a strengthened Labor's Non-Partisan League, and in conjunction with the urban and rural middle classes, the C.I.O. anticipated political self-expression of the American people rooted in the labor movement. As industrial unionization advanced, as groups battered by political issues found their new positions in the transformed political scene, the progressive forces within the disintegrating Democratic Party, in alliance with the already existing farmer-labor groups, would evolve into a national Farmer-Labor Party — an American People's Front. The danger was delay. Reaction, in its headlong race toward Fascism and war, did not procrastinate. In reorienting American life, the C.I.O. vitalized the American tradition of militant democracy, the passionate belief in freedom and progress.

A FEW LABOR TERMS *

Allied Trades Council: An organization of local unions in related trades in one town or locality.

Amalgamation: The merger of two or more local, national or international unions to form a single organization.

Anti-Union Shop: A shop that is "open" to non-unionists but is "closed" by the employer to trade unionists, although often some form of company union is permitted.

Arbitration: A method of settling a labor dispute through hearings and a decision mutually binding by an agency that is acceptable to both the employer and the employees, such as an umpire, a committee or a board.

Blacklist: In its simplest form, a roll of workers' names privately circulated among employers for the purpose of jointly refusing employment to union workmen in general or to individual workers who are held in disfavor.

Business Agent: The paid representative of a local trade union or other labor body, whose function it is to look after all "outside" interests of the union, particularly the relations of union members to their employers. Also called a walking delegate.

Check-off System: An agreement between the employer and the union by which fines, dues and assessments are deducted from earnings and paid by the employer to the union collector.

The term "check-off system" is also sometimes applied to the method of deducting from the workers' wages amounts due the employer for merchandise bought in company stores, rent for occupancy of company houses, fees for company doctors, and similar charges.

City Central: A delegate body representative of the various local unions in one city and the outlying districts. Also, a federation of local unions in one city for joint action on matters of common interest. A central labor union acts as a clearing house for the discussion of matters of mutual interest to its members and encourages

---

* These labor definitions are taken for the most part from W. R. Browne's *What's What in the Labor Movement*, New York, 1921.

the organization of workers. Ordinarily, a central labor union does not have jurisdiction over matters involving trade union autonomy, such as the ordering of a strike, the initiating of a boycott, or the negotiating of a trade agreement.

Closed Shop: A plant in which only union members are employed in those crafts or occupations for which labor unions have been organized in the district in which the plant is located; or a shop in which only members of the union claiming jurisdiction are allowed to retain employment.

Collective Bargaining: The method or process of determining the specific conditions of the labor contract — particularly wages, hours and working conditions — by direct negotiations between the representatives of one or more trade unions, on the one hand, and of an employer or association, on the other, and terminating in a written agreement between both parties.

Company Union: An organization of workers, financed and dominated by employers, within a particular shop or establishment, and having no connection or association with what employers call an "outside union," and no means for *bona fide* collective bargaining. Also called employee-representation plan, yellow union, American plan, etc.

Conciliation: In an industrial sense, the settlement or attempt at settlement of an industrial dispute by mutual agreement between the parties involved, without submitting the case to arbitration.

Craft Union: In its simplest and commonest form, the craft union is made up of workers engaged on a single industrial process, or on several processes so nearly akin that one worker can do the work of any other worker. Organized on a horizontal basis, craft unions cut across industries.

Federal Union: A labor union chartered by and affiliated directly to the American Federation of Labor in a craft or industry for which no international or national union exists. The main function of a federal labor union is to gather and hold together scattered local workers in different crafts or trades until a local trade union is formed, or until workers can be allocated to already existing unions. Federal labor unions pay larger dues to the A.F. of L. than national or international unions.

Federation: An alliance of a group of unions in one or several industries, covering either a single locality, district, state or country.

Industrial Union: A local or national union in which membership is open to all workmen in the industry irrespective of occupation, skill or craft. Broadly, and to some extent theoretically, an industrial union comprises all workers of an entire industry — all who coöperate to produce a common product or type of product, or to render a common service.

International Union: In the American labor movement, there is little if any real distinction between the "national" and "international" unions as types of labor organizations; as a rule, the "international" has local units in Canada and perhaps in Mexico, while as a rule the "national" has not. At best, the American "international" is commonly a "continental" union.

Lockout: The temporary closing down by the employers of a factory or an industry in order to force the workers to agree to conditions dictated by the owners.

Mediation: That form of conciliation in which an outside agency is used as a go-between by the contending parties — an agency which endeavors to help the disputants arrive at a mutually acceptable settlement.

Preferential Shop: A plant in which union members are given preference in employment, by agreement with the union. In some cases, the employer agrees also to discharge future employees within a specified period after they are hired if the new employees refuse to join the union.

Yellow-Dog Contract: A contract forced by the management on individual employees in which the workers pledge themselves not to join a union; and in some cases, pledge not to strike.

GENERAL REFERENCES

Beard, Charles A., and Mary R., *The Rise of American Civilization*, New York, 1930. One Volume Edition

Bimba, Anthony, *History of the American Working Class*, New York, 1936. Fourth Edition

Commons, John R., and Others, *History of Labour in the United States*, Volumes I and II, New York, 1936

Cummins, E. E., *The Labor Problem in the United States*, New York, 1932

Foster, William Z., *Misleaders of Labor*, Chicago, 1927

Foster, William Z., *From Bryan to Stalin*, New York, 1937

Hoxie, R. F., *Trade Unionism in the United States*, New York, 1923

Labor Research Association, *Labor Fact Books I, II, III*, New York, 1931, 1934, 1936

Lescohier, D. D., and Brandeis, E., *History of Labor in the United States: 1896–1932*, Volume III, New York, 1935

Lorwin, Lewis L., with the assistance of Flexner, J. A., *The American Federation of Labor*, Washington, D. C., 1933

Lozovsky, A., *Marx and the Trade Unions*, New York, 1935

Perlman, S., and Taft, P., *History of Labor in the United States: 1896–1932*, Volume IV, New York, 1935

Stewart, Estelle M., *Handbook of American Trade-Unions*, United States Department of Labor, Bureau of Labor Statistics, Bulletin No. 618, Washington, D. C., 1936

Ware, Norman J., *Labor in Modern Industrial Society*, Boston, 1935

CHAPTER REFERENCES

CHAPTER I

Clapper, Raymond, "Labor's Chief: William Green," *Review of Reviews*, November, 1933

Daily Worker, July 7, 1934; September 5, 1935; October 8, 1935

Federated Press Bulletin, September 18, 1929, June 2, 1930; December 14, 1931

Green, William, *Modern Trade Unionism,* Washington, D. C., 1925. Pamphlet

Green, William, *Unions Reduce Industrial Waste,* Washington, D. C., 1925. Pamphlet

Green, William, "Lessons from the British Strike," *Forum,* September, 1926

Green, William, "We Need Peace in Industry," *World's Work,* March, 1928

Green, William, *For Better Understanding,* Washington, D. C., 1930. Pamphlet

Green, William, *Labor Proposes Coöperation,* Washington, D. C., 1930. Pamphlet

Green, William, "Recent Trends in the Organized Labor Movement," *Annals of the American Academy of Political and Social Science,* May, 1930

Green, William, "The Spirit of Labor," *Vital Speeches,* June 17, 1935

"Labor Week in Washington," *Business Week,* October 7, 1933

"Labor's Ultimatum to Industry," *Literary Digest,* December 10, 1932

"The New Head of Organized Labor," *Review of Reviews,* February, 1925

"The New Man At Labor's Helm," *Literary Digest,* January 10, 1925

New York *Post,* October 7, 1935; December 20, 1935; July 10, 1936

New York *Times,* October 10, 1935

"Nothing Radical Here," *Outlook and Independent,* October 14, 1931

Pringle, H. F., "What Labor Really Wants," *American Magazine,* April, 1935

Report and Recommendations of the California State Unemployment Commission, Sacramento, 1933

Reprint of a speech made by William Green before the New York Chamber of Commerce, *Justice,* November 26, 1936

Stachel, Jack, "The 56th Convention of the A.F. of L.," *Communist*, January, 1937

Stelzle, Charles, "The 'Monroe Doctrine' of the Industrial World," *Outlook*, October 28, 1925

Stolberg, Ben, "The End of the Gompers Tradition," *Independent*, February 14, 1925

Stolberg, Ben, "William Green's Convention," *Nation*, November 3, 1926

Stolberg, Ben, "Easy-Going Bill Green," *Today*, May 5, 1934

Sunday Worker, February 9, 1936

Wallen, T. C., "William Green, Labor Conciliator," *Literary Digest*, July 20, 1935

Walling, W. E., *American Labor and American Democracy*, New York, 1926

Woolf, S. J., "William Green Tells Labor's Side of the Story," *Literary Digest*, June 23, 1934

CHAPTER II

Adamic, Louis, *Dynamite: The Story of Class Violence in America*, New York, 1934. Revised Edition

Appeal of Local Union No. 376 to the membership of the United Brotherhood of Carpenters and Joiners of America and to the twenty-second general convention from the decision of General President Wm. L. Hutcheson and the General Executive Board, Brooklyn, N. Y., 1926

"The Carpenters Convene," *New Republic*, December 23, 1936

Constitution and Laws of the United Brotherhood of Carpenters and Joiners of America, as amended April, 1929.

Cummins, E. E., "Political and Social Philosophy of the Carpenters' Union," *Political Science Quarterly*, September, 1927

Cummins, E. E., "Jurisdictional Disputes of the Carpenters' Union," *Journal of Economics*, May, 1926

Daily Worker, August 20, 1931; November 28, 1933; January 10, 1934; June 1, 1936; October 24, 1936; December 4, 1936; April 28, 1937

Federated Press Bulletin, December 11, 1936; December 15, 1936

The General Executive Board vs. Local Union 1051, U.B. of C.J. of A. Philadelphia, 1933

"Golden Jubilee Number," *The Carpenter*, August, 1931

Levinson, Edward, "Bill Hutcheson's Convention," *Nation*, January 2, 1937

New York *Times*, November 2, 1935; January 16, 1936; January 26, 1936; July 10, 1936; August 2, 1936; August 5, 1936; August 6, 1936; August 14, 1936; September 7, 1936; October 16, 1936; November 28, 1936

An Open Letter to the Delegates of the twenty-third convention of the U.B. of C.J., Progressive Bloc, Newark, N. J., 1936

Proceedings of the 21st, 22nd, 23rd, General Conventions of the U.B. of C.J. of A., 1924, 1928, 1936

Progressive Building Trades Workers, *What's Wrong in the Carpenters' Union*, Chicago, 1925. Pamphlet

Ryan, F. L., *Industrial Relations in the San Francisco Building Trades*, Norman, 1936

Seidman, Harold, *Labor's Czars*, first draft of manuscript

Statement by the National Rank and File Committee in the U.B. of C.J. of A., New York, 1935

Steele, James, "The Decline of a Brotherhood," *New Republic*, March 14, 1934

CHAPTER III

Anderson, Paul Y., "So They Found The Body," *Nation*, February 21, 1934

"The Automobile Armistice," *New Republic*, April 4, 1934

Berman, Edward, *Labor Disputes and the President of the United States*, New York, 1924

Bernheim, A. L., and Van Doren, D. (editors), *Labor and the Government*, New York, 1935

Boudin, Louis B., "The Supreme Court and Civil Rights," *Science and Society*, Spring Quarterly, 1937

Brissenden, P. F., "Campaign Against the Labor Injunction," *American Economic Review*, March, 1933

Brissenden, P. F., "The Labor Injunction," *Political Science Quarterly*, September, 1933

Clapper, Raymond, "The Labor Lobby at Washington," *Review of Reviews*, May, 1934

Clapper, Raymond, "Strikes," *Review of Reviews*, October, 1936

Cohen, E. E., *The Yellow Dog Contract*, New York, 1932. Pamphlet

Commons, J. R., and Andrews, J. B., *Principles of Labor Legislation*, New York, 1936. Fourth Revised Edition

"A Conspiracy by Lawyers," *Nation*, October 2, 1935

Daily Worker, May 2, 1933; September 25, 1935

Daugherty, C. R., *Labor Problems in American Industry*, Boston, 1933

Federated Press Bulletin, January 20, 1933; January 22, 1934; August 7, 1935

Garrison, L. K., "New Techniques in Labor Settlements," *Survey Graphic*, April, 1935

Hallgren, M. A., "Labor Under the New Deal, *Current History*, September, 1935

Henderson, H. C., "In A Velvet Glove," *Today*, December 12, 1936

Johnson, E. M., "Minimum Wage Legislation," *American Federationist*, July, 1936

Kiplinger, W. M., "The Political Role of Labor," *Annals of the American Academy of Political and Social Science*, March, 1936

Labor Research Association, *Labor Notes*, October, 1935; March, 1937

Lauck, W. J., "Coal Labor Legislation: A Case," *Annals of the American Academy of Political and Social Science*, March, 1936

Letter from Roger Baldwin to the *Nation*, March 14, 1934

MacDonald, L., and Stein, E., *The Worker and Government*, New York, 1935

"McGrady: America's Champion Strike-Breaker and Peacemaker," *News-Week*, October 5, 1936

New York *Times*, August 1, 1933; August 8, 1933; August 9, 1933; August 19, 1933; September 29, 1933; June 27, 1934; July 16, 1934; July 30, 1935; October 13, 1935

New York *Times Magazine*, October 13, 1935

Perkins, Frances, "A National Labor Policy," *Annals of the American Academy of Political and Social Science*, March, 1936

Perlman, Selig, *History of Trade Unionism in the United States*, New York, 1922

Slichter, S. H., "Labor and the Government," *Yale Review*, December, 1936

Stein, E., Raushenbush, C., and MacDonald, L., *Labor and the New Deal*, New York, 1934

Todes, Charlotte, *The Injunction Menace*, New York, 1932. Pamphlet

"Trouble To Be Shot," *Time*, November 23, 1936

Ward, Paul W., "Please Excuse Miss Perkins," *Nation*, March 27, 1935

Witte, E. E., "What Congress Did for Labor," *New Republic*, July 11, 1934

Wolman, Leo, *The American Labor Movement*, New York, 1927

Young, Marguerite, "Frances Perkins: Liberal Politician," *American Mercury*, August, 1934

CHAPTER IV

Adamic, Louis, "John L. Lewis' Push to Power," *Forum*, March, 1937

Carnes, Cecil, *John L. Lewis: Leader of Labor*, New York, 1936

Committee for Industrial Organization, *Industrial Unionism*, Washington, D. C., 1935. Pamphlet

Committee for Industrial Organization, *Industrial Unions Mean Unity*, Washington, D. C., 1936. Pamphlet

Committee for Industrial Organization, *The Case for Industrial Organization*, Washington, D. C., 1936. Pamphlet

Daily Worker, January 1, 1937; May 13, 1937.

Foster, William Z., *Industrial Unionism*, New York, 1936. Pamphlet

Gebert, B. K., "Steel Workers on the March," *Communist*, May, 1937

"The Great Labor Upheaval," *Fortune*, October, 1936

International Juridical Association, "The C.I.O. Controversy." *Monthly Bulletin*, August, 1936

"John Llewellyn Lewis," *Fortune*, October, 1936

Letter from John Brophy to the *New Republic*, December 25, 1929

Lewis, John L., *The Miners' Fight for American Standards*, Indianapolis, 1925

Lewis, John L., *Industrial Democracy in Steel*, Washington, D. C., 1936. Pamphlet

Lewis, John L., "What I Expect of Roosevelt," *Nation*, November 14, 1936

Lewis, John L., "The Next Four Years for Labor," *New Republic*, December 23, 1936

Mitchell, Jonathan, "John the Giant-Killer," *New Republic*, October 14, 1936

Myers, Gustavus, *History of the Great American Fortunes*, New York, 1936. First Modern Library Edition

New York *Sun*, January 30, 1937

Rochester, Anna, *Labor and Coal*, New York, 1931

Smith, Beverly, "The Name Is Lewis," *American Magazine*, September, 1936

Stolberg, Ben, "King Coal's Boss," *Independent*, July 11, 1925

Stolberg, Ben, "John L. Lewis: Portrait of a Realist," *Nation*, August 1, 1936

Stolberg, Ben, "The Education of John L. Lewis," *Nation*, August 8, 1936

Stolberg, Ben, "The Education of John L. Lewis," *Nation*, August 15, 1936

Tippett, Tom, "The Miners Fight Their Leaders," *American Mercury*, June, 1934

CHAPTER V

Adams, F. P., "Comrade Broun," *Nation*, October 1, 1930

Alexander, Norman, "Not Fit To Print," *Nation*, January 16, 1935

Breines, Simon, "Making Work for Technicians," *Social Work Today*, October, 1934

Broun, Heywood, "Hand and Brain," *Nation*, March 6, 1935

Broun, Heywood, "Because the Judge Says So," *Nation*, March 20, 1935

Broun, Heywood, "White Collar Into Plume," *Nation*, April 10, 1935

Broun, Heywood, *It Seems To Me*, New York, 1935

Browder, Earl, *What Is Communism?* New York, 1936

Buchanan, John, "White Collars Organize," *New Masses*, April 7, 1936

Carr-Saunders, A. M., *Professions: Their Organization and Place in Society*, London, 1928. Pamphlet

Corey, Lewis, *The Decline of American Capitalism*, New York, 1934

Corey, Lewis, *The Crisis of the Middle Class*, New York, 1935

Corey, Lewis, "The Minds of the Middle Class," *New Masses*, April 7, 1936

Corey, Lewis, "American Class Relations," *Marxist Quarterly*, January–March, 1937

Dutt, R. Palme, *Fascism and Social Revolution*, New York, 1934

Edwards, A. M., "The 'White-Collar Workers'," *Monthly Labor Review*, March, 1934

Eustis, Morton, "Theatre with a Union Label," *Theatre Arts Monthly*, November, 1933

"Figures Measure Plight of the White Collar Man," *Business Week*, May 25, 1932

"The Guild Gets the Run-Around," *New Republic*, January 9, 1935

Hamlin, T. F., "The Architect and the Depression," *Nation*, August 9, 1933

Hartwell, A. A., "White Collar Organization Gains," *Guild Reporter*, February 1, 1937

Jackson, T. A., *Dialectics*, New York, 1936

Keating, Isabelle, "Reporters Become of Age," *Harpers*, April, 1935

Langdon, E., "The Teacher Faces the Depression," *Nation*, August 16, 1933

Letter "The First Librarian's Union," in the *Wilson Bulletin*, June, 1936

Lindeman, Eduard C., "The Future of the Professional," *Social Work Today*, June, 1934

Meusel, Alfred, "Middle Class," *Encyclopaedia of the Social Sciences*, Volume X, New York, 1933

MacDonald, William, *The Intellectual Worker and His Work*, London, 1923

Ramsey, David, "Middle Class and a Farmer-Labor Party," *New Masses*, April 7, 1936

Ross, V. P., "Emotional Prodder," *Outlook and Independent*, October 30, 1929

Schapiro, Meyer, "Architecture and the Architect," *New Masses*, April 7, 1936

"The Significance of White Collars," *World Tomorrow*, March 1, 1933

Springer, Gertrude, "Ragged White Collars," *Survey*, November 15, 1931

"Union Label for Pegasus," *Nation*, October 4, 1933

"Unions for Technicians," *New Republic*, January 24, 1934

CHAPTER VI

Allen, J. S., *The American Negro*, New York, 1932. Pamphlet

Allen, J. S., *The Negro Question in the United States*, New York, 1936

Beard, Mary R., *The American Labor Movement*, New York, 1928

"The Blue Eagle and the Black Man," *New Republic*, March 21, 1934

Burnham, G. M., *Social Insurance*, New York, 1931. Pamphlet

Butler, Hilton, *"Murder for the Job,"* Nation, July 12, 1933

Cheyney, A. S., "Negro Women in Industry," *Survey*, April 23, 1921

Davis, J. P., *Let Us Build a National Negro Congress*, New York, 1935. Pamphlet

Feldman, Herman, *Racial Factors in American Industry*, New York, 1931

Ford, James W., "The Negro Masses in the United States," *Communist International*, June, 1937

Frazier, E. F., "The American Negro's New Leaders," *Current History*, April, 1928

Gordon, E., and Briggs, C., *The Position of Negro Women*, New York, 1935. Pamphlet

Greene, L. J., and Woodson, C. G., *The Negro Wage Earner*, Washington, D. C., 1930

Handbook of Labor Statistics, United States Department of Labor, Bureau of Labor Statistics, Bulletin No. 616, Washington, D. C., 1936

Harris, A. L., "The Negro Problem As Viewed by Negro Leaders," *Current History*, June, 1923

Harris, A. L., "Negro Labor's Quarrel with White Workingmen," *Current History*, September, 1926

Hutchins, Grace, *Youth in Industry*, New York, 1932. Pamphlet

Hutchins, Grace, *Women Who Work*, New York, 1934

Johnson, C. S., *The Negro in American Civilization*, New York, 1930

Johnson, C. S., "Incidence Upon the Negro," *American Journal of Sociology*, May, 1935

Keir, R. M., *Labor's Search for More*, New York, 1937

Lumpkin, K. D., and Douglas, D. W., *Child Workers in America*, New York, 1937

National Urban League, *Negro Membership in American Labor Unions*, New York, 1930

Nearing, Scott, *Black America*, New York, 1929

"The Negro in Industry," *Industrial Training Magazine*, January, 1926

"Negro in Industry," *Monthly Labor Review*, September, 1927

"Negroes in the Professions," *Literary Digest*, May 12, 1934

"Negroes Out of Work," *Nation*, April 22, 1931

"Negro Workers and the Union," *Survey*, August, 1935

New Republic (page 137), September 21, 1932

Proceedings of the 55th Annual Convention of the American Federation of Labor, 1935

Randolph, A. Philip, "The Case of the Pullman Porters," *American Federationist*, November, 1926

Saposs, D. J., *Readings in Trade Unionism*, New York, 1927

Senate Documents, 66th Congress, First Session, Volume 12, 1919

Standing, T. G., "Nationalism in Negro Leadership," *American Journal of Sociology*, September, 1934

Wesley, C. H., *Negro Labor in the United States*, New York, 1927

Wolman, Leo, *Growth of American Trade Unions*, New York, 1924

Wolman, Leo, *The American Labor Movement*, New York, 1927

"Women in Industry," *Monthly Labor Review*, September, 1929

Weybright, Victor, "Pullman Porters on Parade," *Survey Graphic*, November, 1935

CHAPTER VII

Adamic, Louis, "Harry Bridges Comes East," *Nation*, December 26, 1936

Cantwell, Robert, "San Francisco: Act One," *New Republic*, July 25, 1934

Cantwell, Robert, "War on the West Coast. I. The Gentlemen of San Francisco," *New Republic*, August 1, 1934

The Coast Committee for the Shipowners, *The Pacific Maritime Labor Crisis*, San Francisco, 1936. Pamphlet

Daily Worker, November 20, 1936; December 17, 1936

Darcy, S., "The Great West Coast Maritime Strike," *Communist*, July, 1934

DeFord, M. A., "San Francisco: An Autopsy on the General Strike," *Nation*, August 1, 1934

Dunne, William F., *The Great San Francisco General Strike*, New York, 1934. Pamphlet

Holmes, Robert, "Thunder in the West," *New Masses*, November 17, 1936

Holmes, Robert, "No Surrender on the Waterfront," *New Masses*, December 8, 1936

Holmes, Robert, "Victory on the Waterfront, *New Masses*, February 23, 1937

Hudson, Roy, "Lessons of the Maritime Strike," *Communist*, March, 1937

International Longshoremen's Association Local 38–79, *The Maritime Crisis*, San Francisco, 1936. Pamphlet

International Longshoremen's Association Local 38–79, *The Truth About the Waterfront*, San Francisco, 1936. Pamphlet

Letter from A. Boyd, Secretary of Waterfront Employers Association, to Harry Bridges, April 14, 1936

Letter from Harry Bridges, President of the International Longshoremen's Association Local 38–79, to A. Boyd, April 14, 1936

"The Marine and General Strike," *The American Plan*, March, 1935

Minton, Bruce, "Ryan vs. Bridges," *New Masses*, July 23, 1935

Minton, Bruce, "Behind Closed Doors," *New Masses*, September 3, 1935

Minton, Bruce, "They Call It 'Mutiny'," *New Masses*, April 21, 1936

Minton, Bruce, "The Waterfront Marches Inland," *New Masses*, September 22, 1936

New York *Times Magazine*, October 25, 1936

"The Red Record on the Waterfront," *The American Plan*, August, 1935

San Francisco *News*, September 3, 1936; September 21, 1936; December 9, 1936

Schechter, Amy, "The Attack on West Coast Labor," *New Masses*, January 28, 1936

Schechter, Amy, "Victory on the Pacific," *New Masses*, May 5, 1936

Schneiderman, William, "The Pacific Coast Maritime Strike," *Communist*, April, 1936

Smith's Weekly (Sydney, Australia), September 19, 1936

Sunday Worker, December 17, 1936

Taylor, P. S., and Gold, N. L., "San Francisco and the General Strike," *Survey Graphic*, September, 1934

Voice of the Federation, April 1, 1937

Yellen, Samuel, *American Labor Struggles*, New York, 1936

CHAPTER VIII

Adamic, Louis, "Sitdown," *Nation*, December 5, 1936.

Adamic, Louis, "Sitdown: II," *Nation*, December 12, 1936

Anonymous, "Labor Can Lead: The Story of Sidney Hillman," *World Tomorrow*, November, 1929

Committee for Industrial Organization, *How the Rubber Workers Won*, Washington, D. C., 1936

Davis, Forrest, "Labor Spies and the Black Legion," *New Republic*, June 17, 1936

Dunn, R. W., *Company Unions*, New York, 1927

Dunn, R. W., *Labor and Automobiles*, New York, 1929

Dunn, R. W., and Hardy, J., *Labor and Textiles*, New York, 1931

Dunn, R. W., *Spying on Workers*, New York, 1932. Pamphlet

Dunn, R. W., *Company Unions Today*, New York, 1935. Pamphlet

Fairley, Lincoln, *The Company Union in Plan and Practice*, New York, 1936. Mimeographed Pamphlet

Fitch, J. A., "Steel," *Survey Graphic*, August, 1936

Foster, William Z., "The Significance of the Sit-Down Strike," *Communist*, April, 1937

Foster, William Z., "The Renaissance of the American Trade Union Movement," *Communist International*, June, 1937

Glück, Elsie, *Introduction to American Trade Unionism*, New York, 1935. Pamphlet

Gordon, E. B., "The Textile Drive," *Communist*, June, 1937

Gorman, F. J., Goldschmidt, A., Salvemini, G., *The Fate of Trade Unions Under Fascism*, New York, 1937. Pamphlet

Gorman, F. J., "The Textile Situation," *Vital Speeches*, October 22, 1934

Gorman, F. J., "Textile and Civil Rights," *Fight*, June, 1937

Green, Leon, "The Case for the Sit-Down Strike," *New Republic*, March 24, 1937

Hard, William, "Hillman and the Amalgamated," *New Republic*, June 2, 1920

Hardy, Jack, *The Clothing Workers*, New York, 1935

Harris, Herbert, "They Fight Their Battles Sitting Down," *Today*, February 6, 1937

Hillman, Sidney, *Reconstruction of Russia and the Task of Labor*, New York, 1922. Pamphlet

Hillman, Sidney, *Labor in the United States*, New York, 1929. Pamphlet

Hillman, Sidney, "Labor Leads Toward Planning," *Survey*, March, 1932

Hillman, Sidney, "The N.R.A., Labor, and Recovery," *Annals of the American Academy of Political and Social Science*, March, 1934

Howard, Sidney, with the collaboration of Dunn, R. W., *The Labor Spy*, New York, 1924

Huberman, Leo, "$80,000,000, a Year for Labor Spies," *New Masses*, June 8, 1937

Huberman, Leo, "The Dirtiest Trick," *New Masses*, June 15, 1937

Keller, James, "The Rubber Front in Akron," *Communist*, March, 1937

Labor Research Association, *Labor Notes*, April, 1937

Levinson, Edward, *I Break Strikes!*, New York, 1935

Luchek, Anthony, "Company Unions, F.O.B. Detroit," *Nation*, January 15, 1936

MacDonald, Dwight, "Espionage, Inc.," *Nation*, February 27, 1937

McKillips, Budd L., "Company Unions on the Railroads," *Nation*, January 8, 1936

Mangold, W. P., "On the Labor Front," *New Republic*, November 20, 1935

Mangold, W. P., "On the Labor Front," *New Republic*, March 11, 1936

Marshall, Margaret, "Textiles: An N.R.A. Strike," *Nation*, September 19, 1934

"The Meaning of the Textile Drive," *New Republic*, September 26, 1934

Mitchell, Jonathan, "Here Comes Gorman!" *New Republic*, October 3, 1934

"More Spies on Labor," *New Republic*, April 22, 1936

Muste, A. J., *The Automobile Industry and Organized Labor*, New York, 1936. Pamphlet

New York *Daily News*, June 21, 1937

New York *Post*, February 19, 1937

New York *Times*, September 2, 1936; September 15, 1936; September 16, 1936; September 22, 1936; September 28, 1936; November 12, 1936; December 30, 1936; January 27, 1937; February 15, 1937

"Picture of a Labor Rat," *Nation*, October 3, 1936

Remarks of Hon. John M. Coffee in the House of Representatives, March 30, 1937, *Sit-Down Strikes Are Legal in Contemplation of the Law*, Government Printing Office, Washington, D. C.

Saposs, D. J., "Employee Representation As Labor Organization," *Annals of the American Academy of Political and Social Science*, March, 1935.

Saposs, D. J., "Organizational and Procedural Changes in Employee Representation Plans," *Journal of Political Economy*, December, 1936

Seidman, Joel, *Sit-Down*, New York, 1937. Pamphlet

Social Economic Foundation, *A Labor Party for the United States*, New York, 1936. Pamphlet

Stark, Louis, "The Meaning of the Textile Strike," *New Republic*, May 8, 1929

Stein, R. M., "Steel Robots That Came Alive," *Nation*, February 5, 1936

Swing, R. G., "Sidney Hillman Turns Architect," *Nation*, April 3, 1935

"The Textile Workers Lose," *New Republic*, October 3, 1934

Ward, Paul W., "Washington Weekly," *Nation*, February 27, 1937

Weinstone, William, "The Great Auto Strike," *Communist*, March, 1937

Williamson, John, "Akron: A New Chapter in American Labor History," *Communist*, May, 1936

Wolf, Howard and Ralph, *Rubber: A Story of Glory and Greed*, New York, 1936

Yellen, Samuel, American Labor Struggles, New York, 1936

INDEX

Actors and Artistes of America, Association, 128–129

Adamson Act, 66

Addes, George F., 108, 218

American Federation of Labor, attitude toward,

craft unionism, 15–16, 24–26, 99, 103–104, 205, 208, 213, 231
    See also Committee for Industrial Organization; Industrial Unionism

dual unionism, 16, 26

employers, 18, 38–40, 179, 191, 201, 209, 213–214, 231, 245
    See also Company Unions

"intellectuals", 11, 116, 129, 151

legislation, 23, 63–64, 66, 68, 72
    See also Labor Legislation

organization, 15, 19, 34–35, 73–74, 85, 100–105, 110, 129, 131, 142, 143–147, 152, 156–159, 164, 168, 178, 205, 208, 210, 213–214, 216, 220, 223, 228–231, 233, 239–240, 244

political action, 10–13, 37, 53, 64–65, 68, 79, 113, 196

progressives, 11, 73, 102, 107, 182, 193, 196, 206–208, 216, 220

class antagonisms, denial of, 11, 97, 196

composition and membership, 18–19, 26, 35, 74, 101, 162, 164, 208–210, 214, 231, 234, 236
    See also under separate unions

conventions,

1934 San Francisco, 24, 102–103, 143, 192, 205

1935 Atlantic City, 25, 30, 85–86, 103–104, 143–147, 205–206, 225

1936 Tampa, 20–21, 27, 105–106

other conventions, 4, 23, 48, 106, 157–158, 213

corruption in, 20–22, 37–54, 61, 128, 201

formation of, 10, 14, 37

Gompers tradition, influence of, 10–22, 37–39, 60, 73–74, 97–99, 110, 115, 123, 128, 163, 168, 196, 203, 206, 220, 228–231, 236
    See also Gompersism; Green, William

American Labor Party, 79, 170, 233, 236–237

Automobile Labor Board, 83, 214

Automobile Workers, United, 27, 86, 103, 109, 215–220

Bar Association, American, 129

Bates, Harry C., 42

Bennett, Harry, 225

Bergoff, Pearl, 209, 224–225

Berry, George L., 51, 56–59

Black-Connery Bill, 78, 113

Black Legion, 80, 225

Blacklist, 71, 78, 81, 86, 177, 180, 189, 191, 201, 218–219, 223, 225–226, 243

Bookkeepers, Stenographers, and Accountants Union, 131–132

Boycott, 71
    See also Contracts; Labor Legislation

Bradley, E. J., 154

Bridges, Harry, 62–63, 163
attitude toward,

industrial unionism, 195

rank and file, 172, 179–181, 189, 192, 199, 201–202

Red scare, 185, 189–191

politics, 185, 193, 196–197

early career, 175–181

1932 and after, 172–175, 181–202
    See also Longshoremen's Association, International

Brindell, Robert, 39, 45, 47–48

Broach, Henry H., 42

Brophy, John, 98, 108, 147

Broun, Heywood, 151

early career, 116, 122

1933 and after, 115–116, 122, 134–142

industrial unionism, attitude toward, 133, 141, 142
    See also Newspaper Guild, American

Brown, Willis K., 49

Bugniazet, G. M., 42

Burgess, R. L., 135

Date Due

MAY 25 '78			
DEC 22 '81			